Alchemy at Work

Alchemy at Work

Using the Ancient Arts to Enhance Your Work Life

CASSANDRA EASON

THE CROSSING PRESS
Berkeley | Toronto

❋

The Crossing Press
A Division of Ten Speed Press
PO Box 7123
Berkeley, California 94707
www.tenspeed.com

Distributed in Australia by Simon and Schuster Australia,
in Canada by Ten Speed Press Canada,
in New Zealand by Southern Publishers Group,
in South Africa by Real Books,
and in the United Kingdom and Europe by Airlift Book Company.

Cover and text design by Lisa Buckley

Library of Congress Cataloging-in-Publication Data
Eason, Cassandra.
    Alchemy at work : using the ancient arts to enhance your work life /
Cassandra Eason.
        p. cm.
    Includes bibliographical references and index.
    ISBN 1-58091-158-7
    1. Quality of work life 2. Self-help techniques. 3. Intuition.
    4. Decision making. I. Title.
    HD6955.E22 2004
    650.1—dc22   2004009765

Printed in the United States
First printing, 2004
1 2 3 4 5 6 7 8 9 10 — 08 07 06 05 04

Contents

Introduction

In that not so distant time before cell phones bleeped louder than birds in the sky and you felt obliged to check your office emails while vacationing on a mountaintop, people worked close to nature. Their toil was directly related to producing food, clothes, and shelter for themselves and their families. They lived in small communities, and they attached their workshops to their cottages.

My maternal great-great-great grandma Anne was a needle maker and had a workroom with a half door leading into her cottage. Her mother cared for her children in the main room while Anne worked. Not that I am advocating quitting your centrally heated office with a view of the Chicago skyline and re-creating an eighteenth-century English hovel.

But the lesson we can take into our modern stress-laden work lives is that our forebears did live more like the birds in the sky, whose call is much sweeter than the most harmonious cell phone ring tone. Their work lives were closely linked to the natural cycles of light and darkness and the seasons. When natural light faded, our kin went home and in the winter slept much longer under their horsehair duvets so they were rested for the longer summer days in the fields or the workshop.

Even if you have excellent workplace conditions, you'll know people in centrally heated offices, stores, hospitals, or factories where neon lighting turns night into day and tinted glass largely obscures the weather and the seasons. Noisy air conditioning and temperature control eliminates extremes of heat and cold while merrily circulating airborne viruses.

Nor do we necessarily have our box of needles or bucket of vegetables to show for a day's toil. We may produce facts, figures, and ideas in a competitive atmosphere to meet targets set by faceless executives hundreds or thousands of miles away or to create a tiny upswing on the money market graphs.

The average caged rat in similar work conditions would be so stressed he could barely bite a chunk out of his fellow inmates. Indeed, stress-related illnesses in offices throughout the world have increased so much that some buildings are called sick because of the high level of absenteeism, psychosomatic sickness, and workplace tensions among workers. Even the potted plants get sick.

Bringing Natural Harmony and Success into the Workplace

Whether you are a workplace-caged rat or your boss brings you fresh-squeezed juice and waffles to start the day, we can all benefit from connecting with the natural seasonal, lunar, and solar cycles that still turn on their annual cosmic wheel just off the freeway. By harmonizing our natural inner rhythms with our daily, weekly, and monthly workload, we can swim with, not against, the tide of prevailing energies.

We can bring the natural world's harmonizing and empowering energies into the office or factory in the form of fragrant plants, miniature trees, herbs, and crystals so the atmosphere is always fresh and ideas bounce off the walls creatively and spontaneously.

Indeed, we can become more successful by developing the natural intuitive powers our ancestors relied on prior to widespread literacy in order to maximize our talents and communication skills, see opportunities and instinctively avoid pitfalls, and supplement our modern sales or presentation techniques with our automatic inner radar. By determining what will be most effective and the precise right time, we stay a step ahead of the competition and opposition.

What is more, a touch of traditional folk alchemy will shield us from negative people and attitudes whether they be Monday morning grouchiness, ongoing harmless but unproductive gossip, or malice and character assassination in less ethically led workplaces where bonuses and promotion can encourage pressure selling and outsmarting coworkers on the way to the food bowl.

Intuitive powers can enable us to tune into the hidden needs and feelings of fellow workers, employers, and employees, thereby becoming aware by signals even deeper than nonverbal indicators of the right time to propose changes or new ideas and the right time to hold back. We can empathize with others, sensing when to ease their workload and when we can push productivity ahead.

Above all we can plan forward, not only by using charts and analysis but also by tapping into the same divinatory methods, albeit refined and sanitized over the centuries, that hunters and gatherers used thousands of years ago to anticipate the coming of the herds. Those same powers are passed on in our genes.

I will be sharing all these techniques and ancient secrets with you in this book so you can take control of your destiny and achieve your potential in your work life. I will suggest psychic shortcuts and intuitive pathways that will have you whistling and singing all the way to the boardroom or to the top of the high achievers' list.

Alchemy in the Workplace

So can we really seriously use psychic powers and alchemy in our working lives without being offered an urgent appointment with the senior workplace counselor?

Most really successful businessmen and women do rely on intuition to make decisions, perhaps affecting millions of dollars and thousands of jobs. The stock market relies heavily on hunches about when and what to sell or buy, usually involving split-second timing before the relevant information appears onscreen through conventional means.

We may find the perfect job because of a chain of seemingly coincidental events. Like animals and children, those most successful in business know within thirty seconds whether a visiting executive, a new colleague, a sales rep, or a deal on an offer is trustworthy and reliable.

There are countless courses and books explaining how we can interpret and control nonverbal signals, so that, for example, a clued-in salesperson can look us straight in the eye and lie through his teeth. But the truly tuned-in people-reader understands the subtle energy patterns around that salesperson and can't be so easily masked or manipulated.

Furthermore, we can draw to us what we need using mind power. If we accept the current scientific view that all matter is in fact moving energy, then we can direct those parcels of energy, initially in the form of thoughts and ideas. Visualization is an accepted successful business technique whereby you picture what you want to achieve and then in your imagination go through the feelings of attaining the goal and anticipate the satisfaction experienced when you hit your target.

Taken just a small step further, by using a series of pre-ordained or sometimes spontaneous words and/or actions, you can increase the intensity with which you focus on your aim so it seems so real that it moves from the realm of thought to a distinct possibility.

Call it focused and amplified visualization or spell casting, you are aiming for your goal by concentrating and releasing psychological and psychic energy to break through the barrier between thought and actuality in a sudden release of energy, like the flashbulb on a camera. So a distinct possibility has now become a fact (give or take a bit of earthly fine-tuning).

Our early hunter ancestors would act out rituals and paint symbols of a successful hunt onto cave walls, concentrating their psychic energy, to draw the animals to the hunting grounds where the hunters would be waiting.

Maybe you want to become head of a department, not spend the twilight hours stalking opossums in the local park. The principle and the process are the same. Whether you carry out success empowerments entirely within your mind or draw them high-tech style on your computer, you can create the psychic environment from which your own ongoing earthly hard work and enthusiasm can be launched.

Psychology and the psychic realm differ only in intensity. The psychically charged crystal or sachet of success herbs that you carry to a job interview or major presentation is a reminder of how great you really are, so you spontaneously radiate "I'm perfect for the job" vibes.

The Rules of Psychic Engagement

Unlike the ruthlessness that sometimes is a feature of less scrupulous big business, workplace alchemy has remarkably moral ground rules.

You can use your psychic powers, such as the natural but underexploited ability called *psychokinesis* (your mind translating your thoughts into actuality, which I mentioned previously), to achieve a desired result with great effect as often as you need.

But you cannot succeed at someone else's expense, as bad vibes like good ones come back to the sender threefold. If someone was demoted or left a position because of her own incompetence or management hostility (the latter may be a warning to think twice about accepting what might be a poisoned chalice), it is fair game for you to focus on attracting a promotion.

However, if you were to wish, for example, that someone would lose his job or become ill so you could take over, not only would the job not bring you happiness, but your own dark thoughts would sour your life outside as well as during work hours. You don't have to be a bad person to have such thoughts—we all do.

You might see a colleague doing nothing all day and getting credit for your ideas and input. Or you might urgently need the extra money that a promotion would bring to pay the mortgage because you are struggling to bring up your children alone.

But to step into the gray area of ill wishing, however justifiable, can cause problems for you as well as the person you are hexing. Take the case of Annie, whose former friend and colleague Sue was unexpectedly promoted over her, though Annie had been with the firm five years longer than Sue. Annie was furious and wished that Sue would lose the job. Annie imagined a ring of fire around Sue's desk, stopping her from entering her workspace.

About a week later Sue did not turn up for work and the

next day she resigned, saying she could not cope with the stress. Maybe a coincidence?

The elated Annie took over, but things started to go wrong almost at once. Annie found the job harder than she had expected; though Annie had a flair for ideas, routine organization was not her field (probably the reason she wasn't offered the job in the first place). Soon the managers were complaining that she was allowing careless work to pass through, and Annie had to work late in the evening to keep up with her mountains of paperwork.

The following week Annie had a minor fire in her house, and though no one was hurt some of her favorite possessions were lost.

Annie asked for her old job back, and an outsider took over Sue's position. Sue moved from the town, and Annie lost a good friend. These things might have been unrelated to Annie's ill wishing, and the nature of the job might have affected Sue also. But I have come across enough real-life examples of how ill wishing seems to set up a negative chain of events to advise caution.

Making Dreams Come and Stay True

Though you can focus on any work-related desire from writing a best-selling novel to being posted to an exotic location, you have to do the groundwork to bring the thought within the framework of possibility in the first place.

This might mean spending hours listening to relevant language tapes, so you would be capable of operating overseas if and when the golden opportunity arose. You have to write and rewrite your novel so it is polished and well typed and then hunt for an agent who reads fiction of the kind you have created. We can't just write a psychic shopping list, perform a chant or two, cast a circle of herbs, and wait for a Hollywood movie mogul whose stretch limo has run out of gas to knock on our door.

Success depends on wanting a dream more than anything else in the world and being prepared in earthly terms to make the golden opportunity work, down to the acceptance speech. Alchemy is like getting a plane to take off the tarmac. But you've got to have an airworthy plane, enough fuel, and a competent pilot to reach your dream destination.

Attaining success is also part of a cosmic balance sheet. If you win the contract or promotion, then you have to give back something in return. It isn't enough to plant a crystal or a flower and go off with a bottle of champagne to celebrate.

The payback has got to be something tangible, like helping the new guy in your workplace figure out the eccentric filing system or spending a lunch break or two with the lady who has been in accounts since Roosevelt was President and socializes every weekend with her cat, but not through choice. That way you are putting back positive vibes so you have credit in your psychic bank account and can draw out favors from the cosmos again when you need a bit of luck or recognition.

Making the Effort

Sometimes we all need a lucky break or a boost of confidence or energy in our career. Psychology and the psychic are, as I said, close bedfellows.

Even if you find psychic and alchemical powers hard to accept, think of those occasions when you wake up on top of the world, happy and confident, and the sun is shining. You go into work smiling, and even the usually gloomy guy in Security grimaces back. The first phone call goes straight through to the person you want to talk to, and you manage to express an idea at a morning meeting that normally you would not dare to voice. But because you sound so confident, everyone else believes you can pull off the project, and the day just gets better.

Contrast that with the days when you wake up and it's gray outside, you trip over the cat, and you break a fingernail opening its food to stop the yowling. The bus is late, your boss snarls, and you spill your first cup of coffee—which is half cold because the machine is not working properly—over your new white blouse just before you are due to give a now coffee-stained presentation, half of which you left behind anyway in the rush.

The difference is the approach, but using alchemy you can instantly tap into positive power and turn even the worst hair day around, whether by drinking water in which you have soaked an empowered crystal or by repeating in your mind a psychic shortcut to an earlier self-esteem ritual (see chapter 5).

Good fortune and success are like a psychic snowball that increases the more you practice, though fortunately it does not melt come the spring. Once you flex your half-developed psychic muscles, you become more aware of undercurrents and sometimes contradictions between people's words, written and spoken, and their unvoiced intentions. On the earthly level, too, you become more focused in areas where logic is needed, more charismatic (which can spill over after hours), and less affected by the mood swings and mayhem around you.

My writing career started with a lucky break when I was forty years old. When he was three years old, my middle son, Jack, predicted to the minute the time when my husband fell off a motorbike while he was falling, forty miles away. My skeptical husband, who as Jack foretold was unhurt, wrote an article in a British newspaper trying to explain away the experience.

A number of mothers who lived near me read the article and told me about their children's psychic experiences of which they had never spoken. I decided to write a book about psychic children, but having written nothing larger than an article I did not know how to go about it. I picked a publisher at random from a directory and sent off a proposal to the editorial director. The same day that my letter arrived on her desk, she had been given a copy of the article my husband had written, had thought that a book on psychic children would be an excellent idea, and had decided to try to track me down through the newspaper. That was nearly fifteen years ago. The book is still in print and has been translated into many languages including Japanese.

My Work Life

I have had a variety of jobs, from selling shoes in a department store where I was about as charismatic as a cactus, to working in a factory lacquering brasses in temperatures hotter than

Hell's Mouth, teaching kids in schools varying from ghetto areas to the sons and daughters of second cousins of the would-be aristocracy, briefly working as a graduate psychologist, and for the last fifteen years as a self-employed writer, broadcaster, and full-time mom of five.

My workplace alternates between the living room table that doubles as the family junk pile and a trailer in a field on top of a cliff overlooking the sea—balancing my computer on a rickety table that also serves as a junk pile—where my kids and their assorted adoptee friends spend the summer.

My broadcasting studio is the phone, when I can unearth it from the family glory pile. My worst moment was when my elderly neighbor two doors down deposited her very large glassy-eyed deceased black-and-white tomcat in a bath towel on my lawn. The BBC local radio station for the counties of Herefordshire and Worcestershire rang me for a phone-in on the return of deceased relatives. I know there are no ideals, but any obstacle can be transformed into an opportunity, given determination and a touch of alchemy.

Using this Book

If your life is hectic, you may need to read this book in your spare time, maybe on a train journey or while waiting for your dinner to cook. You can read the chapters in any order, and there are plenty of references so you can link a section to earlier material if you are interrupted. I have suggested exercises, rituals, and empowerments, many with shortcuts so you can reawaken the necessary power or protection at a minute's notice when you actually need them. At the back of the book there is a summary of relevant crystals, candle colors, oils, and symbol meanings, so you can write yourself a reminder to buy, for example, blue candles if you're working on a nightly ritual to get included on a business trip overseas.

Ideas are directed toward any workplace or career, whether you are salaried, are self-employed, own a company, juggle two careers, are going to college, or are trying to turn a passionate interest into a full-time occupation.

Keeping a Journal

A journal is a place to record decisions you make using intuition or more formal methods of divination. Create either a special folder on your computer or use a notebook. This way you can keep track of your alchemical efforts. You may find that a decision that does not initially seem advantageous, turned out exactly as you predicted three months down the line. You can also scribble down notes about the psychic energy interactions between colleagues or other people you come into contact with as part of an ongoing monitoring process to note new alliances, divisions, and how you used your findings to improve your workplace relations.

Also list any particularly effective empowerments or protective work you carry out and particular combinations of essential oils and crystals that seem potent for you and your business environment.

We always think we will remember details, but given a hectic schedule they may fade. You can also set personal targets and tick them off as you achieve them or note modifications in the light of your growing intuitive powers.

As months pass, whenever you feel despondent or off course, you can read back over your achievements and realize how far you have progressed.

This book is intended to help you develop your own intuitive and instinctive powers so that you can bring every part of your mind into play in your work life. Use the methods in the following chapters to ensure that you stay one step ahead of your competition and feel confident in any situation.

In the next chapter I explain how to use a pendulum for intuitive decision making. We'll use the pendulum to delve into the hidden parts of the mind where the right answers lie. Your pendulum can connect you with the unconscious radar that will guide you to the right choice automatically.

CHAPTER 1

Intuitive Decision Making with Pendulums

Intuition is a spontaneous process, the automatic radar that supplements what is known and recognized by the conscious mind with information we have not yet processed. This information may come in the form of impressions based on our psychically sensitive sensory antennae that extend beyond the limits of the five physical senses.

We may see images in our mind or hear words spoken by our inner voice, "Bid now, go for it, hold back, be silent, wait." Once we start trusting this hidden source of wisdom, we can stay ahead in any situation and avoid pitfalls in our career. In business, intuition is one of the most valuable tools that we all possess, but we have been taught during formal education and training to suppress or ignore it.

Our greatest challenge is recognizing and trusting our invariably accurate intuitive wisdom in those times when we don't have all the facts. It may be that, having listened to everyone's opinion and weighed up the facts and figures, something stops us from coming to what seems on the surface the inevitable conclusion or decision. On other occasions our intuition may guide us toward a seemingly unpromising offer, while warning us against what appears to be a once-in-a-lifetime dream opportunity. Unlike using divination for planning forward, which I describe in chapters 7 and 8, intuitive flashes may not provide a clear picture of the future, just an indication of whether to act now or wait.

The skill of reading people, which I talk about in chapter 3, may help you to fine-tune these intuitive feelings. But often we need to make a snap decision or judgment about the wisdom of an action or trustworthiness of a person or organization, and then we have to go with our gut feeling.

Let me tell you about Amy, who was seeking a job as a production assistant with a record company after finishing her degree in media studies. One day, a well-known company manager to whom she had sent her CV phoned and offered her an immediate interview. When she arrived, Amy was told that she had so impressed the company she was being offered an on-the-road position with a well-known girl band, starting the next evening when she would meet the tour bus for the start of a three-week twenty-town circuit.

Amy was thrilled, but as she sat having coffee in a mall not far from the studio, something felt wrong. The family had jokingly called her grandma a witch, and Amy had inherited the same intuitive sense. Amy described the feeling as being like a mild electric shock that set her teeth on edge, caused a slight churning in her stomach, and prompted a sudden sensitivity in which noises seemed louder, colors more vivid, and smells suddenly stronger.

Though she sat quietly, Amy could not detect precisely what was wrong, only that she had a strong conviction that she should not accept her dream job.

When Amy called the record company, half hoping for some kind of reassurance, the girl who answered the phone sounded indifferent, saying there were a dozen other hopefuls who would jump at the chance. However, Amy was warned she would not get work in the industry once word of her unreliability got around. Amy almost wavered at the threat, but the jarring sensation kicked in. Others who have experienced similar warnings have described it as a jittery experience like having drunk too much coffee.

In fact, a college friend of Amy's, Sarah, took the job and went on the tour in her place. After the first venue, a relatively small theatre in the Midwest, the recording company cancelled the rest of the dates. The first event had been a total disaster, and the band had stormed off the stage.

Sarah was sacked, and the girl band signed with another record label almost at once, blaming the fiasco on the production assistant's incompetence.

In fact it was all a cynical ploy by the first company, who wanted to off-load the girl band, which was having falling sales, and replace them with another more successful girl band. Knowing how volatile the girls were, sending an inexperienced production assistant to a theater where there had been problems with even established, stable bands in the past, was almost guaranteed to bring matters to a head. Both sides threw Sarah to the wolves; the girl band was also looking for an excuse to sign with another label that they believed would represent them better.

Amy got a job not long afterward with another music company where she had to start at the bottom, answering phone calls from young hopefuls. Two years later Amy at last went on the road with an established artist. Unfairly, it has taken Sarah a while to reestablish her career after being involved in such a public disaster.

Most examples of intuitive decision making are more mundane. But the more practiced you are, the more spontaneous and accurate your intuitive responses will be, so you can call on them at any time and be sure of an immediate answer to any issue.

Asking Questions

Even for people who are sensitive to their inner voice, working with a crystal pendulum is a good way of fine-tuning what your inner voice tells you and identifying the options and the real agenda if a matter is not clear.

A pendulum works through the psychokinetic power of which I spoke in the introductory chapter. Your unconscious mind locates the relevant information and transmits it to you by causing the muscles of your hand spontaneously to move the pendulum in a particular direction.

These movements will answer a question with two options, such as yes/no, stay/go, act/wait, speak/be silent, demand/ give, or assert/listen. Alternatively, the pendulum can be used to dowse. Held in turn over a series of options, it will pull down over the option that is best for us, though often not our consciously preferred option. The pendulum is like a very straight-talking friend who won't tell you what you want to hear, but will tell you what is in your best interests to know. This was demonstrated when I was working weekly as a paranormal expert on a traveling cable show in the United Kingdom on an American-owned network.

If the main presenters were on holiday, we would use temporary presenters, often newcomers to television who, if sufficiently talented, already had achieved their first appearance on television. One young novice presenter, Mark, was very self-assured even though it was his first media appearance. By the time I arrived he had upset the stage and camera crews, which is never a wise move.

Mark seized my pendulum and said he was going to use it to ask whether his dinner party that evening was going to be a success. During the advertisement break he condescended to tell me that his real question was whether he would be asked back as presenter the following week, which in his eyes, like the dinner party, was an inevitable triumph.

Back on air, however, the pendulum spun in counterclockwise circles, which was Mark's No response that we had established beforehand. Mark tried to steady the pendulum and physically held it with both hands to force it clockwise, his chosen Yes action. But the pendulum was having none of it and continued to spiral its No Chance reply merrily.

Mark slammed the pendulum on the table and declared that no right-minded person would make a decision based on witchcraft. I don't know how his dinner party went, but I never encountered Master Mark on the television circuit again.

The pendulum confirms the insights we receive from our inner voice, and as your decisions are proved right, your confidence in your own judgment will increase and become more accurate. As well as the pendulum's movements, when using a pendulum you may see images in your mind's eye, hear your inner wisdom speaking as a calm clear voice, or receive impressions as feelings. These impressions will provide extra information on the question or topic under consideration.

All of these phenomena are natural responses, amplified by the crystal, which acts as a receiver of psychic impressions. In the next chapter I suggest techniques for stilling your mind so you can tune into your inner wisdom at times when you cannot easily use a pendulum.

Initially you may find that using some of the calming exercises in chapter 2—to separate you from the more frantic pace around you—can make pendulum readings clearer and more spontaneous. These can all be carried out sitting at your desk, and as a bonus those around you may also become quieter and calmer.

Choosing a Pendulum

Buy a clear crystal pendulum; that's the best kind for decision making. Clear crystal pendulums are also good for locating lost items, such as car keys or papers you took home that were tidied away by a helpful family member. They will also detect negative earth energies in the workplace, which the pendulum and other crystals can then easily neutralize.

Some crystal pendulums are barrel shaped and ridged, an ancient Egyptian design discovered in the ruins of the Temple of Karnack near Luxor, dating from around 2500 B.C.E.

You can also obtain metal or wooden diamond-shaped pendulums, or you can use a favorite crystal pendant or even a key on a cord as an impromptu pendulum.

Buy a small velvet drawstring bag or purse for your pendulum so you can keep it with you in a bag, pocket, or drawer. Once you are experienced with a pendulum, you can substitute a small quartz crystal in your hand when you are talking on the phone; you can tune into your own intuitive feelings and the intentions of the caller according to its vibrations.

Holding Your Pendulum

How you hold your pendulum really is a matter of what feels right to you. Most people hold the pendulum's string or chain between their thumb and forefinger. General agreement ends there. I use the hand with which I write, sometimes called your power hand, winding any extra chain around my index finger of the same hand. Another view suggests that it is better to dowse with the left hand for right brain intuition.

As for the crystal's length, again, experiment. Obviously, you don't want to be trailing miles of string. Recommended string lengths vary between 9 inches (23 cm) and 40 inches (100 cm). In my experience pendulums work best when the chain is short, about 10 inches (25 cm) long, for using the basic Yes/No response. If you are dowsing over a circle or list of options, 6 to eight 8 inches (15–20 cm) seems most successful. For detecting earth energies or looking for lost items, 12 to 15 inches (27–37 cm) seems most effective.

Discovering your Pendulum's Responses

To discover your pendulum's basic movements, choose a quiet time when you are relaxed. You may want to try one of the exercises given in chapter 2 to clear your mind of clutter. In time your pendulum will become so tuned into your psyche that it responds instantly and effortlessly, especially if you carry it with you frequently.

Determining the Yes Response

Even in business, feelings are the channel intuition uses (something feels or doesn't feel right). Therefore, to establish your personal Yes response with your pendulum, visualize a very happy moment in your work life—a sudden triumph or promotion or just the sheer joy of having mastered a difficult skill.

Picture the happy moment, recalling words spoken to you in congratulation or a particularly satisfying response to your suggestion. Wait and the pendulum will start to swing spontaneously in response to the positive images in your mind.

The pendulum will give a Yes response; it may be a single movement or it may continue to swing. Frequently the Yes movement will be a clockwise circle or an ellipse. If your response is different, that means your pendulum is creating its own link with your psyche. Your Yes response will remain consistent once it is established, in personal as well as professional decision making.

Determining the No Response

This time, focus on a moment when you were disappointed at your workplace, when you didn't get offered a contract or sales figures or a commission check was far below what you had anticipated.

A negative pendulum movement is generally the mirror image of the Yes response; for example, a counterclockwise circle or ellipse. But your personal pendulum's No response may be entirely different.

Whatever question has produced the negative response, it is important to reestablish the positive mood and swing (otherwise you'll be left in a sad mood); this can most easily be done by recalling some past success or triumph.

Determining the Ask Again Response

There is a third response, which occurs when you ask an incomplete or badly phrased question. A pendulum is only a tool, though a very sensitive one. It gives you the information you ask for, like the Help function on a computer, where you have to key in the right commands to get the right information.

If your question is ambiguous or cannot be answered by one of two options, the pendulum may indicate you should rephrase your question. Sometimes too your intuition, which controls your pendulum, is alerting you to the fact that your question is off track and you need to think about the real issue that you need to explore (more of this in the flowchart that follows).

Identify this important Ask Again signal by holding your pendulum and thinking of a time of confusion, perhaps when you caught the wrong train or lost your notes just before a business meeting.

Your pendulum may simply not move, cease moving, or continuously circle first one way and then the other. Again, your personal Ask Again reply may be different.

Go back to thinking positive thoughts to restore your personal equilibrium so you don't go around looking puzzled all day.

Testing the Responses

Your pendulum may be a tool, but it is not dumb so don't waste time asking it whether your cup of coffee really is a cup of coffee. Test your responses with a real-life work decision, maybe not one where, if you get it wrong, you'll be fired for shutting down Wall Street. Leave major issues until you are really experienced, pendulum wise. Choose a fairly straightforward matter. For example: "Will this project receive a positive response if I introduce it in today's morning meeting?" You can either ask the question in your mind or aloud if you're alone or with open-minded colleagues. Speak the question slowly, but do not try to anticipate the response. Allow your mind to go blank and do not be too eager for the pendulum to speak.

The response may come after a second or a minute or more. The more definite the pendulum's response as measured by the size and vigor of its circling, the more clearly the answer is either affirmative or negative. As the pendulum moves you may also experience images or hear words in your mind that may clarify the answer. If a positive response seems uncertain, perhaps only a single or a weak clockwise circling, this may indicate that you need to proceed with caution. Asking further related questions may indicate possible hazards you should avoid.

Using Your Pendulum

It is possible to ask both single and multiple questions when using a pendulum. Let's see how this works for both types of questions.

Asking Single Questions

Sometimes a single question can provide the answer to an

option or a dilemma. You can widen the scope of a question by asking: "Should I/can I/will I?"

You will need to phrase your question carefully to avoid having an "either/or" element within the question. For example, if you've got a problem with priorities when everyone wants everything done at the same moment you might ask: "Should I finish my backlog of emails before making my afternoon calls?" You shouldn't, however, say: "Should I finish my emails or make the calls first?" Remember, a pendulum only answers questions with two options or dowses; it does not hold conversations.

You can get more detailed information for a more complex issue by asking a series of related questions, using a flowchart. Let's go back to the example of presenting a new project. "Will this project receive a positive response if I introduce it in today's morning meeting?" "Should I introduce this project at the morning meeting today?" Your pendulum might get you an unequivocal Yes. That is because your unconscious mind is racing ahead like a dog off a leash and alerting you that the energies ahead are very positive.

Asking Multiple Questions

If the answer is No or if the positive response is there but uncertain, you can probe the reasons further in subsequent questions to discover whether the idea itself is unsound, or whether the format or timing is wrong, or whether someone else should bring up the idea. You can ask different questions to identify specific obstacles to your success.

So you might next ask: "Is the firm going to accept the project in its present form at all?"

If the answer is No, the pendulum is alerting you that the idea isn't economically or practically viable. If you are pushing the project as a favor to a close colleague, then your pendulum is warning you that you are temporarily allowing friendship to cloud your business sense.

But maybe you get a qualified Yes response. Next you might want to know whether you need to change the format to garner acceptance. It could be that the project would be better received as a written proposal or an informal introduction, one to one, with the person who has the final say.

If formatting is not the obstacle according to your pendulum, could your timing be wrong? Should you introduce the topic at a meeting on another occasion?

Maybe the moon is *void of course* (see chapter 9) this morning. The moon is void of course between the time it makes its last major aspect (or angle) to another planet as it is leaving one sun sign and the time it changes to the next sun sign. The void of course period may only last a few minutes, in which case it is not a problem. But sometimes it can last for hours or in the most extreme case (which is not that often, fortunately) up to two days, depending on the positions of the planets. But it all means that your idea will not go well or cost cutting is in the air and right now everyone is jittery. In this case, next week or the one after that might be a better time to present your idea, after the dust has settled.

The bonus of using a pendulum to ask yourself questions is that as you develop and modify your questions, you build up a picture of the background to your issue and may, on an unconscious level, spot not only obstacles but also unexplored opportunities. This is how you build up the intuitive aspect of asking questions with your pendulum and making the right decisions.

Using a Flowchart for Personal Work Decisions

If you know that a matter you're concerned about is not straightforward, you can set up a simple flowchart diagram to record your pendulum's answers and keep track of the way a decision develops. A flowchart is a good way to keep track of your intuitive thinking and to guide you to your next question.

When you phrase your question it will elicit one of three alternative possible responses: a Yes response, which perhaps needs expanding; an Ask Again response, which indicates your question is off track and needs reformulating; or a No response, which indicates that in your next question you need to ask why the response was negative.

A group of people can also use the flowchart method to

explore a joint project or issue. Read through the instructions below for creating a flowchart, and then I will walk you step by step through a sample flowchart reading.

To set up a flowchart reading:

1. Choose a time when you are not in a hurry and will not be interrupted. Create a flowchart with three columns, labeling the first column "Yes," the second column "Ask Again," and the third column "No."

2. Ask a question that you have already formulated. Write the question at the top of your flowchart, then blot out conscious thought and wait for the pendulum to speak in its own time.

3. If the pendulum tells you to Ask Again, write a new question in the central, Ask Again, column of the flowchart. If the pendulum's response was Yes, write your next follow-up question in the appropriate box in the Yes column. If the response was No, enter your next question in the No column (see page 22).

4. Let the second question come to you spontaneously. You may find that the direction your question takes starts changing or brings a seemingly unrelated issue to the fore, especially if the pendulum's previous answer was Ask Again.

5. Continue until you have five or six questions and answers or even more if it is a very complex reading.

6. Alternatively, you can list your questions and write the responses next to them in a single column.

Before you try drawing your own flowchart and working with your own questions, read through the following example to see how Hilary's questions led on naturally from one to the next.

Sample Reading

Hilary is in her late forties and lives in London. Her grandmother has left her enough money to pay off her home and to have a small income for the next few years.

She is divorced and her only son, Joe, who is in his twenties, is in a serious relationship and is moving to Canada to live with his new partner, Tricia. Hilary has not met Tricia but disapproves of her because she is nearly ten years older than Joe and has a child.

Hilary has taken courses in aromatherapy and reflexology and treats a few patients at home while working at her full-time post in a bank. She also has a small website selling oils. Should Hilary use her inheritance to quit the job she hates and go self-employed? That was her first question and, though both matters were linked, it was a dual question, and the pendulum wanted her to reformulate and be more specific.

Question 1: Is this a good time to quit the job I hate and go self-employed?
Answer: Ask Again.

YES	ASK AGAIN	NO
	Question 2: Should I quit the bank job? [Answer: Yes.]	
Question 3: Should I set up in full-time self-employment in alternative therapy now? [Answer: No.]		
		Question 4: Should I buy suitable premises first? [Answer: No.]
		Question 5: Should I work at a therapy center for a while to see whether I am really suited for full-time therapy work? [Answer: Yes.]

YES	ASK AGAIN	NO

Question 6: Would it be wise to take further training myself at the therapy center so I am fully qualified and registered? [Answer: Yes.]

Question 7: Should I give some of the money to Joe, though I do not approve of his partner? [Answer: Ask Again.]

Question 8: Should I meet Joe's partner and her young son when they come to London this month?

Understanding the Chart

Question 1: "Is this a good time to quit the job I hate and go self-employed?" resulted in an Ask Again response because, of course, you can only ask an either/or question. This one included two separate questions: was this a good time to quit her job, and was this a good time for her to go self-employed?

So Hilary wrote her next question, Question 2: "Should I quit the bank job?" in her Ask Again column. The answer to this question was Yes, so she wrote her subsequent question in the Yes column. Question 3: "Should I set up in full-time self-employment in alternative therapy now?" caused a strong No response, maybe because Hilary had not really explored the practical indications of changing overnight from a bank career to one so very different. Question 4: "Should I buy suitable premises first?" gave another No response. The next question, written in the No column, was Question 5:

"Should I work at a therapy center for a while to see whether I am really suited for full-time therapy work?" That and the following question, Question 6: "Would it be wise to take further training myself at the therapy center so I am fully qualified and registered?" both received Yes answers.

Then Hilary decided to change tack at the instigation of her intuition, which was formulating the questions. It might seem strange to mix business and personal decisions, but we are not just work machines; we have joys and sorrows, hopes and fears connected with our lovers, homes, family, and friends. If one aspect of our life is wrong, it is hard to shut away those feelings during work hours.

Question 7: "Should I give some of the money to Joe, though I do not approve of his partner?" elicited an Ask Again response because Hilary's wise intuition knew there was more to this issue and told her to think again. So her final question, Question 8: "Should I meet Joe's partner and her young son when they come to London this month?" was entered in the Ask Again column. Since this was the end of the recording session and the final piece in the jigsaw, Hilary's answer was not recorded, but it was a very definite Yes.

Until Hilary resolves the unhappy relations with her son and at least meets his new partner, she will find it hard to settle into work where spirituality is the cornerstone.

The pendulum also alerted Hilary to her own deep awareness that just giving up her bank position and launching into a full-time alternative therapy career was a recipe for disaster.

Hilary was offered a position working part-time at the local therapy center where she took her courses, with the chance to complete the diploma that would enable her to register with an accredited organization. This would allow Hilary to manage financially and discover whether she really did want to work full-time in her chosen field or whether it was just an escape from a job she hated.

Joint Flowchart Readings

Creating a joint pendulum flowchart is a good exercise for a work group, especially when a new person joins a team. The gentle rhythm of creating the chart will help people work together, particularly if one or two coworkers are always dominant or impatient for decisions. Designate one person to act as the scribe. This method will work effectively for up to six people.

To create a joint pendulum flowchart:

1. First, establish everyone's individual Yes, No, and Ask Again pendulum responses using the method described previously.

2. Next, determine the specific area under discussion. The person designated to go first asks a related question and holds the pendulum to answer the question. Everyone discusses the answer's implications before a second person is handed the pendulum to pose the next question.

3. This second response is analyzed, and then the pendulum is handed on to the third person, who formulates the next question, and so on.

4. Continue until everyone has had a turn or until the matter is resolved.

Once you finish the flowchart reading, it is important that you keep track of the decision reached so you can monitor your progress.

Dowsing for Decisions

One of the most common uses of a pendulum is dowsing to find underground water, buried treasure, archaeological artifacts, or minerals within the ground. The pendulum will often indicate a precise location by vibrating and pulling downward, as if tugged by gravity. Wooden and metal dowsing rods have similar reactions.

The same response occurs if you hold your pendulum over a series of options you have written, either within squares on a grid—normally a three-by-three square grid—or in a circle divided into segments. This is a very effective method if you have a series of options and need to choose one or two.

It might be names of people with whom you have the option of working or to whom you might delegate a particular task. It might be a choice of products or suppliers, possible outlets for what you produce, or a series of options about possible actions to take or which accounts or projects will be most profitable to pursue if your resources and time are limited.

The dowsing method works like answering questions by psychokinesis. Your hand responds to the energies of the right decision, and the pendulum reflects and amplifies this knowledge of the best choice, which comes from deep within you.

If you are inexperienced or uncertain about pendulum work, this method never fails. It may even establish the psychic connection that will help you to use the pendulum for answering questions more directly, since the pendulum will suddenly seem unmistakably heavy.

Pendulum Dowsing Using a Grid or a Circle

It is possible to refine pendulum use by incorporating a grid or circle, over which the pendulum can move and determine answers to questions that you have written into the grid or circle sectors.

To dowse using a grid or circle:

1. To use a grid, draw nine squares, three by three, on a sheet of paper in black ink. For the question you are asking, decide what your various options are and arrange them on the grid in any way that feels right. Blank out any squares that are unused with ink.

2. To use a circle, draw a circle and divide it into four, eight, ten, or twelve segments, according to the approxi-

mate number of options you have for your particular question. Again, blank out any unused segments.

3. Hold the pendulum three or four inches above the paper on which you have drawn your grid or circle. Allowing your mind to go blank, pass your pendulum over each area in turn. If using a grid, begin in the bottom left square and move from left to right in a continuous movement over each option. Then travel right to left over row two and finally left to right over row three. If using a circle, proceed from the 12 o'clock segment clockwise.

4. You may feel instantly a definite downward pull, as if by gravity, over one option, but see whether the pendulum will continue. If it does not, you have arrived at your answer. The pendulum may hover over two or three squares, as if uncertain. There may be more than one option to your question, and you may end up combining or reconciling two courses.

5. If your first pass over the chart produces no definite choice, move backward slowly from top right over the three rows of your grid, or counterclockwise over your circle, and the pendulum should respond by feeling heavy over one option.

If you have moved right through this process and felt no vibrations, then there may be an option you have not considered or it may just not be the right time for decision making on this issue. Either try another method (see chapters 7 and 8) or wait until the next day.

Sample Pendulum Drawing Using a Grid

Skeptics say that, when dowsing, of course you will "choose" whichever option you most want. That is rarely, if ever, the case. Let me explain how I ignored the pendulum and lost out financially.

A television journalist, Monica, came to see me about the possibility of my demonstrating dowsing for decisions about health on a midmorning television spirituality show. I decided to illustrate the general technique with an example from my own life. I drew my grid with nine squares, filling in three with options and blanking out the rest.

The week before Monica's visit, I had been offered a lecture tour by a New Age promotions company. Annabel, the organizer, had mailed me a list of various well-known authors and clairvoyants she represented, and I was very flattered to be included. On the show, I would use the dowsing method to decide whether or not to accept the lecture tour offer.

So the three options I drew on my grid were:

Accept all the lectures on offer.		
	Take one date and see how it goes.	
		Leave well enough alone.

To my surprise the pendulum pulled downward and felt heavy over "Leave well enough alone." But ego won the day. In spite of telling Monica that the pendulum had pulled down over the "Leave well enough alone" option, I ignored the pendulum's advice and committed to the whole lecture tour.

The first lecture went well, and payment arrived in the post not too long afterward. The second lecture was less organized, and payment came rather late. At the third event, Annabel was a little worse for alcohol, and the fee remained unpaid. Shortly afterward Annabel's business closed. I later discovered that other lecturers had been trying to sue Annabel for some months for unpaid fees. I was very lucky to escape with one unpaid weekend, but very unwise not to listen to my pendulum.

Speculation Using a Time/Intensity Chart

We all know those times when we are asked to make an assessment, whether of the time necessary to complete a task, the true monetary cost of time spent carrying out a project, or what the financial returns or number of products sold are likely to be. You may have done all the necessary mathematical calculations and studied tables of probabilities and risks until your eyes misted over and yet you are still uncertain. This is where the great businessperson, using a hunch, will pluck figures out of the air that invariably are spot on.

You may not have reached that stage of trusting your intuition, but it can be invaluable to be able to name a realistic figure, whether you are balancing the books of a school budget, or assessing as I do the realistic time needed to complete a book, building in unknown variables such as family crises, crashing computers, and cancelled interviews. Or you may want to calculate traveling time with a truckload of urgent supplies, given the vagaries of traffic, weather, and industrial action at some continental ports.

The basic reason for charting this type of information is to help you identify both opportune periods of time and the relative importance of an appropriate action. It sounds complicated, but it is really just a series of ascending numbers that can relate both to a period of time—days, weeks, months, and so on—or a degree of necessity—how important it is for you to know the result—on a scale of 1 to 10 or 1 to 12. To use a time/intensity chart:

1. Draw a large circle on a sheet of paper and divide it into either ten or twelve segments. The circle's divisions will vary according to the question you are asking. If your question can be answered in terms of the number of months until something will occur, your circle should have twelve divisions, one for each month of the year. If your question can be answered in terms of monetary figures or on a scale of importance, your circle should have ten divisions.

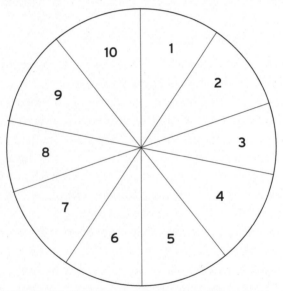

It may be self-evident from the question whether you are dealing in hundreds, thousands, or millions of dollars. But if in doubt, use the ordinary pendulum questioning method; for example, Will the answer be in hundreds of dollars? If the pendulum indicates No, ask next whether it will be in thousand of dollars, increasing the unit of measurement until you get a Yes response. If the parameters are larger than you anticipated, you may have hit upon a winner or have a substantial debt.

2. Clear your mind and ask the question you would like answered.

3. Pass the pendulum clockwise over the numbers in turn slowly, until the pendulum pulls down over one number. If the pendulum pulls down over two numbers, it may be giving you either a price range or an approximate time scale if there are a lot of variables or other people involved in the project.

4. If there is no response the first time, repeat the question a second time; normally this method will work fairly quickly.

5. If there is still no response, look through your more logically created facts and figures to see if there are any potentially unconsidered snags that might make a fixed time scale or budget impossible to estimate.

Dowsing in Practice

You might start with questions that have a lot of considerations, which may be in the back of your mind and can't be settled with a simple yes or no. For example, appropriate dowsing questions I have encountered in the workplace are:

- "Should I apply for promotion?" This will lead into asking when would be a good time and how to ask or maybe whether there are other options, such as moving to another firm.

- "Should I report petty pilfering that is going on in my department?" You might have to ask whether you should tackle the thief, tell the boss, tell a colleague, or maybe secure your own property and let matters take their course if you suspect Security may be on to the thief. You might also consider in what areas the firm seems to condone dishonesty while cracking down on others.

- "Should I write a novel?" "Should it be for pleasure, in the evenings toward eventual publication, give up my day job and work part-time? etc, etc?"

Working with a pendulum can help you increase your ability to make decisions based on your intuition. After having formulated your original question, allow your intuition to guide you through your follow-up questions; they may surprise your conscious mind. You are the clerk; write down and organize your pendulum's responses. The method may look complicated on paper, but in practice it is easy and very effective for those tangled issues where we may be denying the strength of our feelings or ignoring our wise inner voice.

In the next chapter we will work on ways to create an oasis of inner calm so you can become aware of your unconscious wisdom and intuitive powers and remain serene even in the most fraught situations. The grounding, centering, and stilling technique is especially useful in preparing you for the pendulum work already described in this chapter.

CHAPTER 2

Creating an Oasis of Calm: Relaxation Techniques

Some offices (including several well-known media offices I have visited) resemble the parrot house at the zoo, with people chattering, screeching into the phone, flapping from crisis to crisis, and repeating ceaseless high-powered jargon for the pleasure of hearing their own voices. Uproar may give the impression of fruitful activity, but the impetus for decisive action becomes dissipated and diluted.

In contrast, the hawk, who has given its name to powerful business people as well as more warlike elements in government administration, hovers silently over land, sometimes for hours, before swooping swiftly and decisively in response to the smallest movement in the grass far below.

Watch televised images of people at the stock exchange. Almost everyone is leaping up and down, waving their hands, or making megaphone-like calls. But there will be one or two who are motionless most of the time, their fingers poised over the computer send button or the number for speed dial. When they wave, it is for bids that make large sums of money instantly or to offload a sinking ship in an eyeblink. Though they are not joining in the conventional mayhem, their pay is usually the highest in the room.

A calm workplace is equally vital to the self-employed man or woman working from home with a thousand and one distractions: vacuum salespeople, callers from organizations who want to save your soul or cut your electricity charges, neighbors who pop over for coffee and free counseling because "I knew you wouldn't be doing anything," and family members needing their teeth fixed, their laundry collected, and a ride home because it is raining. You may see yourself as a hovering hawk or as the gentler dove, sky dancing harmoniously in collective flight as part of a flock or sitting tranquilly alone, observant and ready to take to the air when danger strikes. Whichever of these images is appropriate, developing both inner and outer stillness is the key to clear, concentrated thought and focused action. Furthermore, not only is stillness, ultimately, the way to create an efficient and harmonious workplace, it is vital for the success of all the techniques described in this book.

Relaxation Techniques for Busy People

Relaxation is easy if you have the time to float in a warm tub filled with oils or to sit cross-legged on soft cushions with equally serene-faced devotees in an incense-filled room, listening to the sounds of a rainforest CD.

Of course if you work from home or in a setting with like-minded people and liberal smoke alarms, you can burn incense or oil and play dolphin or ocean sounds, maybe as part of a regular pre-work session while the phones are switched to silent. When I worked as a teacher, I always started the day with a quiet session. The kids in the inner-city schools, who were constantly surrounded by noise and traffic pollution (one playground overlooked the main traffic route to London Airport), became more able to concentrate and less hyperactive.

Let's imagine a less idealized, more hyped-up setting than an early morning meditation session as everyone tumbles in from the subway, eating bagels while shedding coats and performing acrobatics to get to their phones before they stop ringing. The real test is staying relaxed as others panic, phones scream, faxes clatter, and the "You have urgent mail" light on your computer blinks excitedly enough to serve as an entire city's Christmas decorations. If you stay calm, you not only fix everything in half the time, but those around you also ease up.

The principle behind relaxation is to deliberately tense your muscles in turn and then relax them. This method also works wonders before an important meeting. You can relax at your desk, sitting in an airport departure lounge when there is a delay, or in a cab in traffic snarl ups. Relaxation techniques are especially effective if you can work outdoors; for example, you can take a short break in the local park or at a workplace green area.

Even if you have a queue of people waiting to be served or have their queries answered, if you feel yourself getting overheated or panicky, use a prearranged signal with a colleague to have them take over for two or three minutes while you sort some papers and yourself. In an emergency go to the bathroom for a few minutes of peace, running the cold tap for background ambience while you splash cool water on your pulse points and breathe easy.

There are a vast number of relaxation techniques available that can be learned relatively easily. If you practice yoga, Ta'i Chi, Zen meditation, or Reiki, for example, you already have your own way of relaxing and breathing. If not, I have taught the following method to people who are tense from their day at work but who have no knowledge or background in alternative therapy.

To relax using a simple breathing technique:

1. Stop whatever is making you tense, and in your mind picture your body's outline etched in light, marking your space and separating you from the source of your tension. Breathe in very gently and slowly through your nose and out again so one breath follows another in an unbroken stream. As you do so, picture two beautiful butterflies, one resting on each foot.

2. Hold your feet as still as you can as you gently inhale, and then as you relax and exhale, imagine the butterflies slowly moving upward.

3. Keep up the breathing rhythm as you see the butterflies land on your knees. As you inhale, hold your knees motionless so as not to disturb the butterflies. Then exhale gently and slowly as they move off into the air again.

4. Continue as the butterflies land together on your navel, then separately on your hands, separately on each breast, together on your throat, separately on each shoulder, together at the top of your spine, and finally together on the crown of your head.

5. Maintain the gentle breathing pattern, and visualize the butterflies moving down again, stage by stage, to your feet and then finally flying off, leaving you totally relaxed.

6. If you are leading a group, you can describe the path of the imaginary butterflies. You can also substitute dragon-flies, beautiful brown moths, tiny angels, fairies, bubbles, or feathers for the butterflies. You can even draw a body outline on your computer and, working with just one visualized butterfly, move the cursor slowly up and down the drawing of a body while breathing gently.

The butterfly technique is quick and effective, but if you can't spare even the two minutes for this method, here are some other methods to try.

Breathing Techniques

Work on establishing a regular breathing routine. A few slow deep breaths are good before you confront someone who has been negative toward you or who has unfairly criticized you, or before you launch into a verbal or written complaint or attack, however justifiable the cause. Breathing exercises can also be helpful before an interview, if you have to address a group, before what you know will be a difficult phone call or meeting, or before dealing with the general public in any way. These techniques are also good if you are feeling intimidated or cold-shouldered by someone at work but know a complaint would be counterproductive in stopping their pettiness.

I always practice breath control before I talk in a bookstore or at a festival or go on air on the radio or television, knowing I have only a few minutes to make a good impression. In any studio, especially before a live broadcast, everyone gets very tense and rushes around like headless chickens.

I also use breathing techniques if someone has been dismissive or critical, which really upsets me even after fifteen years of writing, so I can avoid showing that I am rattled.

There are many ways you can practice breath control, but the best technique is the one that suits you and fits into your life.

Establishing a gentle slow rhythm of in and out breaths may be a better choice for you than worrying about counting breaths or getting a more complex technique exactly correct. I still get blown off course by self-styled experts who describe a technique in incredibly obscure technical language and express surprise when I do not use it. Again, if you are studying body energies or martial arts, your own tradition will have its suggested methods.

To do a breathing exercise:

1. Straighten your spine, relax your body, and tilt your chin slightly downward.

2. Breathe deeply and slowly from your diaphragm, just above your navel. This prevents the shallow breathing that can cause hyperventilation and panic attacks if stress increases. When you breathe slowly and deeply, anxiety and stress automatically will subside. You can breathe in this way without panting or lifting your shoulders up and down, so no one except you will be aware of what you are doing.

3. Hold your hands in one of the following recommended positions: palms downward on your thighs or knees, hands resting on your lap palms up, or hands cupped one on top of the other with your power hand (the hand you write with) underneath. You may be able to adapt these to breathing sessions at your desk, but they will

not be as vital. However, a full lotus position or lying flat on your office floor at moments of stress may alarm more traditional colleagues and employers.

4. Breathe in through your nose, counting in your mind "one and two and three and four."

5. Now hold the breath, this time counting in your mind "one and two."

6. Then breathe out through your nose as "one and two and three and four."

7. Pause for "one and two" before repeating the cycle.

Repeat this cycle up to ten times, slowing the count even more if you wish.

Pranic Breathing

Prana is the Sanskrit word for the "life force." In pranic breathing you inhale this vital essence from natural sources, such as the earth, the air, the sun, flowers, trees, and crystals. Pranic breathing is very helpful if you work where there is no fresh air coming in through windows, only air conditioning, if the nature of the work generates a lot of tension, or at times when there are urgent deadlines. Prana can be absorbed most readily and easily through natural fragrance; therefore, this is the relaxation aspect I am concentrating on in this chapter.

Indoors or out, fragrant plants can fill us with calm and gentle optimism. The ancient Egyptians believed that the spirit or essence of a plant contained magical healing powers given to them by the deities. This spirit was transferred into fragrance that, when absorbed by mortals, increased their personal perfection. Pranic calm can be stored in advance. It is absorbed quite spontaneously when we work in the garden or go to the forest or shore. Five minutes in the local park, city square, or any other green space will, even on a chill and damp winter day, top up that power, connecting you with what the medieval German mystic Hildegard von Bingen called "the Greening Principle."

In appendix III, I have suggested plants that can bring calm and gentle confidence to a workplace. Here I am focusing on your personal store of prana, which you can keep in your workspace. You can replace or supplement conventional, unscented office greenery with fragrance, especially from herbs and flowers that grow in your local region.

To practice pranic breathing:

1. Focus on a scented plant or herb. Inhale slowly through your nose, drawing in breath to fill your lower abdomen, continuing to breathe until your diaphragm and chest are full of pranic breath. (You can also work with an aromatic fruit such as an orange, lemon, or lime by piercing its skin to release the citrus smell.) You may visualize this breath as golden or pure light or the color of the flowers or herbs you are using as a focus.

2. Exhale any fear, worry, or tension slowly as a sigh (silently if necessary in your surroundings) through your mouth. You may see this exhalation as a dark mist.

3. Aim to establish a regular slow rhythm of breathing without focusing on counting. If you prefer, use the Far Eastern method of inhaling through your mouth and exhaling through your nose, though I learned the nose/mouth pattern in acting classes.

4. If you are in a long meeting, see if you can place flowers or a bowl of fruit in the center of the table for quick pranic top ups.

The fragrances you use in conjunction with pranic breathing need not be anything expensive or rare. Try the following for your own pranic breathing practice:

- Miniature roses, flowering lilies, hyacinths, lilac, pots of lavender, lemon balm, lemon verbena, and sage all induce harmony without sending the pranic breather to sleep.

- Tiny indoor bay laurel trees and orange trees in blossom or any fragrant flower in season, preferably still growing in a pot, will fill you with pranic tranquility even when you do not have time for organized breath work.

- Essential oils can also restore harmony. For focused breathing, add a couple of drops of oil to a cup of warm water and place it on your desk or workbench. Orange, neroli, or lemon verbena are especially good for creating an atmosphere of quiet optimism and, as a bonus, they silence passing grumblers. For background tranquility, if you sit near a radiator you can balance your saucer of oil in water on top of the radiator or soak a cotton wool ball with the oil and put it on the radiator.

Pranic breathing can be a truly calming and fragrant relaxation technique that can be performed easily in the workplace, providing an excellent effect and considerable benefit.

Crystal Calm

Crystals have been used to transmit harmony and balance through the ages. Because they have been formed within the earth over millennia, they are a very stable form of energy and a balanced source of the life force. If you see an aura photograph (taken by a special technique called Kirlian photography) of the psychic energy field around a crystal, you will find that a crystal emits moving colored lights just as people or animals do. You can draw on the calming properties of crystals when you are stressed by holding a crystal, having it on your desk, or drinking water in which a crystal has been soaked. A number of healers and crystal researchers have discovered some kinds of crystals to be more calming than others, and I have listed them at the end of this section.

For the workplace, crystals are a very portable source of harmony and one that will keep working in the background while you are working. What is more, since they are so beautiful they will not attract adverse comments from skeptical colleagues; they are ornamental as well as calming.

In appendix I, I describe crystals you can use in your work space to protect you both from human hostility and from the psychic and psychological pollution of technological noise and equipment. In chapter 11, I describe how you can empower crystals to attract good fortune and success into your life.

Often the same crystals can be used both to create an atmosphere of tranquility and as a focus for pranic breathing. This is done by holding the crystal between your hands and visualizing its color as colored light entering your body. When using the crystal to instill tranquility, however, if your crystal has absorbed fear or negativity and left you feeling serene, you need to wash the crystal under running water or bury it for a while beneath a living plant to restore its energies. You can do the same with your crystal pendulum when it has done a lot of work.

You do not need a large or expensive crystal. A small dish of crystals in your work space emits the same power as more costly polished specimens (see appendix IV for color meanings so you can also use your crystals to balance bodily and psychic energies). Crystal energies are transmitted quite spontaneously whether you touch the crystals or not because the psychic energy field is wide and very open, even in a small crystal. Over the days and weeks they lower not only your stress levels, but those of the people around you. Indeed you will find colleagues quite naturally drawn to touch or pick up your crystals while they are talking, and they will become visibly more tranquil and happy. They are picking up the energies through their fingertips by a process known as *psychometry*, or psychic touch, which is an extension of physical touch.

We have small psychic energy centers in our hands called *chakras*, and these enable a crystal's power to be absorbed rapidly. Drinking water in which crystals have been soaked is calming, though it has not been verified scientifically. It would seem that we pick up the essential power of a crystal rather than any physical property in it. But as with many spiritual matters, the effects prove the effectiveness, such as when you notice that someone for whom you have made a cup of coffee with blue lace agate water is much kinder in their words and less critical.

The following crystals will restore harmony to the most hectic lifestyle or stressed individual:

Purple amethyst

Dark gray apache tear (transparent obsidian)

Calcite in all colors

Blue celestite (the angel stone)

Blue lace agate

Green or purple fluorite

Green jade

Creamy or blue moonstone

Pink manganocalcite

Pink rose quartz

Golden brown rutilated quartz

Gray-brown smoky quartz

Grounding, Centering, and Stilling

Another technique for avoiding stress or being drawn into panic or conflict is the triple technique of grounding, centering, and stilling the mind.

Grounding is a method of settling ourselves when there is a lot of stress or chaos or a deadline that makes us panic so we cannot think. It is like the grounding wire on an electrical plug, connecting us with common sense and perspective. It also will slow us down if we start running around like a scalded cat.

Centering is a technique that focuses your mind on the most important matter at hand and detaches you from the distractions of other people or tasks that are claiming your attention. It also stops free-floating anxiety.

Finally, stilling the mind will take you a step further. When your conscious mind is focused, it will lead you inward so you feel quiet and calm. At this stage you may receive the added input from your wise inner voice and the signals picked up by your unconscious radar that are not accessible to the conscious mind.

You can use all three methods in succession or separately, according to the situation and the kind of input you need. So how might this all work on a day-to-day basis? Well, when you first arrive at work, the method can be adopted to separate you from the journey to work and any lingering concerns you have about unfinished chores and free-floating anxieties from home, such as whether you put your child's comfort blanket toy in the day care bag or whether the florist remembered not to put red flowers in your mother's birthday bouquet (she hates red flowers). The world will tell you soon enough if you got it wrong, usually as a reproachful text message when you've almost added up the longest column of figures in the world.

It is worthwhile getting to work early so you can have five or ten minutes either outdoors or in your workplace while it is still quiet. Switch off your cell phone (the world will still turn) and leave your work phone on divert or silent.

Grounding, centering, and stilling can also help midday— especially if like me you work alone at home—helping to distance yourself from irrelevant interruptions or to push away the morning's frustrations that niggled away your whole lunch break (if you got one).

You should repeat the exercise when you get home, leaving work worries, if not work, at your front door.

The grounding, centering, and stilling technique can be a good prelude to the type of pendulum work described in chapter 1 and indeed any time you need to contact your inner voice.

Grounding: Rooting Ideas in Reality

Grounding will drive away the anxiety that fills our minds with unnecessary clutter and rarely provides solutions to problems that might not flare up anyway.

You can use grounding to ensure that you are connected to the real world with its often necessary reality constraints. It will help you set targets for yourself and others that can be achieved and put into action ideas that will translate into actuality within the scope of budgets, time, and resources.

If at all possible, do your grounding work on grass, earth, or even a child's sandbox in the park. If you are indoors, remove your shoes so you make contact with the earth, however many floors below it may be. Leaning against a tree or even a sturdy green plant makes the earth connection more powerful.

To ground yourself:

1. Stand with your hands hanging loosely by your sides, fingers pointing downward, with your legs slightly apart. Straighten your back, relax your muscles, and lower your chin slightly.

2. Slowly raise your hands above your head while breathing in through your nose to a count of four, "one and two and three and four."

3. Then with your fingers extended upward and your arms in a curved position aiming inward, imitating the shape of a tree, hold the position and breathe for a count of two, "one and two."

4. Slowly lower your arms downward toward the earth while breathing out for a count of four, so when you reach four your arms are by your sides with the fingers pointing down toward the earth again. Exhale through your nose or mouth as you prefer.

5. Rest for a count of two, then repeat the cycle for a second and possibly third time or even more, pressing your feet hard down on the ground as you exhale.

6. On your final out breath, picture your worries pouring out through your feet and your fingers, letting them flow into the soil to be recycled into positivity.

You can use the grounding technique on its own, or you can modify it for sitting at a desk or workbench. For example, if you are in a hurry and feel you can't settle down to breathe, sit on a chair, raise your arms as though stretching, then lower your arms and press down on the chair as hard as you can with your hands and perineum (seat) and try to push through the floor with your feet. Repeat this two or three times, picturing negativity flowing downward from you and out through the floor. Don't worry, your negative energy won't land on the people working on the floor below; Mother Earth has effective filters. This is a good tactic if you have to go and see someone or take a call, and you know there may be a confrontation or you might receive misdirected anger. If you are actually on the phone or talking to someone and that person is being unfair or unnecessarily sarcastic, obviously you can't start waving your arms about like a windmill. Press gently but firmly with your free hand and perineum on your chair, press your feet on the ground, and allow any anger or angst to flow downward into the earth, leaving your psychic and mental field clear.

Centering: Finding Your Focus

My down-to-earth mother used to accuse me of having a flea brain as my thoughts and conversation flitted from one topic to another. But then I had not learned centering.

Centering is the logical progression that follows on from grounding and enables you to focus on the matter at hand, which is an excellent aid if you need to prioritize or if people are constantly interfering and making conflicting demands. Like grounding, centering brings quiet to your inner space so you can hear your inner voice or get accurate pendulum readings.

Centering can also be used separately from grounding. It automatically filters out irrelevancies from conversations, memos, emails, and so on so you can see as though highlighted with marker pen the main argument or crucial fact that someone has possibly buried beneath a load of business speak in the hope that no one will notice.

To develop this faculty, follow up your morning and midday grounding with this exercise. In practice, the last stages of grounding and the first stages of centering flow into one. As with grounding, if possible stand on soil, sand, or grass to make a direct connection with the earth. If this isn't possible, at least remove your shoes.

To center yourself:

1. Hold your arms by your side and point your fingers downward.
2. Picture all the energies that are not yours (for example, the pressures of others, work demands that have to wait while you fix more urgent needs, smoke screens, and sales hype) leaving your body, flowing downward and

out through your fingers into the earth where they will be absorbed.

3. Create an arch of imaginary light all round you with your hands, fingertips extended, stooping down to include your feet. (You can visualize this if you are in a confined space or situation.) All your real priorities and concerns are within this enclosed area of light. If any of those free-floating anxieties you grounded pop back up, they are now outside your immediate circle of awareness.

Alternatively, you can move your arms together in opposing directions like a crystal windmill (this takes a bit of practice) whose sails catch the sunlight (again visualize if necessary). Centering is gently energizing as well as calming. If a new stressful priority turns up, your automatic radar will alert you on your inner screen that you have urgent new mail.

If you find centering difficult or you need some quick immediate centering because everyone is yelling at you or piling work on you, inhale slowly and say *center* or *focus* silently on your in breath, extending every syllable, and then exhale the word again (silently if you are not alone), pausing on every syllable. Repeat this ten times, and you will be centered. Centering can be a good technique when you get home. Contrary to popular opinion, the most successful entrepreneurs do not focus on work 24/7 and by switching off the internal work machine, you will be relaxed and eager for the next day.

Stilling the Mind

You now have two strong barriers against chaos in place, but you can add a third to ensure that whatever the crisis or deadline you stay cool. Stilling the mind can also be used alone just before a pendulum reading or divination, when you are receiving conflicting opinions, or in a meeting where there is lots of cross talk and numerous undercurrents.

Perhaps the most useful technique to add to your psychic/psychological armory, stilling enables you to switch from your everyday mode to a higher state of consciousness so you can pick up information not available to the conscious mind and make intuitive leaps from A to Z without going through the intervening stages. Stilling allows original creative thoughts to emerge if a discussion is going around and around the same trackways and getting nowhere fast.

You can also use stilling to shield yourself from being affected by the mood swings and tantrums of drama kings and queens or from being blown off course by less than subtle pressure. I find it useful if a domestic crisis of a member of my often angst-ridden family suddenly bursts into my workspace, demanding I mediate, negotiate, or fix it *now!*

I often still my mind to prevent draining my energy during a particularly stressful or delayed journey. I know if I arrive at a lecture after agonizing for hours over a grounded or cancelled plane, I will feel like last week's wet dishrag, and the plane won't come any faster for my fretting.

On the other hand, when action is needed and everyone is telling you it's not their problem, a still mind is the perfect launching pad for a focused, calm but assertive counterdemand that the perpetrators sort their own backyard. This is far more effective than yelling, bursting into tears, or, like I do, backing down sulkily as I hear my mom's voice in my head telling me that nice girls never make a fuss.

Sit or stand, preferably in natural sunlight or, if not, where a pool of artificial light such as from a lamp falls on you. If you work at home, you can use candlelight. If you are in a dingy place, picture yourself in a pool of sunlight or moonlight or in the middle of a rainbow.

To still yourself:

1. Do nothing except listen to your breathing; do not try to control, count, or change its rhythm. If you have erected mental or protective boundaries around your self, now is the time to push them away, so you are not aware of anything except the gentle flow of light and a sense of floating on a sea of gentle energy waves, just being, not thinking, reacting, or even feeling. Alternatively, imagine yourself floating on the backs of cotton wool clouds you see from an aircraft window.

2. If thoughts intrude, gently push them away as though launching a toy boat on a pond; watch them sail off.

3. Visualize your problems tied to a helium balloon and floating away, or set them on a fluffy cloud and blow it away with the lightest of breaths.

4. Then picture a sky full of stars and watch them go out one by one until you are enclosed within a velvety blackness. Or imagine pouring a jug of clear water into a stream drop by drop until it is gone and there is only the rhythm of the stream. Or picture yourself on an empty train that slows down and suddenly stops in the middle of the countryside, and gradually all sound and motion ceases.

Of the various techniques I have described in this chapter, one or two will become your favorites. As you use them, an oasis of calm will develop around you and your work space. That is just about you; but in most working situations, you are also part of a team. This brings with it other considerations, of course.

Getting to Know Your Fellow Workers

Team-building exercises are sometimes planned at vast expense by organizations eager to help workers really get to know their colleagues and to encourage coworkers to operate as an effective team. Groups of unwilling men and women are forced on a precious free weekend into eyeball-to-eyeball competition with one another in six feet of mud and slime, puffing and groaning through activities better suited to an Arnold Schwarzenegger movie, supervised by a misogynist ex-marine whose attitude problem probably earned him an early discharge. Dirty, wet, and cold, you return to work on Monday morning vowing life-long revenge on the computer analyst who dropped you into an alligator-infested pond when the rope bridge he had insisted only he could lash together disintegrated beneath your feet. As for your opposing team, can you ever again share ideas with the woman who smirked when you collapsed on a log, revealing a split wider than the Grand Canyon in the back of your combat shorts, too late realizing that the decaying wood was hosting the 2003 Ant Olympics?

Wouldn't you have preferred a weekend spent with work colleagues walking quietly through the forest or on the shore, just being together? There you could allow the frantic activity of daily interactions to fade into companionable silence and enjoy a chance to talk heart to heart.

Maybe you can suggest informal trips, like the old-fashioned work outings for occasional weekend days or even overnight camping trips on a long weekend. Inviting families, not just for the obligatory often-fraught Christmas party, but for social events, can help you to see the people you work with more sympathetically. It also enables newcomers at a company to make friends. You can even have one or two days a year when younger family members are invited to try Mom's or an older brother's job under supervision and see how their firm operates. This scheme has been very successful where I live, not least improving workplace interactions.

Other people will be positively affected by your new air of tranquility. Their voices will become softer, and even the most hyperactive roadrunner will slow down and start listening. Your work output will actually increase as a result of your ability to focus amid distraction and to speak calmly and rationally when tempers get overheated and constructive debate turns into hand-to-hand fighting. You may become drawn into more formal mediation and your opinions taken far more seriously because when you do speak, your words are measured, focused on the current topic, and not biased by emotional appeals or critical observations that make people feel bad about themselves and rarely work tactically.

You will also be able to distinguish between opinion and fact and to add your increasing intuitive awareness to your more conventionally acquired skills.

In the next chapter we will explore the art of reading people on a level even deeper and more subtle than body language.

CHAPTER 3

Reading the Signs: Recognizing the Aura

He's in a black mood today. She was green with envy. I was so angry I saw red. I'm feeling blue. She is such a gray person. These common expressions demonstrate how we perceive moods and more permanent character traits in terms of colors.

What such judgments are actually unconsciously detecting are the colored bands of energy that are around a person, which are especially prominent when an individual is experiencing strong emotion. These psychic energy, or aura, signals cannot be masked easily and so are a far more accurate tool in reading people than the nonverbal body language signs that we can more readily modify.

Imagine how useful it would be if you could gauge your boss's mood as she was walking across the car park. You would know that this morning was not the best occasion to ask for a raise in salary or a long weekend to visit your sick grandma or stay with your new lover. By lunchtime a sunnier hue might have emerged.

When meeting a new client you can tell instantly whether a hard statistics sell, an empathic "How is your ma?" approach, or a one-day-only bargain offer is the best approach. So too when interviewing a candidate for a position or meeting new colleagues, you could assess beyond any surface nervousness or interview technique whether he or she is a *people* person, good with facts and figures, or creative but potentially temperamental.

In this chapter we will learn how to read other people's moods and more permanent character auras and how to understand workplace interactions in terms of the unconscious signals that pass spontaneously between individuals in groups. Subtle group interconnections may also explain the cause of sudden collective tension or a personality clash at a time when external pressures are low.

These hidden personality indicators can help identify people who might work together well and pinpoint those who would benefit from more responsibility or who might conversely be happier working in the background.

The Key to Reading People

The human aura has been defined as a bioenergetic field that surrounds the body in an ellipse, though it can most easily be observed around the head of the subject being studied, like a halo. Saints and very spiritual people are invariably pictured with golden halos since their auras are so pronounced that most people can perceive the ring of gold, even if they are normally unaware of aura energies.

A personal individual energy field is constantly changing as it interacts with what is called the universal energy field, which is made up of the energies of other people, flowers, trees, plants, animals, and solar, lunar, stellar and planetary vibrations, as well as less positive noise and pollution. In practice we are influenced by those with whom we most closely live and work, their thoughts as well as their actions, by our immediate home and work environment, and by sensations that bombard us while traveling.

Personal aura energies are perceived as rainbow-colored swirling bands of light, and they can vary both in terms of predominant color and intensity of color. These light bands contain a great deal of information about a person's character, mood, feelings, stamina, and energy levels.

An aura also forms an early warning system of potential problems so you can detect whether you, a colleague, or an employee is suffering as yet unexpressed stress and needs support before actual signs are manifested as irritability or a drop in production.

Individual auras vary in size and density under different conditions. It is estimated that they extend from between an inch to about three feet all around a person, approximately the extent of an average extended arm span.

Seeing Auras

Though everyone's aura contains some degree of each of the seven rainbow colors plus white and sometimes pink, gray, brown, and even occasionally turquoise or the less positive black, for reading people in the workplace we will concentrate on understanding the significance of the two predominant color bands of someone's aura. These bands are called the Personality Aura and the Mood Aura.

Most people can already sense or *see* auras to some degree, whether in the mind's eye or externally as a halo. When you were a child you may have colored cows green and cats purple, even though you had a full set of crayons, because you saw a multicolored world of psychic as well as physical hues. The ability is still there to be rediscovered.

The Personality Aura

The Personality Aura is seen as a relatively permanent aura color, sometimes with streaks of less prominent colors interwoven. It doesn't generally change unless you have gone through a major life event such as falling in love, having a baby, or changing your career. The Personality Aura predominates when a subject is relaxed and is not being affected by any major mood stimuli. The color will be matte and even. You can see this Personality Aura band of color in the background even when the Mood Aura is active, unless a mood is so extreme that it swamps everything.

The Mood Aura

The Mood Aura reflects the subject's emotions or preoccupation at the time of its observation. The Mood Aura is much more transient than the Personality Aura, and the color will swirl like colored mist, full of movement, flickers, flashes, and twinkles. It will be superimposed over the Personality Aura. At times of lesser levels of emotion or concentrated thought, the Mood Aura may appear like faint mist, through which the Personality Aura shines.

There may sometimes be more than one color in the Mood Aura, especially if a person is experiencing conflicting emotions or trying to integrate different demands. The shade or intensity of a color in either the Personality or Mood aura is significant. When reading the Personality or Mood aura, watch for:

- Harsh metallic colors. They indicate an excess of a mental quality or hidden aggression.
- A pale color or one that disappears around part of the head, especially in the Personality Aura. This suggests that the strength of personality has become eroded by other people or by circumstances or that the person is exhausted.
- Jaggedness, dark streaks, or spots. These are signs of stress, and the subject may have a lot of headaches or be irritable with mood swings.
- Holes in the color of either aura. This says that vital energies are seeping away.

If you know the person whose aura you are studying as a friend, you can chat with them about their general health and feelings, but never be tempted to play doctor or guru.

Collective Workplace Auras

In business (and also in families), the accumulation and combination of individual auras and the nature of the business forms a collective aura in which one or two colors predominate. Sometimes the workplace has a permanently relaxed people-centered green aura or a purposeful orange aura in which everyone is individually working on their part in the creative process. Less positive rival factions may only be able to darken the air with spiteful yellow and angry red temporarily. If you work in a workplace with a predominantly orange and green or a blue aura, then efficiency and harmony will go hand in hand. A brown aura will indicate practical activity, but whether it is a rich golden brown or a turgid brown depends on the nature of the interactions and the overall ambience of the business. (I will define the meanings of the colors later in this chapter.)

In meetings or conferences too, the collective aura can be like a refreshing mist or, more negatively, like a dark cloud and can influence positive or less fruitful decision making and working conditions.

An office atmosphere will change according to events, and even two or three new personnel can quite dramatically alter the overall ambience (see chapter 6 for more information about identifying specific workplace interactions). A meeting's agenda as well as the personalities of those present will set the initial color mix, but this may change if a meeting proves especially stimulating or controversial. If you have a high-ranking bully with a harsh red aura attending then that will obviously be an overwhelming negative factor. However, a number of calming purple or blue auras can more than counter any empire-building tactics and allow reason to prevail.

Collective auras, like individual ones, can be modified, such as with the presence of crystals or flowers; I have written about this in detail in chapter 6. So, for example, you can put masses of pink rose quartz crystals on the conference table in advance to soothe Attila the Hun from the design department.

Developing Aura Reading Skills

Next I will suggest specific easy techniques for discovering both Personality Auras and Mood Auras. You can adapt these techniques for discovering collective auras by focusing on the area about four feet above the height of the tallest person in a room.

First activate your innate aura sensitivity by gaining general impressions of individual auras. Study random subjects at work, especially when they are communicating on a subject they feel very passionately about; the topic need not be work related. You may sense rather then see colors around people. For example, if a woman has just returned from maternity leave, look around her head for a gentle pink glow of love, especially if she is showing you photographs of her baby. Fathers may exhibit a rather deeper pink.

A keen environmentalist will exude green if he or she is trying to ensure wildlife habitats are not destroyed by unnecessary building projects. Instead of allowing your eyes to glaze over, intently study the computer devotee who is surrounded by yellow sunshine while expounding on the virtues of a new software program and explaining precisely how you can save ten seconds getting connected to the Web.

Spend two or three weeks people watching in a variety of situations while they are concentrating on a difficult task, relaxing in the canteen, attending meetings, talking on the phone to the head office, or interacting with a difficult client or their lover. Study those who come occasionally into your workplace or whom you meet in connection with your job as well as people you meet daily, from the most senior executive to the equally valuable person who delivers the post.

Aura reading requires that you get used to seeing auras in a variety of situations. The Mood Aura is usually seen first; it sparkles, flashes, and twinkles. The more stable Personality Aura is usually seen the second time you look (or when you are more experienced); it appears as a color behind and beneath the Mood Aura, closer to the head.

If you find perceiving different auras difficult, concentrate on a space about six or nine inches beyond the subject so the subject is only vaguely discernible at the side of your vision, but you can still see the person's general outline. While the head is, as I said, a source of stronger overall impressions, you may detect radiance around the whole body, with more intense colors around the head, hands, and feet

Scribble notes or images in your journal, using pencils in different shades. Record not only the colors you see or sense but also the feelings, the intuitions, the images, and maybe even words that spring to mind. For aura reading is not just about detecting colors but about discerning what the aura is telling you about the possessor and his current worries, hopes, and dreams. Notice any dramatic changes in a particular person's aura, and try to understand why this should occur during the period of observation. After two or three weeks you will be ready for closer observations of two chosen subjects.

Ongoing Method of Aura Reading

You will need two subjects to study in an ongoing survey. The longer you persist, the more you will learn about aura variations generally as well as about your subject specifically. Their Mood Aura will be your main concern once you have established their more stable Personality Aura. Your first choice should be a colleague, someone you work with regularly and closely so you can monitor them several times during a day. If you work alone, then practice on a family member or friend. Study your subject in a variety of moods—under stress, talking about family or a lover, elated about a sudden success or temporarily depressed after a confrontational call or exchange, concentrating, telling a joke, daydreaming, or relaxed. Note the changes in their Mood Aura and any times of day, days of the week, situations, or visits from individuals that seem to evoke a particular color. After the weekend, Monday morning may show quite a dramatic swing depending on whether your subject has been rock climbing, spending time with his elderly grandmother, or dating a new partner.

Over the observation period, note briefly in your journal, if possible, the setting and circumstance surrounding each mood along with the date and time. This need only take a minute or so. If there are hardly any mood changes, the subject may be very serene within. However if the subject's Mood Aura is permanently dull red, for example, your subject may be permanently angry at the world. Equally, if her Mood Aura is constantly changing, you may be observing someone who tries to please whomever she is with, which a very pale Personality Aura would confirm.

Ideally for such an intimate prolonged study, you should ask your subject's permission. When you explain your project, your subject may decide to study you in a similar way. Exchanging information can be very positive as well as revealing.

Your second subject should be someone who is more distant from you emotionally or physically, an employer or employee with whom you may only exchange pleasantries or from whom you receive orders, or a sales representative or delivery person who visits your workplace two or three times a week and stays for a few minutes to talk. Observe him or her once every two or three days at different times of the day or when there is obviously something bubbling under the surface. After the brief observation, a subtle "How are you today?" or "You look stressed" may reveal some background information for your journal.

Again if you work alone, choose a professional whom you can observe at different times of the day or evening, for example, a fitness coach or someone who works different shifts in a local store or garage with whom you have a chance to chat.

Keep up the ongoing monitoring for three or four weeks, especially for the second less-known subject, until you can establish a pattern. For example, you may learn that the delivery person who stops for coffee two or three times a week and always has a bright red aura on Wednesday sees his girlfriend on Wednesday night. With subtle detective work in conversation you may discover that his rich golden brown aura on Friday reflects payday, when he deposits money in his savings account toward buying his own place. Most important, from day one record your personal impressions of the significance of your subjects' different aura colors. You will be surprised by how closely your intuitions match what you uncover with tactful questioning.

Other Methods of Aura Reading

Because aura reading often needs to be fast, and because background noise and the activity of other people around you may serve as a distraction, instant methods are essential. The advantage of instant aura reading is that you do not have time to rationalize or doubt the evidence of your inner eye. These are methods I have taught and used successfully. After a few weeks you may find that you no longer need to initiate specific techniques to *see* an aura, but that you are automatically aware of the auras of those around you.

At this stage you need only focus on a person or interaction to bring this information from the background into your conscious awareness.

Reading Auras Instantly

For in-depth aura readings, try the following technique. It works equally effectively for studying your own aura.

To read an aura instantly:

1. Stand or sit so your subject is framed against soft light, if possible. In front of a window or in a doorway is ideal. (When you are studying your own aura you can use a mirror.)

2. Focus on your chosen subject without being too obvious. Look at the area around the person's head, though as I said earlier, the aura does surround the entire body as an ellipse.

3. Close your eyes for a few seconds, open them, and blink. You will get a vivid impression of their aura, either externally or in your mind. Your first impression will be of their flashing Mood Aura.

4. Repeat this and the second time you will become aware of their more matte solid Personality Aura.

As with your more general observations, scribble down not only colors but also any intuitive impressions you receive. What do you sense the colors are saying? Is your subject tired after a night out (paleness in the Mood Aura) or more permanently exhausted (which would be reflected in the Personality Aura)? If the subject reflects anxiety, is it purely work related (red or blue) or is it a personal problem that may concern an unsatisfactory interaction with a colleague or employer (green)?

Aura Reading Using the Psychic Camera or Flashbulb Technique

In psychology, for a number of years it has been recognized that while human memory normally tidies up recollections, even in a short space of time, the flashbulb memory preserves even minute details. For example, a person will remember what they were doing the moment they heard of the first moon landing, of John F. Kennedy's assassination or Princess Diana's death, or when they received sudden personally good or bad news. Even years later people can recall that moment in minute detail. The intensity of the emotion generated freeze-frames the entire context of the incident.

The same technique can be applied to aura reading, in which you symbolically freeze-frame your momentary perception of an aura by building up an imaginary light bubble around the image. The only necessity in this technique is that your subject must be relatively still and positioned in fairly bright light. You need only focus on one part of his or her aura in your psychic view finder, so you can look either to the side or slightly above or beyond the subject to avoiding the impression of staring.

To use the psychic camera or flashbulb technique:

1. Visualize the light surrounding your chosen subject increasing in intensity so the whole outline of his or her head and body becomes pure white.

2. Focus on this visualized light, breathing in very slowly through your nose and deliberately hold it for a count of "one and two and three."

3. Breathe out again through your nose or mouth, "one and two and three." With each out breath, imagine increasing the intensity of the light around your subject, as though you were blowing up a psychic balloon of light. You can breathe silently and subtly so your subject does not think you are hyperventilating and dials 911.

4. Continue to fill the psychic balloon. Increase the intensity and the light sphere in your mind with each breath sequence for about two or three minutes in all.

5. Project a final flash of light, from your mind to your subject's aura, freezing the aura image within the intense flash of power and whiteness. The white light will break up into the colors of the aura when it flashes. (It may help to count "three, two, one" in your head just before you project the psychic beam.)

6. You may momentarily see white light circling the aura like a camera flashbulb, as your power meets the outer aura field. You have not affected the subject's aura at all, merely touched it with the light.

Now you can read the aura at your leisure, for the image remains in your imagination even if the subject bolts. You will tend to see both the Mood and Personality auras, generally with the Personality Aura as an inner ring of color. You can differentiate the auras by the intensity and movement of the two bands. Scribble down your impressions as soon as you can.

Aura Reading Using Psychometry

Psychic touch is called *psychometry*, and it is a valuable psychic tool for gaining impressions through intuition. As well as around the head, an aura also can be detected emanating from the palms. So when you shake hands with someone, through psychic touch you are receiving impressions of that person's aura. This is an excellent way in business of picking up aura impressions, often accompanied by a great deal of other information that floods your mind.

To read an aura using psychometry:

1. You will need a partner. Hold your palms vertically facing each other. Move them together until they are almost touching and then away again, first slowly and then faster, a dozen or more times. You will feel as if your hands are being attracted to stick together.

2. Around your fingertips you may detect light or bands of color. Again, two bands will predominate, usually the matte, more stable Personality Aura color is closest to your physical hand, framed by the moving, sparkling Mood Aura.

3. Moving quickly, grasp the other person's hand in a hand-shake very lightly so he or she is applying the pressure. Look at the colors emanating from the person's fingers into yours. You have only a second or two before your own aura energies respond and mingle with your part-ner's. The joining of energies through hands is a good way of monitoring the two-way effect of more formal relationships.

4. There may be a tingling sensation, which can be harsh if the other person is feeling hostile or threatened, warm during a positive encounter, or weak if the subject lives mainly in his or her own world or has many people con-stantly drawing energy off him or her.

Once you know the technique, you can read a person's aura just by shaking hands with him or her. The less formal practice of kissing even relative strangers on the cheek or hugging when greeting them will also emit a burst of aura color from another person's face.

Aura Color Meanings

When presenting a color's meaning below, I have also suggested colors to counter any negative collective auras. You can use the same remedies to calm or energize your own Mood Aura if it becomes unbalanced.

White is the color of limitless potential and boundless energy. It is a highly evolved color, indicating a person who has successfully integrated the different aspects of themselves and who will always seek what is of worth rather than material success.

In business, each day is a new adventure and a new begin-ning for this person, and no task is dismissed as impossible or idea as unworkable (at least not without careful consideration).

A too-brilliant white can hurt even the inner eye when per-ceived and can lead to pushing ahead regardless of consequences and eventual burnout. A very pale misty white indicates unrealistic expectations, and a murky white masks feelings of alienation from others.

Counter too much negative white in a group interaction with bright yellow for logic and golden brown for grounding ideas in reality.

Red is the color of movement, of a survivor, and it indicates a person's desire for change and for translating ideas into action.

In business terms, red means that viable proposals will be in production on the factory floor almost before the end of a meeting. If there has been inertia or lack of enthusiasm, the presence of a crusading red individual aura will inspire even those dozing their way to the weekend.

When the red is dull or harsh, it may indicate suppressed fury, an irritable nature, and resentment. Scarlet flashing auras directed toward another person, rather than toward a project or worthy cause, do not make for harmonious work relationships for anyone, as inappropriate workplace passion between two members of a team can disrupt even a normally smooth running department.

Counter too much negative red in a collective aura with a rich yellow for positive ideas and creativity (which mingled with the red makes the integrating orange). Alternatively a clear but dark blue will introduce a calming element that directs thoughts to the level of official concerns.

Orange is the color of confidence, joy, independent thought, and strong identity.

In business, a warm rich orange indicates the ability to integrate different demands, a steady creativity, and an open-minded approach. It is an excellent aura for harmonious business interactions, all partnerships and cooperative ventures, and for any self-employed and marketing personnel.

A dull or murky orange can indicate that someone is feeling very territorial about their rights and responsibilities or has an oversensitive ego. In contrast, a pale orange may be manifest by someone who defines his or her worth and identity only in terms of their job description.

Counter too much negative orange in a collective aura with

a clear blue for inspiring group loyalty and rich indigo to melt rigid demarcations.

Yellow is the color of logic, focus, concentration, and financial acumen, especially in speculation and technological expertise.

In business, yellow promotes clear and concise communication, strategic thinking, and the rapid assimilation of knowledge and expertise in any field. It is also good for regular short-haul business travelers and for sales representatives.

Irregular harsh streaks of yellow can indicate hyperactivity and impatience with teaching others. Mustard yellow may mask jealousy or a potential gossip. A metallic yellow haze conceals secrets or less than honest intentions; make sure you keep classified information well protected.

Counter too much negative yellow in a collective aura with green for empathy with others, with brown for a steadying influence where risk is involved, and also with brown to ensure motives and words are of the highest intent.

Green is the color of loyalty, trustworthiness, empathy and sympathy with others, tact, and generosity with ideas, resources, and time.

In business, green encourages a people-centered and environmentally aware atmosphere.

An employer or coworker with a rich green aura will always remember that other people have lives and problems in and out of work that can affect efficiency; this aura is good for all caring professionals and in jobs that require imagination.

Yellowy green can be a sign of possessiveness and unwarranted jealousy about friendships or favoritism between others. Pale green suggests emotional dependency. A cloudy green aura can indicate that the distinctions between work and social life are blurred, causing confusion about roles and appropriate work behaviors.

Counter too much negative green in a collective aura with deep blue and bright yellow to prevent personal issues or rivalries from hindering impartial decision making.

Turquoise is the color of wisdom and experience, even in the young, indicating a person's ability to do many things simultaneously and to demonstrate good organizational skills.

In business, turquoise is a good aura for those who assume leadership because they will explain their goals clearly and motivate a team without being autocratic. They will also remain impartial and judge each person on his or her merit.

There are no negative connotations with turquoise, and a group exhibiting a turquoise aura will ensure effective collective decision making and true equality in the workplace.

Blue is the color of idealism, of wise leadership qualities whatever the person's age, of natural authority, and of an ability to see different sides of an argument and varying opinions.

In business, a rich blue indicates an ability to see beyond the immediate and to put together different aspects of an issue to envisage the whole picture and long-term results. Blue auras offer assurance that the possessor will put principles before personal gain; this is good for all managers, executives, and those who travel frequently overseas on business or who work permanently abroad.

Harsh blue can be a sign of someone who is autocratic and has little time for human weakness. Dull blue represents over-conservatism and a concern for the letter rather than the spirit of the law or task.

Counter too much negative blue in a collective aura with pink for tolerance and gray for being prepared to compromise rigid principles where they would cause hardship or resentment if applied.

Purple, violet, and indigo are colors of intuitive thinking, of trusting instincts, and of cultivating a calm personal inner center and thereby a harmonious working atmosphere.

Surprisingly, purple can be a successful aura for creative ventures in business, especially those involved in any New Age business or in any trade that balances profitability and maximum output with good work conditions and the spiritual needs of all involved.

When the purple becomes too pale, drive and incentive may be lacking. If a purple aura is blurred, the owner is spending too much time on daydreams and illusions. An inky purple means that a person is feeling isolated and may need support.

Counter too much negative purple with white and red to get things moving in the real world.

Pink is the color of the peacemaker and wise counselor, mender of quarrels and rivalries, someone who will bring together people whose ideas and priorities may be very different.

In business, a pink aura is good for anyone involved in health or childcare, therapies or counseling. But whether the business involves caring for others or not, this individual aura of calm will permeate the entire workplace.

If the pink is misty, you may be dealing with someone who sees other people's point of view so much he or she is unlikely to reach any decisions without firm direction.

Counter too much negative pink with a confident orange or a power red.

Brown is the color of the office homemaker and nurturer of wounded feelings and egos. It augurs stability, realism, and the patience and perseverance to carry even a tedious task efficiently through to the end.

In business, brown promises sound financial sense and an ability to work with details, and it can be a good counterbalance to the yellow aura speculators who thrive on risk. Plans will be carried through within budget and on time with the minimum amount of drama when a brown aura predominates, so this aura is a good choice for a project manager.

Harsh brown suggests someone who is obsessed with money or material concerns to the exclusion of everything else. Murky brown can indicate narrow horizons. Very pale brown says that a reliable worker is being relied on too much and needs a rest.

Counter too much negative brown with yellow and green.

Gray is the color of compromise, adaptability, and the ability to merge into the background, the color of someone who can be trusted with secrets.

In business, a gray aura shows the possessor has the ability to make things happen unobtrusively and to negotiate behind the scenes, to be a good foil for a flamboyant figure, and to be helpful taking care of confidential documents and sensitive material, which is excellent for any form of investigator or treasurer.

A dull gray may suggest depression, while a very pale gray can be a symbol of indecision and an unwillingness to challenge the status quo, even if it is inefficient.

Counter an excess of negative gray with an infusion of orange and red for assertiveness and confidence.

Black is not a color that is particularly helpful in the workplace. The possessor may deliberately or spontaneously be shielding him or herself from intrusion—so this is not a subject to read or to work with easily.

A matte black indicates exhaustion or depression. It is more often seen as black spots or streaks than as a blanket black aura.

However, a harsh metallic black can suggest that the person is potentially a psychic vampire. This person will offload problems, ignore any positive suggestions, and put the most negative interpretation possible on the motives and actions of others. If possible this is a person to steer clear of or to pass on to the work counselor.

Workplace Interactions

Earlier in this chapter I wrote about collective workplace or meeting table auras. Before we talk about modifying auras, I will take the subject of workplace interactions a stage further to explain how collective auras build up and also how underlying currents between people can affect you as well as the general office atmosphere.

One of the most potentially useful things you can do is to plot the interactions and connections between the auras of people you work with. This can give you a great deal of information about the underlying dynamics of any workplace and can be especially beneficial if you are new to a firm or have a managerial role and need to decide on the best combinations of workers in a team.

Of course I am not suggesting you put down your tools while you make a detailed study of the interconnections in your workplace. It will not do your career prospects much good if you sit coloring circles during a major meeting. So plan to spend part of a lunch hour or coffee break, maybe taken early so you can study people in situ while they are still working. Two or three different sketches over a period of time will give you a pretty good idea of what is going on around you.

Though the dynamics may change according to what is happening, the basic Personality Aura connections of people in your workplace endure over months unless there is a major upheaval in the office or a personnel change. Imagine the connections between people as various strong, straight strands of color with the more transient Mood Aura moving like a snake, twined around the connecting energy lines.

You can also study the auras of a regular group of people who attend, for example, a morning meeting. By plotting the interconnections you can understand why one team member regularly undermines a colleague or supports another regardless of the viability or validity of what is being said. The true leader of the meeting may be someone totally unexpected. Use your intuition as you plot the group's auras to work out the source and nature of the antipathy or perhaps strong attraction between two unlikely people. If one person is absent or an executive comes from the head office to join in once a week, you may see some major changes in the power structure on those occasions. This also applies to general office interactions.

Spend some time studying your results. If you have done several drawings at different times, see how the absence of a particular person changes the group's dynamics, especially if it is one of your key people to whom a number of people react positively or negatively. If someone who is disliked is not there, does the scapegoat for negative emotions change? If the leader is absent does someone else become the focus?

Once you understand the hidden dynamics of your workplace, you can on a conscious level understand where power lies. Whether you are organizing the workforce or are a part of it, you can maximize the group's resources and avoid unwittingly encouraging factions or rivalries.

To plot your group's aura interconnections:

1. Draw a diagram of your office, marking with a circle the spot where each coworker usually sits or stands.

2. Using a set of colored pencils (with two or three shades of each color), mark the rays passing between different people as lines of color, thus starting to create a web between the circles. (You can use a paint program to create the diagram on your computer screen.) You will look very busy and important creating your interconnected web with different circles marked with numbers (code them so you know who each circle represents but so no one else does unless you are exploring this with a colleague).

3. Color in each circle as you study that person's Personality Aura. Then add the Mood Auras. You may decide to print out sheets of the finished diagram in black and white so you can regularly update the Mood Auras.

4. Now look to see whose aura out of everyone's in the room or work area is the brightest and note the extent of its rays. This person is the focus in your workplace. You may be surprised at who it is.

5. Draw lines to join this main aura to the other auras with which it is connecting and note whether the rays are proceeding in both directions; that is, are their rays being reciprocated by the person to whom they are directed? If it is a two-way interaction, you will have parallel lines between the people's circles. Now draw in the rays that are traveling to the focal aura but are not being reciprocated.

6. Draw an arrow on one end of each of your lines, depicting whether the line is leaving or coming toward a person.

7. Next, look at the second brightest aura in your diagram and plot that person's connections in the same way. Continue until you have interconnected everyone's auras, although you may find even in a group that one person has no connections at all or sends out aura colors while receiving none in return. One or two people may be

receiving rays from a number of others, which they may or may not be returning.

8. First analyze various Personality Auras, ranking them in order of brightness. Then sort them according to their color, the influences they exert, and the ways they are influenced. Who is constantly sending out rays and who receives many energies? Are energies sent out and received in equal proportion by each individual? Note rays that move toward an aura but do not reach it; the person may be deliberately blocking emotional contact. Is there a psychic vampire who sucks energies from others into a dark aura?

Using Your Insights for Positive Interaction

Now compare what the auras tell you with what you observe in overt office relationships. The aura readings of two or three significant characters may reveal two- or even three-way tendrils of mutual dependency in a seemingly victim/villain(ess) scenario. Perhaps an employer and employee or two colleagues display open antipathy to each other or toward a third party seemingly without reason. If there is a lot of scarlet between two auras, there may have been a secret affair that petered out, while the apparent underlying emotion still wields a fair amount of power.

Observe any significant interactions that occur during the day. During an argument or criticism one aura may become significantly paler or less vibrant, and the weaker of the two or three may not be the obvious bully. Sometimes color may be leaking out and being absorbed by the stronger individual. See what happens to the respective auras when the bully bullies his or her favorite victim.

Monitor too over a period the aura links of a colleague who suffers one disaster after another and to whom everyone lends a sympathetic ear. You may find that that the aura of the person you thought was unlucky may actually be drawing strength from the friends or colleagues acting as counselors. Such a person is called a psychic vampire, and when you identify one—most offices have one—he or she may be totally unaware of what they are doing. You will actually see the energy being drawn across the lines to them as though by suction.

What can also be significant is the strength of the rays traveling between people whom you thought shared no real interaction. Vibes traveling one way may be positive and unfulfilled admiration or a love interest tinged with envy and resentment—an unconscious form of psychological and psychic attack.

Modifying a Collective or Personal Aura

If you know that people will be unenthusiastic on a Monday morning or when certain people get together there will be mutual antipathy or that a particular proposal will cause hostility whatever its merits, you can prepare the room or meeting place in advance with more positive colors. The difference will be quite dramatic.

You can also use this method in one-to-one encounters in the workplace with colleagues, employers, or employees who have set their minds on being negative or obstructive. Turning them into toads (see the next chapter) may seem more satisfying but may not be a good long-term career move.

Most important, you can cheer up your own aura or calm yourself down when you start seeing red.

The easiest method for modifying a personal or collective aura is either to set a pot of relevantly colored growing flowers or a bowl of fruit in the center of a table. For example, green grapes can soften a dark red mood or oranges (or orange juice) can fill everyone with confidence and overcome a dull gray winter morning gloom.

If you are uncertain which way the mood will swing at a meeting, prepare a vase of variously colored flowers, a bowl of different colored fruits, or a dish of crystals of many colors. Focusing on each relevant color in turn, use the pranic breathing method (see chapter 2), and breathe the necessary antidote color around the table or toward each of those causing the disharmony (you'll know them by their color on your diagram; see the previous list of color meanings).

Eating or drinking the color essence of a fruit or crystal water is the most instant and powerful method of lifting collective or personal gloom or irritability. Since crystals do contain powerful energies, absorbing crystalline color by seeping them in water and then drinking the water or splashing it on pulse points transmits the desired energies to transform private angst or mood swings. For example, adding sparkling yellow citrine to your morning bath or shower will send you to the office sparkling. Add a few drops of the empowered water in which the crystal has soaked to a jug of drinking water or make coffee with it for everyone to lift collective gloom. Even a small crystal has almost limitless power to turn a mood around.

To make crystalline aura waters:

1. Use spring water (still mineral water). Place the water in a small wide-necked, clear glass bottle. Even a few drops will carry the essence; you do not need to use liters for greater effect.
2. Add the relevant crystal. It only needs to be tiny.
3. Cork or put the lid on the bottle and shake the bottle nine times.
4. Leave the bottle outdoors in a sheltered place or on an indoor window ledge for a sun and moon twenty-four-hour cycle (from dawn to the next dawn or, Celtic style, from sunset to sunset) or for eight hours if you are in a hurry.

Crystalline Rainbows

The following crystals are especially potent for modifying a negative collective or individual aura, for along with their colors they have individual energies to dissipate the murkiest fog or workplace gloom. For example, making coffee every day—with blue lace agate water—for a bad-tempered boss with a persistently metallic harsh red aura will transform him or her if not into a teddy bear at least into a tame bull. You can also set citrine on window ledges to reflect yellow sunlight's optimism or hold a crystal and breathe in the light to empower or calm yourself (and then, as I suggested, blowing it around the office or meeting table).

Amethyst (purple) Counters negative red or blue. Reduces stress, irritability, and obsessive traits.

Agate, blue lace (soft light blue) Counters negative red or yellow. Turns anger into calm and angry words into gentler ones; deflects criticism and sarcasm.

Amber (orange) Counters negative green or yellow. Builds self-esteem and confidence and prevents panic in crises; encourages creative solutions.

Citrine (yellow) Counters negative gray or brown. Increases confidence and optimism, overcomes inertia, and transforms negative thoughts and words into positive ideas and enthusiasm. Make *sun water* with citrine by leaving the bottle in sunlight from dawn to noon.

Jade (green) Counters negative red or blue. Deters bullies, prevents overreaction under provocation, and prevents mood swings.

Moonstone (cream or very pale blue or yellow) Counters negative white, yellow, or orange. Prevents harshness, overreliance on logic, insistence on impossible deadlines, and general inflexibility. Make *moon water* by leaving the bottle in moonlight overnight during the full moon so the water turns silver.

Rose quartz (pink) Counters negative red, blue, orange, or white. Reduces obsessive behavior and encourages conciliation, tolerance, and compromise. Works well for large formal gatherings such as shareholder meetings or visits from the head officers; stops bullying.

Sodalite (dark blue, indigo) Counters negative orange or red. Calms potential conflicts, deflects unreasonable demands, overcomes fears and panic, and allows considered responses.

Turquoise (turquoise) Counters any negative color or harshness in the aura. This power stone brings the confidence to speak out and to stand up against bullies or anyone pulling rank or backbiting; encourages altruism, idealism, and integrity.

Auras in the workplace are not yet recognized in the same way as nonverbal signals or body language for detecting and interpreting hidden signals from clients and colleagues alike. Yet as you work with auras you'll become more aware of both the possibilities and pitfalls in individual interactions. What is more, you can even understand the group dynamics in an unfamiliar workplace and so ease your way into a new team or post. By modifying a temporarily or more permanently hostile, unenthusiastic, or overcompetitive collective aura, you can reduce your work stress and increase your productivity.

In the next chapter we will explore ways of using our mind's power to overcome obstacles in our path and to attain what it is we most need or desire in our career.

CHAPTER 4

Visualization and Magic to Get What You Want

We all know those media moguls, tycoons, and lesser drama queens and kings in all walks of life who stamp their hooves and scream, "I want it and I want it now." Their minions might quake at these oversized toddler tantrums, but in fact such tactics are often counterproductive. Polite requests usually produce far more permanent results from those who inspire mutual respect and loyalty.

There is nothing wrong with knowing what you want and striving to attain it. Had humankind not shown ambition we would still be living in caves. It does not matter what your current career aim is, whether you want to grow and sell the largest freshest tomatoes in the Western hemisphere, organize an efficient clean water supply to a remote Indian village, hit your weekly sales targets, or write a best-seller with film and merchandising rights presold to Warner Brothers. Having a game plan and successfully carrying it through underpins every business venture from the individual working in the back room at home to a multinational conglomeration in a glass-and-steel industrial palace.

But in career and creative ventures alike, the best plans or ideas in the world rely not only on hard work and presentation but also on the more elusive luck factors—being in the right place at the right moment and maximizing every opportunity, unexpected as well as expected (more of anticipating those one-off chances in chapter 7).

I have already talked about the impetus needed to get a plane off the tarmac or a project off the ground in a concentrated burst of energy and of using psychokinesis, mind power, to draw what you want to you. So let's move on to visualization, an accepted but maybe not fully exploited business practice of focusing on a particular aim and anticipating and experiencing the steps needed to attain a desired result in advance, switching on the "choose me" neon sign. The process kick-starts motivation, strengthens determination, reinforces dedication, and temporarily excludes from our vision other more vague or less urgent wants and needs.

Visualization

Remember in childhood when you walked in circles saying "I wish, I wish" over and over again in your mind, imagining it was the first day of a vacation at the ocean. The daydream seemed so real you could smell the salt and taste the crunchy sand in your picnic even though you were still sitting in your backyard.

Childhood visualization or imagining was rooted in recalling previous good experiences mingled with some ideal scenario you'd maybe seen in a movie or read in a book. Workplace visualization is no different and is not only an effective individual personal focusing technique, but can be adapted by an imaginative manager or team leader as a collective exercise.

A group working on the same project can be led into creating, out loud, a joint vision of a successful outcome to a venture that relies heavily on cooperation. It is far more effective than pep talks or company memos. It is also a good way of encouraging shy but very talented people to express their ideas in a relaxed situation where rigid demarcations do not exist within the experience.

Group visualization can be initiated sitting around a circular table or during one of those ideal corporate bonding weekends. In ancient times, when a group met they would pass a wooden stick called the speaking staff—made of hazel, a tree of wisdom—from one to the other so whoever was holding the stick, whether of high or low status, could speak without being interrupted.

You can either use a crystal sphere or some symbol that you select to represent your goal as the speaking staff. Outdoors you could create a staff from a fallen branch.

The crystal sphere speaking staff is also a good device in meetings where one or two people tend to dominate the conversation or talk others down. Of course you need to set a time limit for speech as some will still monopolize the stage.

Whether you are visualizing alone, with a work partner or colleague, or in a group, the basic technique is the same. Though the essence of visualization is spontaneity, by defining your focus and the desired end result in advance you can create powerful parameters within which to weave the steps to a successful outcome.

If working alone you may find it helpful to speak aloud. The ancient Egyptians, who were master magicians and ran successful businesses for four thousand years when most of the world was still living in huts, believed that speaking words aloud had the power to bring wishes and desires into reality. There are four key stages to successful visualization: defining the goal, choosing a focus, endowing the idea with reality, and retaining the power. Let us take each in turn.

Defining the Goal

Your goal may seem self-evident, but sometimes we have only a vague woolly idea of precisely what we are aiming for in the long term, whether a private ambition or as part of a project involving different departments or companies.

Being unfocused is like trying to throw a ball made of cotton wool as opposed to a hard rubber or leather. The ball goes all over the place or sticks to your hands, and it is hard to get much impetus behind the effort. Like all psychological and psychic work, successful visualization occurs most readily within the sphere of human emotions and real desires, rather than a vague dream or hope. So if you really care about something then you will define your goal and its values clearly.

Another key to successful visualization is when the dream or desire is already rooted in tangible earthly efforts or it at least forms the impetus for sustained effort in the following days and weeks. If you want to be a musician to the exclusion of everything else—as opposed to just thinking it might be fun to be a rock star one day—you will practice endlessly and take temporary jobs to support yourself so you can quit at short notice to go for auditions and on last-minute tours.

If you are organizing a group exercise, it is up to the facilitator to initiate enthusiasm by briefly describing the benefits that ultimate success would produce. Also, group visualization should not be diluted by preceding or following it with discussion of policy or complaints about failing to meet targets.

Choosing a Focus

A tangible focus can make individual or group visualization easier, whether it is an estate agent blurb with a photo of the ideal homestead for growing sunflowers, an image or costing program of people enjoying clean water in a remote village, or a car similar to the one being manufactured (even if the final product is still under wraps) so workers can see what their department is contributing to. Advertising the goal is important not only for potential buyers but also for those making a product.

If your focus is less tangible, endow a crystal sphere or other symbol with the goal you want to visualize.

To endow a crystal with your particular focus:

1. Place the crystal or other symbol where you can easily see it, such as in the center of a table for group work.

2. If you are working alone, hold your hands so you enclose the crystal. Take time to allow impressions to form in your psyche. These may appear as words, images, or feel-

ings and may add a new dimension to your original definition of the desired outcome. This new material from your wise deep unconscious mind is not so bound by the limitations of time and space.

3. If you are working in a group, use the speaking staff method. Allow each person in turn to hold the symbol or crystal—serving as a speaking staff—and define the ultimate goal as he or she sees it. Each person should be given the opportunity at this time to express the ideas and feelings about the project or product that the crystal evokes in him or her. When each person has finished speaking, he or she should hand the symbol to the person sitting to his or her left. The process should continue without comment from anyone else until everyone has had a chance to speak.

This method is remarkably effective for bringing even the most disparate individuals into cooperative decision-making mode. The crystal acts as the psychological authority so colleagues become equal while they are speaking.

Endowing the Idea with Reality

This is the next stage of visualization, and it is important that the following steps are followed:

To endow your idea with reality:

1. Place the crystal or other symbol where you can see it.

2. Begin with gentle regular breathing, while focusing on the symbol or crystal. If in a group, allow individuals to create their own breathing rhythms.

3. If working alone, use your imagination to re-create and move through the various stages you will experience, from anticipation to triumph, taking as long as necessary on each new step. As a group leader, you could map out in advance a scenario with nine or ten stages, allowing frequent pauses so individuals can silently weave their own imaginative experiences into the basic framework.

4. Combine feelings evoked by past successes and the idealized best possible outcome, allowing your unconscious
   mind to cast up related fragrances, sounds, touches,
   and even tastes to make the visualized aim as three-
   dimensional as possible.

If in a group, the first time you use this technique you may need
to guide the visualization. If, for example, you are working with
a crew on a future documentary, use a phrase such as, "Picture
the sun shining and everyone smiling as the cameraman gets a
close-up of the hibiscus growing around the village . . . the scent
is rich." However, if you have quite a self-confident group, you
can continue the talking stick method, having them continue
to build up the joint vision by continuing to pass the symbol or
crystal around the group.

Whether alone or with others, be as specific about your
goal as possible, describing aloud the color and make of the car
you want, the kind of dwelling you seek, and so on.

Now it is time to move to the last stage in the visualization.

Retaining the Power

Finally, while the sense of well-being is still at a peak, create for
yourself or suggest to the group that they create a personal
secret shortcut back to the positive emotions felt at the climax
of the visualization. In your mind, suggest a trigger to remember
those feelings such as: "When I touch the center of my brow
with my right index finger, I will recall the joy/calm/assurance
of success I am now feeling."

This helps to translate the power of the visualization to success in the real situation over the next days or weeks.

You may repeat and modify the whole visualization process
as a long-term project progresses or if initial aims are modified
by circumstances.

Workplace Magic

Workplace magic is just the next station on from visualization.
You still work with a goal and use a tangible focus. The main

difference between visualization and this type of magic is that you carry out a series of ordered progressive steps so a symbol becomes endowed with power (this happens to some extent in visualization if different people are holding and passing a symbol around while speaking). This power, which is accumulated energy, is released into the cosmos in a sudden burst of power to transform the thought or need into manifestation or at least a distinct possibility in the material world.

I discuss spell casting and divination using state-of-the-art technology later in the chapter, so you can practice alchemy subtly but effectively at work. I will also describe more traditional magical methods in the form of spells or rituals for early mornings before work, in evenings, or on weekends to positively influence your career, whether you are working toward an improvement the next day or carrying out a spell once a week to further a longer term career ambition.

Try a spell or two. You may find they are considerably less wacky than popular media hype would imply. They are also remarkably effective because they amplify your existing natural mind power as opposed to summoning up weird entities. In chapter 9, I have given times of the month, the day, and the seasons when particular kinds of magic are especially effective. But if the need is urgent any time will work.

Psychic Cookery

Think of spells like cookery recipes. You decide what you want to make in advance, anticipating the end result as you did in visualization. As with ordinary cookery, collect together the raw ingredients of the spell in advance, in this case the symbol you have selected and other materials like colored candles or incense, which are easily obtained close to your home or by mail order if you live in a remote area.

Following the steps of a recipe or the stages of a spell combines the ingredients (different energies) in a way that ensures they mix well. In doing so you are combining energies and breaking down their separate components, recombining them in a new perfected whole.

This combination and reformation method was developed by the medieval alchemists in their dark mysterious laboratories as they extracted from the *prima materia* the raw potential of their ultimate goal, by heating, distilling, and recombining the basic elements to create the philosopher's stone, which would turn ordinary metals into gold and, it was believed, grant immortality.

More mundanely, cooking a dish or spell gives you your desired end result, a perfect cake or casserole or the job of your dreams.

The Positive Power of White Magic

Of course, you could bake a cake that contained an ingredient that made the recipient sick. Magic is the same. You can in theory do really horrible spells to make bad things happen to rival colleagues or firms. However, not only does negative magic play havoc with your own psyche, but as Annie found with her ring of fire in the introduction, bad wishes tend to attract bad fortune. It's like opening a channel or door normally kept closed by positive thoughts and actions and then not being able to limit the nasty visitors to only those you actually invited (a problem medieval magicians experienced when they summoned up demons to do their bidding). Better to do magic to improve the quality of your own work so what you design outsells other similar products on merit. Alternatively focus on increasing your own ingenuity and productivity magically so you deserve and achieve success in the real as well as the magical world.

How to Cast a Spell

Spells can be as simple or as complicated as you want, but they usually involve the same four stages in the same order: defining the focus, activating the spell, raising and releasing the power, and grounding the power after the spell.

A spell also generally has two main components— repetitive words or phrases to create a rhythm to build up energies and actions that likewise tend to be repeated or follow a sequence and also become more intense as the energies increase.

The most basic spell involves writing on paper what it is you want and burning the paper in the appropriately colored candle while reciting your wish. You then either scatter the ash of the burned paper to the winds for a fast result or bury it beneath a fruit tree for slower growth. You met color meanings in the previous chapter, but you can read their career significance as candle colors in appendix IV. For example, green candles can be used for all matters of gradual growth, whether an increase in prosperity, a particular long-term project such as passing examinations, or for more harmonious relationships in the workplace. Blue is for getting a new job or promotion, while yellow is for mastering a technological skill or improving sales figures.

Whether you choose an almost instant or a more complicated spell, which is not necessarily more effective, try to work when you are relaxed (use the techniques given in chapter 2) and will not be interrupted. Get everything ready in advance.

In traditional societies the women, especially at home, would perform rituals to keep absent husbands, brothers, and sons safe while they were at sea or hunting.

If you have work colleagues you meet regularly in social situations who are open-minded, you can suggest getting together occasionally for a common aim, anything from helping your department or workplace through a time of crisis to sending calm or healing energy to a sick or stressed-out colleague who is struggling to cope.

Who knows? One day a collective office spell to overcome an obstacle such as delayed essential supplies or to send energy to an area or person that needs it, such as the sales force before an overseas conference, may become a commonplace event after a morning motivation meeting. Until then you may need to be more circumspect.

As I said earlier, anything positive you direct toward the cosmos comes back threefold as unexpected benefits or bonuses so spells for other people's success are especially potent in terms of your own future career path.

To perform a spell you will need:

A table to work on

A candle in your chosen color (see appendix IV); you can substitute beeswax or plain white for any color

An incense stick in your chosen fragrance or a smudge stick

A small quantity of salt, potpourri, flower petals, soil, or colored sand

A small amount of mineral water that has been left in the sunlight or moonlight, water steeped with rose petals or commercially prepared lavender, or rose water

Dishes for the salt (or potpourri, etc.) and the water

Candle holders

A deep vase or incense holder

A suitable symbol or crystal to represent your wish (see appendix I)

Matches

As with visualization, the process of casting spells includes four stages: defining the focus, activating the spell, raising and releasing the power, and grounding the power after the spell.

Defining the Focus

Defining the focus for a spell corresponds to the first two stages of visualization (defining the goal and choosing a focus): determining what you hope to achieve and what symbol you are going to use to represent that aim.

Your symbol might be a job description of your ideal position taken from a journal or an idealized position vacancy that you have written yourself; it might be a photo or newspaper article about someone who is already successful in your chosen field. Alternatively you could focus on a pot of flowers that you put on your work station or a sachet of herbs that you can carry with you after the spell as a good luck charm (see chapter 11 for more about good luck charms). Each flower and herb has a magical meaning (see appendix III). Basil is a symbol of improved finances, and rosemary represents enhanced memory and concentration, while marigolds are good for resolving legal matters satisfactorily.

Crystals too can provide a focal point for magic and then also be carried as a charm after a spell. Again each crystal kind has significance; for example, lapis lazuli is used for promotion or to help you cope with unexpected leadership challenges. Tiger's eye brings you courage to go for what you want or an influx of money or credit when your company urgently needs it.

Raid a child's toy box or an old silver charm bracelet for a model boat or plane if you want to travel more in connection with your job or to get a position with a ferry or an airline company, on an ocean liner or in the armed services.

A key and tiny padlock could unlock a career avenue that has been closed to you or right inequalities that, in spite of legislation, are still perpetuated at unofficial meetings on golf courses or in locker rooms.

Holding your symbol, name aloud the intention of your spell and any specific details, such as a time scale within which you need a result (such as within a month). If relevant add the location to which you wish the fulfillment of the spell to take you (a transfer to the New York or Sydney office or the small town where you would like to open your grocery store).

Activating the Spell

This step corresponds to the visualization process, but it involves externalizing the visualized energies into physical actions and/or spoken words. Group visualizations do of course involve speaking aloud, but in this case the words increase in intensity and speed as the spell progresses. Once you have decided on a basic format that you're comfortable with, you can allow spontaneous words and actions to inspire you during your spell or you can write down the chants you will use in advance.

A symbol can magically be filled with energy in any number of ways, the most common being using the four ancient natural forces, earth, air, fire, and water. The ancient Greeks and the medieval alchemists believed as do magicians and witches to this day that these four forces in different combinations make up the psychic and psychological building blocks of all life forms, including the human personality. The psychotherapist Carl Gustav Jung, who was a pupil of Freud's, also subscribed to this view in relation to the human personality. The earlier practitioners went so far as to ascribe physical as well as temperamental attributes to the four elements, for example, a choleric temperament for those with an excess of fire in their bodies.

By combining the four elements within your chosen symbol through ritual, a fifth element called ether or *akasha* is created, providing a burst of energy to act as a catalyst that enables something entirely new to be manifested as reality, for example, your wish.

In chapter 6, I describe ways of balancing the four elements to create a productive and happy workplace. You can also read more about spell casting and different ways of increasing energies in the books listed under Useful Reading. But here we will concentrate on passing a chosen symbol through or over the magical substances of earth, air, fire, and water in turn to endow your symbol and your wish with their powers (see below). Use a table for your four elemental substances, and set the symbol of your wish in the middle of them. In this way you are creating a magical space in which you can raise your power to achieve your goal. After you have used a substance, return it to its place on the table.

Earth brings stability and ensures the practical success of spells. Its direction is north.

1. Use salt, potpourri, flower petals, soil, or colored sand as a magical earth substance.
2. Set your chosen earth substance in a dish to the north of your table (use an approximation or a compass as you prefer).
3. Scatter a circle of salt or petals clockwise around your symbol to endow it with the power of earth.
4. As you make your circle, create and recite an earth power chant, for example, "I call promotion with the power of earth."

Air gets the energies of a spell moving and can bring swift results to a spell. Its direction is east.

1. Use incense sticks or cones, a small smudge stick, or feathers to swirl around as your magical air substance.

2. Light the incense or smudge stick and set it or the feathers in a tall metal container to the east of the symbol. (In appendix III, I describe the magical meanings of different incense so you can choose the right one for your needs. For example, allspice will attract prosperity, strengthen business links with profitable outlets, bring about necessary changes, and encourage single-mindedness of purpose.)

3. Having made a circle on the earth of salt or petals, now create a clockwise circle of smoke or waft your feathers around your symbol.

4. As you make your circle, create and recite an air power chant, for example, "I call promotion with the power of air."

Fire burns through any obstacles to success and adds inspiration and clarity to your spell so you can see and draw to you the positive outcome. Its direction is south.

1. Use candles as a magical fire substance.

2. Light a candle in a deep, safe holder using an appropriate color if you wish (see appendix IV or use white or beeswax). Set the candle to the south of the symbol.

3. Following your circle of air, pass your symbol through or above the flame or carefully make a clockwise circle with the candle around your symbol.

4. As you pass your symbol through the flame or make a circle, create and recite a fire power chant, for example, "I call promotion with the power of fire."

Water helps the energies to flow from thought into reality and also ensures that a spell remains positive. Its direction is west.

1. Use still mineral water, water that has been left in the sunlight or moonlight, water steeped with rose petals, or commercially prepared lavender or rose water as a magical water substance.
2. Set your chosen water substance in a dish to the west of your symbol.
3. Sprinkle a clockwise circle of the chosen liquid around the symbol.
4. As you make a circle, create and recite a water power chant, for example, "I call promotion with the power of water."

You have now endowed the symbol of your wish with the four elemental powers. Because they have been combined within your symbol, you now have created the fifth element, ether. Ether is the elemental energy that can translate your thoughts into reality by empowering your symbol.

In the next stage we will increase that power so that it breaks through the barriers of the material world.

Raising and Releasing the Power

This third step is the most active and powerful part of a spell, building up the speed and intensity of the action you started in the previous stage. In practice, the stages run into one another. Combine the four chants and recite them one after the other, maybe adding a connecting empowerment before you start the next cycle of chanting with earth again. So after saying, "I call promotion with the power of water," you might add, "Earth, air, water, fire, bring to me what I desire," and then go back to "I call success with the power of earth," and so on. You could repeat the five chants in order, faster and faster.

At the same time, you are going to enchant your symbol. This is very easy and involves holding your hands, palms down, a few inches above the symbol. Move your left hand in counterclockwise circles, and at the same time move your right hand in clockwise circles. Move them faster and faster as you chant faster and faster until you feel the power welling up in you.

You will sense when you are ready to release the accumulated power into the cosmos. Finish the chant cycle and bring your hands together in a clap on the final "Bring to me what I desire." Then say: "The power is free as I count three—one, two, three—so shall it be, three, two, one (blow out candle), the spell is done."

Grounding the Power after the Spell

To bring yourself back to earth, sit quietly while inhaling the incense you lit and picturing the fulfillment of your dream. When you are ready, clear and wash any tools and sit quietly, perhaps playing gentle music or tending plants, making plans for practical steps to achieve success in the everyday world.

Technological Magic

Though you will usually carry out work-focused rituals at home and can't readily light incense or candles at work, the computer is a wonderful magical tool with its design and draw programs, a variety of clip art packages to serve as symbols, and a screen saver that can connect you instantly to the energies of your power animal (see chapter 12 for identifying your personal power totem).

Sending an Affirmation Email

We all get a buzz when we receive a positive email. Each night before you go home, send yourself an email to be read first thing the next morning when you switch on your computer.

To send an affirmation email:

- Remind yourself of what you have achieved, even on a bad day or one that had constant interruptions.
- State what you have to look forward to in the coming day (if things are doom and gloom, be creative).
- Include lessons learned. For example, "I will not waste time worrying about the spiteful remark Elaine made about my presentation. Instead I will recall the good things that

Jim, whose opinion I value more, said about my efforts and will do even better in the future."

- Define your immediate goals.
- Define your long-range goals.
- List some ideas for furthering both short-term and long-term goals in the day ahead.
- List three things that you can't or didn't manage to achieve and that still irrationally take up brain slots: for example, becoming a ballerina, prom queen in 1994, or as good a cook as my sister, Alice, according to my mom.
- List six strengths you possess.
- State three more qualities or skills you would like to develop or achieve.
- Add a PS: "I am not single-handedly responsible for the world turning, nor am I the office doormat, so I will remember to say no sometimes when people try to wipe their shoes on me."

If you are really feeling low, send yourself an e-card and some jokes. Some days you may only want to include a few of these aspects or incorporate others that are more relevant. If you don't have a computer, leave yourself a message on your cell phone to listen to before you start work. You can also link with colleagues to send a daily encouraging email or text message.

Attracting Spells

Computers are excellent both for spells to attract good things into your life and to banish doubts, fears, or negative influences. You can use the whole computer screen or draw a circle—a symbol of power and protection—within which to weave your alchemy.

To create a computer spell:

1. In the center of your computer screen or circle, write a word or phrase to represent what you want to attract into your career or general life. Alternatively, draw an image or take one from clip art to represent the goal. You

can also use a scanned photograph or digicam image on your screen. For example, you could draw a bird or boat to represent overseas travel or a more permanent posting or perhaps the national flag if it was a particular country or state emblem you wanted to trade with or live in.

2. Create a mantra to express your need, such as "Power of fortune increase see, in California may I be," and say it over and over in your mind (or aloud if you are alone), speaking faster and faster each time. Feel the sensation of power and excitement rising within you.

3. As you increase the speed of your mantra, increase the size of the image or word gradually so it fills your whole screen (or circle, if you are using one).

4. When you cannot enlarge it any more, end the spell with the following chant: "The power is mine, as I count nine, one, two, three, four, five, six, seven, eight, nine."

5. On "nine," press the *print* button so the image will emerge in a tangible form that you can pin on the wall as a reminder of your power when you get discouraged.

Computers are ideal for spell casting because you can use the mouse to manipulate images, create a magic circle with the four elements on screen, or use focused imagery as a way of concentrating your energies through mind power. This is just as effective as a more conventional magical spell, and a lot easier to carry out in the office. If you want to make the spell more complex, using a circle on the screen, label the four cardinal points, north/earth, east/air, south/fire, and west/water.

To create a more complex computer spell:

1. On your computer screen, set a small version of your image, word, or phrase in the center of a circle and, using your mouse, move the image around, passing it in order through the four cardinal points, beginning with north at the top of your circle. At each point, chant, for example, "I call California with the power of earth."

2. As you move your symbol to the east, build up the chant: "I call California with the power of earth, I call Califor-

nia with the power of air," until at the west you incorporate all four elements into your chant.

3. Next, increase the size of the image until it covers the
four marked directions and the circle, repeating the
chant.

4. Finally, erase the circle while saying: "The power is free,
the power's in me, earth, air, water, fire, let nothing stop
what I desire."

5. Wipe out the image because the power is within you.
Repeat when necessary as you take steps toward fulfill-
ing your dream.

Some chants sound like doggerel and for that reason are very
good for making a pattern of sounds to increase your inner
source of power. If you prefer you can use simple words or create beautiful poetry for your spells. Do write down in your journal the ones that work well as the words can so easily slip away
in the flurry of life. If you are working in a communal office you
can recite the chants in your mind.

Banishing Magic

We cannot banish people from our workplace and life by magical means because that interferes with their free will. But we
can banish the negative influence they may be having on our
career and our sense of well-being.

We can also banish obstacles to success, whether these are
imposed by circumstances, other people, or our own fears. In
the same way we can rid ourselves of attitudes and weaknesses
that hold us back, such as indecision or timidity, and the old
voices from the past that can still haunt us and make us anticipate failure because we messed up mathematics in the third
grade and our teacher said we would always be useless with
figures. Even a doctorate in nuclear physics may not counter
Miss Wallbank's poisoned chalice twenty-five years ago.

The key to successfully banishing magic is positive intent.
Don't do your computer-banishing spells when you have just
had an argument, been the subject of a spiteful remark, or been
treated unfairly. Negativity tends to spill over into a spell.

The other important success factor is to replace what you are banishing with something positive, as otherwise the banished factor tends to creep back into the vacated space.

To perform a banishing spell:

1. Create a symbol of whatever you wish to work with—whether a word, phrase, or image on your computer screen. Be as ingenious as you like; for example, use a photograph of a flock of cackling geese to banish spiteful workplace gossip or a mountain made up of rocks to overcome a pile of debts taller than the Sierra Nevada. Enlarge the image so it fills your computer screen.

2. Create a banishing chant that is fun and makes you smile. My favorite, especially if I am a bit scared of what I am banishing, is based on a childhood rhyme: "Spite and gossip go away, don't come back another day. Far from here may you stay. Out you go, 'cause I say so."

3. Repeat your chant (silently if necessary) as you diminish the size of the image or words until they are barely visible on the screen.

4. Now count backward and say: "The spell is done, as I count one. Three, two, one, be gone, be done. Now there is none. I have won."

5. Hit your print button as you say "won," and when you have the tiny printed image, cut the paper into tiny pieces and bury or burn them.

If you need to repeat the spell, each time begin with a smaller image on the screen as the power over you or fear diminishes. Finally, decide how you are going to replace what you have banished, perhaps with an affirmation of power or confidence written on another document file that you created at the same time on your computer. Alternatively put the image of a beautiful flower or place in the new file, or maybe a digicam photo of your children, partner, or dog that represents more positive energies that bring blessings into your life. If you are using a picture of what makes you happy, you might like to adopt it as a temporary screen saver.

If you use the techniques in this chapter, you will see how simple magic can really be the alchemy of the workplace. Since alchemy is all about transformation, we are in effect using our own mind power to change life to what we want.

In the next chapter we will focus on all-important workplace protection, both to stop malice between colleagues or bullying and to neutralize any negative energies that flow beneath and affect even the top floors of the tallest building.

CHAPTER 5

Workplace Protection

Who needs psychic protection at work when we've got legislation, equality commissions, and workplace counseling services? Probably we all do, as long as there are people and communal workplaces.

Let me tell you about Marnie, the new teacher in an inner-city school where many of the staff were approaching retirement. Every time Marnie sat it was in someone else's special chair, every time she made a drink she was using someone else's personal mug, and every time she tried to make an innovation in her teaching program, she was told: "That doesn't work. Forget the fancy trash you learned at college. This is the real world and the kids aren't worth it."

Marnie discovered that new teachers stayed a year at most, and the school not surprisingly had a recruiting problem. When she tried to establish a work experience program with local businesses for younger children to give them an incentive to study, she was blocked by the other staff.

Marnie went home, intending to resign the next day though she loved the kids whom she found willing to listen to new ideas. As she sat watching an electric storm through her apartment window, Marnie was fingering her clear crystal pendant given to her by her grandma. On impulse she opened the window and set the pendant on the ledge to catch the full force of the storm as she thought about how her grandma had always taught her to go back in fighting whatever the odds if a cause was worthwhile.

Marnie scribbled down the plans she wanted to implement. Next morning, clutching her storm crystal, she went to see the head teacher and put her plans for how she wanted to teach her classes and her ideas for motivating the younger kids with experience in the world of work.

To her surprise, the previously lethargic head, who mainly kept the door shut and ignored what went on, agreed to back and finance her from the school budget for setting up job placements. Ignoring the other staff, Marnie went ahead. Fortunately it was a hot summer of electric storms, so she regularly topped up what she regarded as her protective storm crystal and succeeded in successfully placing the first batch of kids.

Marnie took her breaks in her main classroom to avoid unnecessary negativity and brought in her own travel kettle and mugs. She didn't miraculously, as in the movies, turn the school around, but she did succeed in her own small area. Two years later she had her own mug and chair in the staff room.

Short of the guillotine, no workplace legislation would have been effective against such entrenched attitudes and bad practices that were tacitly ignored all the way up the tree to the education offices, where complaints fell on deaf ears and earned the protestor the mark of troublemaker. People just moving on does often, as I have found, keep the lid on bad workplaces. Sometimes, like with Marnie, all you can do is protect yourself psychically (see later in this chapter for ways of empowering crystals with the weather) and clean up your own personal pitch.

Most employment experiences are more positive than Marnie's, with an encouraging boss and cooperative coworkers. Equality and working conditions legislation on both sides of the Atlantic is easing out the last pockets of discrimination, prejudice, and open bullying. But even with a high level of legislation in the workplace, sexual harassment can be a problem, especially if you are young and even though you hold a student of the year award from Harvard and work twice as hard as your coworkers.

There may be entrenched workplace predators, not only elderly Lotharios but young bloods eager to test out their sexual allure, who regard a new arrival as prey to be stalked. Some guys, especially in a mainly male environment, assume that all women up to the great-grandma stage are there to be groped. They may make offensive remarks best left for the locker room as part of ordinary conversation and assume a business trip with a female executive means a double room booked in the name of Smith. Men, too, can suffer from bosses who assume that personal assistant duties extend beyond the office.

Official complaints may be counterproductive or not taken seriously. Even if you are successfully pursuing legal or official harassment channels, psychic protection is a fast and effective way of getting those who behave inappropriately to back off. For really threatening guys, I would recommend a phallic-shaped crystal or stone twisted counterclockwise once sharply as their octopus arms approach you.

But you cannot legislate against personalities and more subtle forms of criticism or gossip that often emanate from one or two individuals who may have worked with a company for years and consider it their personal territory. For sensitive individuals, constant subtle bitching or a sarcastic manager perhaps under pressure from higher up the food chain can interfere with con-centration and chip away at self-esteem. Jobs involving customer care bring many rewards but also stress when things go wrong, even if the faults were not of your making. Customers or clients offload sometimes justifiable complaints about mistakes and poor service either face to face or by phone or angry fax or mail. You smile, placate, and promise improvements or recompense until you feel your face will crack, while your stomach rides a diges-tive roller-coaster and your head pounds like a steam hammer.

Even the self-employed working alone can receive negative feedback, as I often experience when three organizations demand that work be finished at precisely the same time and the bank hassles me because none of the three companies have sent me payment for two months. On a bad day my gallstones play their own internal ball game with my liver.

Even friendly office encounters can on occasions intrude, when you need time and quiet to settle to a project or meet a deadline. A particular person may parrot on about a new lover who rivals Brad Pitt as you add columns of figures again and again—and get interrupted in precisely the same spot so you forever associate three thousand and forty-two with "blue eyes you could drown in." An older colleague may watch constantly over your shoulder, offering so many helpful suggestions that they become counterproductive because they prevent you from developing your own style.

Basic Workplace Protection

Karma will eventually sort out the acid-tongued harpy more effectively than backing her against the filing cabinet with a stapler or muttering vile incantations as you pour the coffee. In the meantime most of us at some time need psychic workplace protection, just as we need to block junk mail from slowing down our computer. You don't want to hurt or offend anyone while using psychic self-defense, but at certain times you do want to create a space around yourself where you can work undisturbed and not have to defend your position like Custer's last stand.

In chapter 2 we worked on creating an oasis of calm as a major way of establishing a peaceful working environment. Psychic protection is just one step forward in your line of defense.

If you do work in a harmonious setting, protection will only need to be very light, maybe a dish or two of protective crystals to counteract noise and the general mental and psychic pollution of phones, faxes, computers, photocopiers, air conditioning, and hissing coffee machines, though of course it is hard to imagine life without them. But if you do need some defense, there are a number of very subtle and easy ways you can protect your space and person against anyone with less than positive intent.

The Power of Light as a Psychic Shield

Light shields are an effective way of keeping your workspace open and welcoming, but can be activated when you are under sudden attack or in danger of unwanted intrusion.

The psychic shield technique is ancient. On his travels through the Near East, the ancient Greek general Alexander the

Great discovered a valley filled with huge diamonds. However, the diamonds were guarded by poisonous serpents. Alexander ordered his soldiers to polish their shields so that they became like mirrors. Then as the men advanced, the serpents saw their own reflections, became confused, and stung one another to death, so leaving the way clear for Alexander to obtain the treasure.

For thousands of years the Chinese have used mirrors as just one element of feng shui to deflect harm or bad vibes from their homes and workplaces.

To obtain the protection of light:

- Use any shiny object as a shield: the mirror of an open makeup compact, a small ornamental or swivel mirror (octagonal ones with Chinese I *Ching* designs called *baguas* on them are especially protective), a stainless-steel cylinder-shaped pencil holder, a desk organizer, or a pair of spectacles facing outward between you and the direction from which a potential intrusion will approach. Tiny mirrors on a prism hung in a window behind you will also reflect back any negativity moving toward you.

- If the approaching person is unfriendly or super critical, subtly project in your mind a light source from the mirror shield on your desk, visualizing it as a metal shield so any negative words bounce back to the speaker. If you sit and smile calmly, the person may move back involuntarily as the reflected force of his or her own tirade or sarcasm hits him or her fully and rebounds.

- Should someone be bitchy, be unfairly critical, or try to bully you, whether the president of a multimillion-dollar corporation or someone who resents you joining the firm, and in spite of your mirrors you feel intimidated, as the person leaves pick up a tiny mirror or the spectacles and hold it toward his or her retreating figure and say out loud (or to yourself if you can be overheard): "You can have that back." You are not cursing the person, just sending back the negativity that rightly belongs to him or her and emanates from some inadequacy in his or her makeup that causes the person to offload unpleasantness. It is the single most effective tactic you can use in any area of your life. When possible, splash water on the reflective surface you used.

- When you need to enter the lair of the office dragon or an autocratic executive, wear silver- or gold-colored earrings, a shiny pendant, bracelet, or shiny buckle, put your spectacles on a cord or chain around your neck or on your head, or carry a folder with a metallic cover or edges. Silver and gold are both very protective metals.

Remember what I often forget, there is never any justification for rudeness, diminishing another person's self-esteem, or pulling rank, so you are quite justified in sending back in your mind, like lobbing a tennis ball back, unnecessarily negative feedback or personal character assassination whatever the source.

Crystalline Protection

Light-reflecting crystals on your desk or workbench are another excellent way of setting up a protective force field.

To enact crystalline protection:

- Choose clear quartz crystal, sunny sparkling citrine, warm glowing orange carnelian, or amber—all symbols of courage and confidence, the latter said to contain the souls of many tigers. Keep these in a dish in your workspace so you can run your fingers through them to keep your defenses charged.

- Buy two or three small clear quartz crystals with points at one end that you can set along the three outer sides of your workstation. Turn them point outward when trouble or intrusion appears on the horizon. If you have the point facing inward the rest of the time, the crystals will transmit positive energies toward you during the day.

- If possible, set your crystals to allow natural sunlight or at least artificial light to make them sparkle.

- Use a tiny clear crystal sphere to hold up between your hands to fill you with confidence and optimism if you are expecting a difficult call or face-to-face meeting. Picture the crystalline sphere enclosing you during the conversation.

- Wash your protective crystals regularly under running water, especially after a hostile assault, and allow them to dry naturally.

- Have also within your work area darker semitransparent stones to filter out depressing comments or discouraging remarks that can sap energy and enthusiasm. I call these my "moaner stones"; they absorb unhelpful responses that come by phone or email as well as teenage angst or whining cats passing through my workspace.

- Especially effective are gray or brown smoky quartz, golden rutilated quartz with its tightly packed needles of light, rainbow or gleaming black obsidian, or its softer sister, Apache tear, formed according to legend from the tears of grieving Apache women after their men leapt from a cliff rather than be taken prisoner. These darker stones should be rounded and can be kept permanently on display in a dish or protective semicircle in your workspace to absorb noise pollution, stagnant energies, highly contagious inertia, and serial complaining. You need to wash these regularly and bury them in the soil of a potted plant for twenty-four hours over the weekend on your day off if they have had to absorb a lot of doom and gloom.

- Gentle-hued stones will not only deflect negativity but soften passing or encroaching resentment, anger, and plain cussedness. Try a mix of soft purple amethyst, any of the fluorites, blue lace agate, water ice calcite in pastel shades, or pink rose quartz in a third small dish. Hold one of these gentle stones or place it close to your computer or phone while downloading unknown emails or answering the telephone to the general public. A rose quartz circled counterclockwise will absorb any negativity if a call turns unexpectedly unfriendly.

- Kunzite or sugilite, both recently discovered stones, should be kept in a car or van for you to use in connection with work to keep you safe and prevent road rage; also use it while commuting.

- Green-and-black malachite crystals will guard you from the more adverse effects of modern equipment. Have one at each of the four corners of your computer or any machine you regularly use.

- Agates, amber, deep red garnet, rainbow laboradite, and turquoise are pollution absorbers and also good traveling companions, whatever the mode of transport. Deep blue sodalite or blue lapis lazuli are very protective if you fear flying, and moonstone or aquamarine will offer assurance at sea or overseas.

- Darker stones such as smoky quartz will help you lower your profile when necessary.

- If you cannot display your crystals because of the nature of your work, keep rounded ones in a drawstring bag or carry a single gently protective crystal, such as rose quartz, and a more active one, like citrine, in a pocket or on a pendant or belt buckle.

- A clear crystal point can be carried and held in the hand, point outward at times of psychological threat. Your crystal pendulum will double if you grasp the crystalline part.

In chapter 3, I talked about the power of crystalline waters. Keep with you one or two protective crystal waters from the list above to splash on your pulse points or drink if you feel under pressure.

Empowering Your Protective Stones Using the Weather

At the beginning of this chapter I described Marnie's storm crystal. She discovered how to empower it quite by chance or, as I prefer to believe, by tapping some ancient folk memory passed on to her genetically.

Clear quartz crystal is by far the most receptive stone to fill with weather energies, though smoky quartz and rose quartz respond well to rain, citrine to sunlight, and moonstone to the moon. In fact you can empower any crystal for an urgent need using the power of the natural elements.

To empower a crystal:

- Leave your crystal outdoors for the duration of a storm to protect you from intense negativity from a number of people at once, from entrenched attitudes that are holding you back, and from those who are determined to thwart your efforts or undermine your confidence.
- Use rain to refresh your crystal and to guard you against others' inertia, lack of enthusiasm and effort, fault finding, and general moaning, and to stop you from becoming exhausted from acting as office cheerleader (maybe you should also think about handing over the role occasionally).
- The wind in a crystal will blow away pettiness, gossip, jealousy, and those who try to make you feel guilty for not living the workplace as they do, 24/7.
- Snow will melt away anger, bullying, irritability, unreasonable demands, and hyperactivity in others who disturb your calm. Use two or three ice cubes in warm weather and let them melt around your crystal.
- Use sunlight for countering any form of negativity, secret factions, rivalries and plots, and to protect you against those who drain your energies.
- Use moonlight for protection against those who trample on your dreams or whose reality principle is in fact the negativity principle and also against those who are perpetually sarcastic or acid tongued.

Empowered crystals, especially quartz crystals, are one of the most efficient and unobtrusive methods of workplace protection. You can empower a single quartz crystal in more than one kind of weather if you have a number of problems at work and need to make yourself a psychic powerhouse. Or you might have your citrine sun crystal, your rose quartz rain crystal, and your moonstone moon crystal in your workplace as well as a multipurpose clear crystal. Crystals just go on working in the background, leaving you to cope with the business at hand. After just a few days you will experience more positive vibes around you and so will know the crystals are doing their jobs.

Creating a Visualized Psychic Force Field

Hopefully you will not need to cast a field of protective light around yourself very often, but it is a method I have used successfully over the years, especially when working in radio or television. Some presenters can be quite hostile and totally closed to whatever I say on New Age matters before I even speak, and they make unnecessary personal attacks on my integrity.

The technique of using a psychic force field is effective as well if a particular person deliberately bugs or needles you so you will sooner or later lose your temper or if that person frequently takes credit for your work and ideas. The force field will not harm the other person, but will merely make them back off and leave alone what is not theirs. Enclose your computer with a protective field to prevent a virus attack since even the best virus defense system in the world cannot evade each new nasty invasion. The protective field will also deter hackers (and not least, curious colleagues who may want to read your private emails and creative folder of ideas). Surround your written and printed files before a presentation to ensure you get a fair hearing so you stand or fall (as I like to do in broadcasts) on merit and performance not on preformed prejudice.

The force field is also a good way of stopping theft of your most precious tools or equipment, from your backup hard drive to your car or van. Lisa, who drives a van and has to park overnight at motels, carried out the ritual monthly and takes the empowered model of her van into her motel room at night. In several years her goods have remained safe though other vehicles nearby have been robbed.

I also cast my psychic field around essentials like my passport and airline tickets as it seems to stop me from mislaying them.

To create a psychic force field:

1. Work in a pool of sunlight or arrange lamps to enclose you or the equipment or data you want to guard. If the item is large, for example a car, you can use a symbol of it instead, such as a toy car or a representative crystal (for example, turquoise for forms of transport). A golden

fiberoptic lamp with moving beams is especially good for creating a force field.

2. Carry out the visualization whenever you want it to start. If it would be difficult to work in the office, work at home using a symbol to represent your wish.

3. Extend your arms above and around yourself and the machine/files/symbol so the subject of the ritual is enclosed in an invisible inner circle within the actual pool of light. If you are using a symbol or crystal, draw three clockwise circles around it instead, still within the actual pool of light, using the index finger of your power hand, the one you write with.

4. Say either silently or aloud, if possible: "I draw this light to me, I draw this light through me, within me to the ground, above and around, protect and surround me/this machine. Keep harm away, dangers allay, gently but forcibly, light so I call thee in three. One, two three, guarded be."

5. Now declare your time scale. "I ask that this protection remain for—." (Generally you can set a protection to last for about a month and then you need to reempower it.) If this is a short-term need, for a particular trip or special project you are working on, you can set any time scale from a few hours to however many days.

6. Encircle yourself or the artifact three times more or make three extra circles around the symbol, counting aloud and repeating: "One, two, three, danger do not trouble me."

7. Now turning around nine times clockwise within the pool of light, shake your fingers and picture sparks showering from them and creating an electric fence around you, your equipment, or its symbol. If you used a crystal or symbol, you can now set it on the piece of equipment at work and it will be protected. Lisa keeps the model van in the glove box while driving.

8. Whenever a threat becomes more acute, shake your fingers and in your mind call the force field of sparks to be instantly activated.

As with your mirrors, you will not harm any assailant, merely stop them in their tracks; looking puzzled they may head off in another direction or change to a less aggressive tack of questioning or find their hacking program quietly shuts down.

Herbs for Protection

In chapter 2, I suggested using herbs to create an oasis of calm. Most of the plants I mentioned have built-in protective properties. For example, basil calms fears of plane travel, and others such as bay, fennel, orange blossom, rosemary, sage, and thyme, have their own special uses and adaptations.

To use herbs for protection:

- Keep a pot or dish of protective herbs on your desk or in a small purse to carry with you. Replace them regularly, scattering the old ones to the winds in an open space after work.

- Dried chopped nettles are very defensive, and you can buy them ready prepared from health stores or, wearing strong gloves, you can finely chop garden nettles and leave them to dry on a rack. A few in your protective dish of herbs or in a tiny purse in your drawer, tool bag, or car will deter most forms of potential harm.

- Keep rose or lavender water in your drawer for instant protection. Guys sometimes prefer a cedar or sandalwood cologne, which is equally potent. A single drop on your pulse points will activate your innate protective instincts.

- Herbal teas, whether made fresh or as herbal tea bags, are an instant source of protection, and if you don't enjoy drinking them you can inhale the fragrance. You can also subtly scatter a few grains of herbal tea in a clockwise circle around your desk if things are getting nasty (break open a sachet of herbal tea bags if necessary).

- A coffee or tea diffuser can be used to prepare teas made with fresh herbs. You can have a few small pots of herbs on window ledges for instant use as well as ongoing protection (one teaspoon of dried herbs or three teaspoons of fresh herbs to a cup of hot water, stirred and left for five minutes; strain off the herbs before serving). Offer herbal teas around at meetings and tense times.

Use the following herbal teas for these specific uses:

- Chamomile tea deflects spite or unfair criticism and calms irritability.
- Elder flower tea prevents extremes of emotion and over-the-top reactions.
- Hibiscus tea, much loved in modern Egypt, brings optimism and deflects negative responses.
- Lavender tea stops unkind gossip, teasing, and subtle bullying.
- Lemon tea cheers up moaners and prevents fault finding and those who set obstacles in the way of every plan.
- Peppermint tea prevents whispering campaigns, tale telling, and subterfuge.
- Rose hip or petal tea encourages conciliation and compromise and is healing after harsh or unfair words have been spoken.

Defensive Oils

The oils I mentioned in chapter 2 are also protective, and you can add these to a diffuser or a cotton ball, or use them in a spray. Use the following oils when you need especially potent psychological and psychic filters against negativity:

- Cedarwood replaces hostile words and thoughts with optimistic thoughts and encouraging words.
- Geranium deflects overaggressive competition and encourages cooperative effort and shared credit for results.
- Lemongrass repels spite and underhandedness and is as effective in neutralizing harm done by human snakes as well as its traditional association with repelling poisonous reptiles.

- Pine cleanses a soured or hostile atmosphere and returns hostility to the sender.
- Rosewood prevents hyperactivity or excess pressures that can make a workplace stressful and encourages equality if there are cliques or invisible barriers to success.

Smudging the Workplace

In Native American traditions, smudge or smoke magic is used to cleanse artifacts, people, and places. Incense has served a similar purpose in other societies.

If you operate from home or are part of a very small office, you can regularly smudge around your space and your equipment to cleanse stagnant energies and to cast a smoke spiral of protection around your business.

At a New Age festival or alternative therapies event you will often see stallholders smudging around their tables and boxes of goods before unpacking them. This creates a protected space so crowds and noise will not affect the atmosphere of the area within which they have set up a temporary base and maybe treatment bench. The practitioners will then smudge again before packing away (and at the end of each day in a longer event) so they do not carry away other people's negative energies and, if they are directly involved in healing, to cleanse accumulated angst and pain.

I smudge myself before a major event when I will be meeting and hopefully helping a lot of people with their problems so I do not become overwhelmed and ineffective. I smudge at the end of each day in order to relax in the hotel and not go over and over things I did wrong/could have done better and any negative reactions I received.

In larger workplaces, smoke alarms have made physical smudging difficult, and more conventional staff members may feel uncomfortable if you waft smoke around them and their desks or benches. Use instead a representation of the workplace to smudge two or three times a week around your own area and equipment and perhaps weekly around your department and/or the whole building (see page 108 for how to make a map of your workplace).

If there is going to be a crucial decision or meeting that will affect everyone's well-being, especially if the intervention is coming from outside the firm, you can cast a screen of protection using your map. This is also a good idea if there is industrial espionage or, on a smaller scale, so your own ideas are safe from plagiarism or a colleague who always takes the credit for innovations you proposed informally.

Using Smudge Sticks

Smudge sticks are made of sagebrush and cedar in America, Canada, or Australia. The bundles of dried herbs are tied together in a wand, and sold in health as well as New Age stores and extensively by mail order. If you cannot obtain a smudge stick, substitute a firm sage or cedar incense stick that you can waft in the same way. Work outdoors in a sheltered location if possible.

To smudge in the workplace:

1. First draw a plan of your office, if possible with a stick in sand or earth. Working with natural earth substances brings added grounding and shielding powers. If you cannot find a suitable outdoor space, acquire a deep tray like a child's small sandbox about two feet square, or larger if you prefer, so you can kneel and smudge all around it. You can also use children's clay, making thin clay wall outlines and balls of clay for people and objects and drawing the various essential machines in the clay with a knife. Set the model on a large metal tray if indoors.

2. Mark the outline of the work building in the sand, clay, or earth. If representing more than one floor, place each one in separate but adjoining squares within the main outline. Then mark in the different work areas and any equipment you use, making your own area disproportionately larger and more detailed.

3. Use small crystals or glass nuggets to represent significant people.

4. Surround your own area with a circle of small malachite crystals if you can obtain them (or any other protective crystal).

5. Light the tip of a smudge stick, using a taper from a lighted candle and as the flame subsides, blow gently on the tip until it glows red. Holding the smudge stick in your power hand (the one you write with) and fanning the smoke with either your other hand or a feather, first pass the smudge around the edges of the plan counter-clockwise, creating small counterclockwise smoke circles, and then around each of the work spaces and major pieces of equipment.

6. Allow the smudge to find its own rhythms and pathway and spiral over each crystal representing a person, increasing the circles over anyone who generally displays a negative attitude. Circle your own space three times counterclockwise.

7. As you smudge create a mantra or continuous chant that becomes mesmeric. One of my own favorites is: "Nothing harm, peace calm, troubles cease, live in peace." You may find yourself swaying as you smudge.

8. Picture the actual setting with everyone relaxed and har-monious.

9. Repeat the circles, this time moving clockwise and mak-ing clockwise smoke circles just above the plan over each of the areas. This will infuse the workplace with positive energies, for you must always replace what you have taken out to avoid leave any space for the old stagnation or hostility to return.

10. Next set your work bag and shoes on the ground and this time, standing up over them, create smoke figures in the shape of the number eight, combining clockwise and counterclockwise movements, still chanting. (You can smudge your shoes and bag whenever you know you have a difficult day ahead and when you return home after a bad shift, even if you do not have time to smudge the workplace plan.)

11. Finally put your tiny smudged crystals in a circle around you on the ground to symbolize unity and smudge yourself from the floor to the crown of your head with counterclockwise spirals, followed by clockwise spirals down to your feet again. Follow with a third clockwise spiraling upward ending with a clockwise smoke circle around your head. You can do this again when you are in a hurry without the rest of the exercise.

12. If the smudge goes out at any point, relight it and continue with a loop where you stopped in order to rejoin the energies.

13. Wrap the crystals or glass nuggets representing your colleagues in a pink scarf and leave them in a drawer until your next smudge.

Take your own malachite crystal into work and place it in your personal workplace, remembering to wash it frequently and to take it home when you need to smudge again. You can either destroy the model after smudging and re-create it the next time or leave it in place. The advantage of re-creating it is that as you do so you can allow your own negative feelings to drain away into the creation.

Negative Earth Energies

You may work in a brand-new city warehouse or a barn conversion or the tallest skyscraper in town. But you may still suffer from sick building syndrome where there are frequent absences, a high staff turnover, and stress beyond that expected by the nature of the work. Usually the problem is more subtle than that and confined to one or two small areas. For example, the place you sit may feel cold and seem dark even in the height of summer with light pouring through the windows, or you may not like working when the office is deserted.

There are a number of explanations for what is usually a case of negative earth energies. Sometimes the workplace is built on land where there are very strong earth energies that are not meant for dwellings, and we may feel constantly enervated or conversely exhausted.

Look for a clue in the name, perhaps a city square or district called Temple or a Native American name that may indicate the area was once a sacred site or hill or even a burial place. Earlier settlers were sometimes unaware of or indifferent to the significance of these old sites and occasionally erected warehouse or big old houses that were converted or knocked down and replaced by twenty-first century wonders. But the earlier energies remain no matter how many times the rebuilding.

True negative earth energies can also be caused by major construction works such as building a motorway, by an excess of electricity pylons or cell phone masts in the vicinity, or by existing or former mine workings. Industrial estates can become psychically as well as physically polluted by these entities. Workplaces built on reclaimed docklands or on the site of former abattoirs, mental hospitals, prisons, workhouses, or where slaves lived or were buried or orphanages where children were badly treated can also be affected by sad memories ingrained in the land. Again, a name may give a clue to the unhappiness seeped into the soil.

Certain spots where natural subterranean energy lines converge or cross beneath a building may likewise account for a place where more arguments than might be expected flare up or people occupying a particular desk seldom stay with the company long. Conversely you may get a desk where everyone who sits there or their partners get pregnant soon after joining the company. That's a surge of positive earth energy and can be helpful if someone wants a baby. Just warn the new occupants. Under Useful Reading at the end of this book, I have suggested some titles if you want to know more about these energy lines and grids.

Detecting and Neutralizing Negative Earth Energies

Start by playing psychic detective. Is there a place in an office where even a healthy plant dies, where a number of people seem to get unreasonably irritable or visitors comment on feeling cold? Does a particular fax machine or photocopier constantly break down no matter how often it is fixed, a computer attract more than its share of system failures, or a certain phone constantly cut off callers? What about the desk where people don't stay or the area of the storeroom where things go missing or get dropped? People may blame the office ghost, but often it is an energy problem (that could of course activate the energy of some deceased discontented worker or resident on the land years before). Even if there is any paranormal activity, it will disappear once you have neutralized the energies. Note these problem areas on a scribbled plan, plus any spots that seem inexplicably dark, cold, or unfriendly.

To investigate negative earth energies:

1. Using your crystal pendulum, stand just outside one of the trouble spots. Start to move directly inward toward an imaginary center of a circle. Allow your pendulum to swing freely, and as you enter a trouble spot you will find that the pendulum begins to swing quite violently counterclockwise.

2. Walk inward in a direct straight line as though walking along the radius of an invisible circle, and you will reach a peak of pendulum negative swing activity that forms the center of your invisible but very real negative earth energy spot. Here the pendulum will swing first one way, then the other in very rapid succession, and you may get nauseous.

3. Walk outward in a straight line in the opposite direction from the invisible radius you entered, and the pendulum activity will decrease until it ceases. That takes you to a point on the circumference of the troubled circle energy. If you move inward in a straight line at any place on the invisible circumference, negative activity will increase.

4. Mark on your workplace plan the approximate diameter of the negative energy, which may be as little as one or two feet in circumference to between four and six feet in circumference. Some researchers have identified trouble squares rather than circles, but however the trouble spot

is divided, it will still have a concentration in the center. In the middle of one of these spots, you may feel your teeth on edge and a mild electric shock that lessens as you move outward.

5. Repeat these steps until you have created a detailed plan with all the negative energy spots marked.

If there are areas where the negativity remained particularly strong throughout the whole circle, this active circle may indicate an epicenter where energy lines intersect, causing a power overload (even fifty floors above the ground). You would not often have more than one of these overload spots per room or maybe none at all in the building. But clear that up and the energies in the room will also dramatically improve almost at once.

Curing the Trouble

Although we may not fully understand earth energies in spite of numerous theories, there are a variety of tried and tested methods by which you can successfully neutralize areas of negativity or excessive power.

To cure the trouble spots:

- If your desk or chair is over a place of negativity or hyperactive power, try to move slightly so you are not sitting in the center of the energy and so phones, computers, and so on are nearer the perimeter or preferably outside the negative area. If this is not possible, place an amethyst, amber, or smoky quartz crystal on your desk or workbench or on a piece of equipment over the center of the negative energy. Wash this frequently under running water.

- Phone calls (a case for a cordless) and personal interviews at work should, when possible, be carried out from a place of more positive energies.

- Should there be other negative spots in the room where you often stand or sit, wear or carry in your pocket an amethyst, amber, or smoky quartz.

- Fresh flowers or a potted plant above a place of lesser negative power will also absorb any bad feelings. African violets or aloe vera is especially effective. You may need to replace these frequently as the spot is not conducive for growth. Try to rotate hardworking plants, and bury jade or moss agate in the soil of the pot to strengthen the roots.

- If you can, set small amethysts on window ledges or near other difficult areas.

- If your colleagues are cynics, not helped by all that subterranean negativity (you may have had to come in on Sunday morning to use your pendulum), take your workplace plan home and cleanse the spot from there. For practical reasons, for example, if you work in a hospital or daycare center or top security establishment, it might also be easier to carry out your earth energy neutralization at home remotely. Since the energies are psychic not physical, you can transmit positive power remotely.

- To cure the trouble remotely, position a small amethyst on top of each trouble spot as drawn on your plan. Wash the amethysts weekly and let them dry naturally before returning them to the plan. Smudge around the edge of the plan once a month, counterclockwise and then clockwise. If possible keep the plan where natural light will fall on it, if necessary hanging rainbow prisms at the window.

Before long you will notice a distinct improvement in the atmosphere, and returning visitors will comment that the place has been painted or that there are new larger windows.

In the next chapter, having got rid of any bad atmospheres, we will work with balancing the energies so there is the right mix of creativity and harmony in your office.

CHAPTER 6

Getting the Balance Right: Workplace Energy Patterns

Helena, who lives in southern Sweden, works as a junior editor in a publishing company in a corrugated metal warehouse on a bleak industrial estate of uniform units. But the main offices and visitor areas are filled with crystals, dream catchers, prisms, comfortable chairs, and soft music.

Birds in an indoor aviary chorus in the reception area while often as not someone's dog will have come visiting for the day. The fragrance of coffee and fresh flowers pervades the air, even in the packing department. If time is short, the publishing director and Helena join the stockroom team to get orders to the post. The whole place is full of laughter, and people seem to flow from one area to the other. People take turns collecting young children from the local schools in the people carrier and caring for them after school if childcare arrangements fall through.

If someone has a domestic emergency it is dealt with sympathetically, and immediate time-off is offered without silences, sarcastic remarks, sighs, or hints of disloyalty and a lack of commitment, which nothing can legislate against.

A small room off the main offices has a bed and couch if anyone has a headache so they can rest and not need to go home, thus avoiding taking the whole day off. Everyone eats in the huge kitchen at convenient times (or when they are hungry or thirsty). There is always bread, cheese, butter, jam, milk, juices, and fruit supplied by the company. The publishing director shares mealtimes with the workers, and decisions are discussed, any problems are ironed out, and future work schedules are devised over coffee and cakes at a weekly meeting in the kitchen attended by all the staff.

Efficiency is high, tensions are nonexistent, and days lost to ill health are remarkably few. Staff turnover is very low.

A positive workplace atmosphere resides not only in physical comforts but also in mutually supportive relationships. I can still recall being a single parent sobbing my heart out while pushing my sick infant son in his stroller to the child minder because my boss was so sarcastic and my mainly older colleagues were silently reproachful for days afterward on the rare occasions I had phoned in and said my son was unwell.

Even in the largest corporation headquarters, an open-plan office can become by mutual agreement a series of individualized mini-homes away from home where staff feel comfortable and relaxed and give their best. Look into the cab of any long-distance lorry driver and you will see what I mean.

Making a Home Away from Home

If you are responsible for personnel, small but significant features do dramatically improve worker commitment, whatever the nature of the business. Consider: comfortable seating and flowers in rest areas; new magazines and daily papers; on-demand juices and fresh coffee; hot chocolate for cold mornings; bread and butter, jam, honey, and fresh fruit for snacks; a fridge, toaster, and microwave; a small garden created out of a delivery yard; and good quality soap and towels in the bathroom.

The extra expenditure is more than covered by increased output, fewer disputes, a low staff turnover, and diminished petty thieving and vandalism, because people feel that their workplace is an extension of their home. If you do work in a restrictive environment—and the same applies to impersonal hotels on business trips—try to imprint something of your own personality on the space, so it becomes part of you and will energize you at flat times (see chapter 2 for suggestions).

If you work from home, try to keep computers, faxes, and work tools separate from your living area or sleeping area (or cover them over at the end of your working period). Draw a line between collecting the laundry, dealing with family problems, and work time and space (even high-flying parents working from home may suffer from the twenty-four-hour family taxi service syndrome). Whether working in or outside the home, and especially if you are caring for children full- or part-time, establish a lunch break or at least some time for yourself each day during working hours. If you are sick or have a crisis, don't beat yourself up or stagger in with a temperature that would melt the polar ice cap.

Efficiency and creativity do decline rapidly if you become a work machine, and before long you are cast in the role of St. Matilda the office martyr (or Gertrude the walking germ factory). After all, years on no one will recall that you were the only to make it in when the 1999 hurricane ripped up the freeway (and then you had to turn around and go home again because there was no power).

The Elements and the Workplace

Positive changes can also balance the overall energies of business premises. They may not instantly transform colleagues into the Brady Bunch, but they will spontaneously and rapidly improve tempers, iron out hyperactivity, and maintain a lively creative atmosphere.

As I described in the previous chapter, the ancient elements—earth, air, fire, and water—are part of our psychic and psychological makeup, and each offers us qualities and strengths to meet particular challenges and opportunities.

The workplace, too, contains furnishings, equipment, and decorations that reflect in differing quantities these four elements. If you are working with the Chinese system, five elements are reflected (see chapter 8). These elements can be modified or supplemented to create the right elemental mix.

Working with the Four Elements

Ideally, all four elements should be represented in a work space, though in differing proportions according to the nature of the business or your career. Later in this section I list specific objects and materials associated with each element. By displaying these objects or using these materials, you can positively affect the balance needed for different professions and situations.

If you have a career in a caring profession, such as medicine, teaching, social work, childcare, charity work, alternative therapies, customer service, the hospitality or tourist industry, or in a partnership, water should predominate. Of course you would still need air for focus and for effectively channeling necessary expertise, earth to ground theories in good practice, and fire to inspire you and those you are working with to try new approaches and to see alternatives when you hit a major obstacle or client resistance.

For a career in technology, science, computer programming, pharmaceuticals, research, sales, accountancy, advertising, sports, dance, insurance, taxation investigation departments of any kind, or any form of speculation, you need a predominance of air. For media and creative activities, publishing, the music industry, any of the armed or rescue services, the travel industry, or work involving frequent business trips, metalwork, inventing and patenting, work in the fuel industry, troubleshooting, or self-employment, a predominance of fire is good. For law and justice, real estate, pension funds, manufacturing, crafts, government and international organizations, banking, agriculture and horticulture, work with animals, decorating and renovating properties, mining, environmental work, and the care of senior citizens, earth should be the major element.

Changing the Elemental Mix

On occasions, the mix of elements will need to be altered. For example, you might require additional fire power in your normally watery office if you have to get a project finished urgently. Water will calm down stressed individuals trying to meet a deadline and tripping over their feet in haste. Likewise, extra air will bring sudden focus and concentration when creativity is in overdrive, and extra earth ensures somebody actually makes sure the materials are available and time scales are feasible to complete an order before committing to an early deadline.

Below I have listed crystals, colors, and various materials that can be used to increase a necessary element or temporarily change the elemental balance.

Earth

Colors Green and brown

Character The Facilitator

Qualities it brings to the workplace Stability, common sense, practical skills, systematic approach, gradual increase in prosperity, realism, awareness of limitations imposed by time and resources, loyalty, ability to maintain the flow of regular work and orders, patience and perseverance, attention to detail, and tolerance.

Crystals Most agates, amazonite, aventurine, emerald, fossils, jet, malachite, moss agate, obsidian, tree agate petrified wood, rose quartz, rutilated quartz, smoky quartz, tiger's eye, and all stones with holes in the center.

Substances and materials Salt, soil, herbs, flowers, miniature trees, coins, fruit, nuts, seeds, potpourri, potted plants, colored sands and ornamental gravel, anything made of wood, clay, fabrics, or ceramics, cushions, mosaics, paper, account files and books of all kinds, animal symbols and images, forest or animal call music, and anything green or brown.

Air

Colors Yellow and gray

Character The Organizer

Qualities it brings to the workplace Logic, clear focus, an inquiring and analytical mind, ability to communicate clearly, concentration, versatility, adaptability, power, ability to deal with two or more thoughts or projects at the same time, curiosity, commercial and technological acumen, money-spinning abilities, ingenuity, sales and marketing skills, and ability to work under pressure.

Crystals Amethyst, blue lace agate, clear quartz crystal, citrine, danburite, diamond, sapphire, lapis lazuli, sodalite, sugilite, and turquoise.

Substances and materials Feathers, feathery grasses, stainless steel and chrome, paper clips and knives, fans, pencils and pens, pins, scissors, all technological equipment including computers and phones, tools or instruments, ceiling mobiles, wind chimes, keys, fragrances and fragrance sprays, open windows, bird and butterfly symbols and images, bird call music, and anything yellow or gray.

Fire

Colors Red, orange, or gold

Character The Creator

Qualities it brings to the workplace Creativity, originality and fertility of ideas, enthusiasm, inspiration, leadership, breadth of vision, courage, ability to generate enthusiasm in others, ability to transform a raw idea or product into a marketable creation, ability to see possibilities in even an unpromising situation or project, and willingness to accept it when work is leading nowhere and to jettison unproductive ventures.

Crystals Amber, blood and fire agate, bloodstone, *boji* stones, carnelian, desert rose, garnet, hematite, jasper, lava, iron pyrites, obsidian, ruby, and topaz.

Substances and materials Lights of all kinds, especially fiberoptic lamps, prisms, crystal spheres of all kinds that reflect rainbows, essential oils, natural sunshine, rainbows, oranges and all orange fruit, sunflowers and all golden or orange flowers, gold foil, anything made of glass, radiators, stoves and furnaces, dragon images, music from hot lands, and gold jewelry or anything that is gold, orange, or red in color.

Water

Colors Blue and silver

Character The Integrator

Qualities it brings to the workplace Intuitive understanding, empathy and sympathy with others, negotiation and peacemaking skills, imagination, ability to work with others, gentle good humor, uncanny power to anticipate the needs of a situation and thoughts of other people, openness to new ideas and opinions, willingness to deputize for others, acceptance of people for who they are and not for their status, and networking skills.

Crystals Aquamarine, calcite, coral, fluorite, jade, kunzite, moonstone, milky quartz, opal, pearl, selenite, and tourmaline.

Substances and materials Milk, water, tea, coffee, juices, seashells, kelp (seaweed), water features, vases and all containers, nets or webs of any kind, dream catchers, fish in tanks or sea creature and dolphin images, sea, river, or dolphin music, silk scarves, transparent drapes, silver bells on cords, Tibetan singing bowls, anything made of silver or copper, silver foil, and anything blue or silver colored.

Earth, air, fire, and water are key elements, as potent and relevant as they were for the ancients and the alchemists.

Tune into Your Needs

If your office seems out of balance, for example, everyone is unreasonably irritable, you can use some of the above materials to subtly correct the balance. Even if you can only change the balance in your own workspace, the effects will be experienced more widely, often quite rapidly.

You may already have some elemental crystals for calming or protective purposes. You may keep a set of one or two of each of the elemental crystals in a drawer or locker to top up your existing crystal dishes as required.

You could instead keep small, colored ribbons or colored wools that you can knot into a single strand around your chair or workbench or in a driving cab (or use different colored watch-bands) to give you a gradual infusion of elemental strength.

Alternatively, if you know what kind of a day lies ahead, you can dress in particular elemental colors or wear the appropriate metal to swim with the prevailing tide. You can also make different elemental crystal waters (see chapter 7) and keep a small bottle of each to drink or splash on pulse points.

An excess may affect everyone, but it will be most noticeable in individuals who display that element prominently in their character normally. The excess may also be obvious during a meeting or through remarks made and behavior observed during a break. The excess may be a permanent feature or may have been triggered by an event, such as a wave of redundancies or a lost order or even new people joining the team. Elemental imbalances tend to spread like wildfire but are easily remedied. The following list suggests ways you can assess whether a particular element is in excess in the people in your immediate environment.

Earth excess Inertia, sluggishness, stinginess with money from a usually generous person, obsession with details, inability to grasp the wider picture, unwillingness to consider alternative approaches, obsessiveness with tidiness, excessive home-making or nest building, pessimism, or territorial tendencies (that's been my mug since the Boston Tea Party). Counter with increased air.

Air excess Super criticalness, sarcasm, or wittiness at the expense of others, unusually rushed or inaccurate work, incoherence, unwillingness to explain thinking or ideas, crankiness, gossiping, liberalness with the truth, poor timekeeping, lost data or forgotten appointments, or changed focus midway without reason. Counter with increased earth.

Fire excess Irritability and impatience, temper tantrums, autocratic acts, unrealistic work pace for self and others, sudden loss of interest in a project, inability to switch off from a subject or from work, increasing accident proneness, empire building, carelessness with property, unnecessary risk taking, inappropriate sexual remarks or jokes, or inflamed office passion. Counter with increased water.

Water excess Overemotional response to professional matters, manipulative behaviors, favoritism, role taking such as being a helpless little girl or big sister or dad knows best, attention seeking, flirting, constant need for reassurance or praise, excessive socializing and you're-my-best-buddy syndrome, sense of rivalry, jealousy, or oversensitivity to constructive advice. Counter with increased fire.

Does Something Sound Familiar?

You may, as you read the list of excesses, identify your employer, partner, colleague, new recruit, or yourself as possessing the more negative aspects of an element (three or more excessive attributes mark an elemental obsessive). Such characteristics are fairly fixed and will need a slow gradual effort to modify an excess elemental balance. However, you may identify a temporary and usually quite dramatic element swing in your own or a colleague's behavior perhaps because of a problem at home or worries about the future.

Since it's hard to identify our own more permanent excesses, ask a friendly but honest colleague which of the four elemental characteristics you show and then read the list of excesses. Use the three-or-more rule and adapt the following elemental obsessive therapy or ask a friend to reprogram you.

Modifying an Elemental Obsessive

There are times when it becomes essential, for your own state of mind and your working situation, to change a colleague's overcompulsive behavior. You can start in small ways, such as altering the color of his or her mug (hard to do with an excess of earth) or using counterbalancing crystal waters in a drink you offer.

Other ways to modify an elemental obsessive:

- Place a substance from the remedy element as near your colleague's workspace as possible. For example, you can use earth potpourri for an air obsessive.
- Offer relevant cure crystals in the form of a gift or put them under the carpet or behind the back foot of the person's workstation.
- Write memos or messages for the obsessive using the appropriately (counterbalanced) colored paper and pens.
- Rig the Christmas present lottery so the water obsessive gets a red (fire) scarf or gold earrings or a Bedouin drum music CD.

It's a bit like shifting a mountain with a dessert spoon unless the elemental shift is a temporary one, but if you persist, your chronic earth character may give half a dollar to someone's birthday collection or your watery willow will express an opinion without expecting a round of applause.

Workplace Harmony and Activity Eastern Style

You can use the Eastern energy balancing system called feng shui (meaning wind and water) alongside the Western elemental one that I described in detail previously.

However, the Chinese system uses five elements—earth, wood, metal, fire, and water—and they are linked in a complex interaction of creating, destroying, helping, and hindering. Therefore I will concentrate in this section on encouraging the free and harmonious flowing of the life force, called chi, through the workplace (and home). If you want to know more about the fascinating five elements and the more complex system of feng shui measurement of the different areas of your business premises, I have listed a number of books under Useful Reading. You can also find many excellent web pages and online courses on

Feng shui. Feng shui was originally created more than five thousand years ago as a method to ensure that ancestral tombs and other revered places—and more recently ordinary homes, gardens, and workplaces—were built to harmonize with the landscape and the natural contours of the land. There are two formal systems of feng shui: the Form School and the Compass School, which involves precise measurement.

The folk system of feng shui that coexists in China and other Far Eastern lands alongside the more formalized methods concentrates on practical ways of ensuring that fresh but not too powerful life force energies flow freely within workplaces.

Many ordinary people in both the East and West practice folk feng shui in their homes and businesses, and this is the kind of practice described in more popular journals and books. I will therefore concentrate on describing general folk principles and recommended good practices in relation to the workplace and leave you to move on to the complex methods if and as you wish.

The Flow of Chi

A regulated flow of chi promotes growth, health, and vitality. When this positive energy becomes blocked, problems can occur, such as a general feeling of malaise or dis-ease, and can prevent opportunities from flowing into your business. If, however, chi flows too fast or intensely, it may lead to anger, hyperactivity, and an inability to relax, and it may carry away prosperity and well-being.

Good chi does not flow in straight lines, but circulates gently within and around a building to avoid "stale air." In contrast, adverse or bad Ch'ichi—or Shasha—does travel in a straight line, accumulating in poisoned arrows, which can be created by the sharp corners and diagonals of adjoining buildings or badly positioned furniture within a work space. The former are generally deflected by hanging workplace logo banners or mirrors on the outside of the building to reflect back the bad energies (but few workers are going to hang their feet out of a twenty-fourth floor window to launch the company flag to improve sales).

However, you can easily move furniture. If you catch yourself on the corners of desks as you pass through an office, the room's feng shui is probably wrong as well.

After entering through a building's main doorway, chi should be encouraged to flow in gentle wavy lines through the various rooms or work areas. See if you can walk from your building's entrance through the various areas without walking in a straight line.

The level and intensity of flow should vary according to the purpose for which the room or premises is used. An advertising agency needs more vigorous chi flow than a residential home for senior citizens. In workplaces as in homes, chi can be encouraged to circulate freely by using mirrors, crystals, water features, and wind chimes to gently push it on its way.

Checking the Flow

For a more detailed assessment of your chi factor, walk through your workplace from the front door with your pendulum. It will swing gently clockwise as it follows the undulating, positive chi.

To check the flow of chi:

- Follow the natural progression of rooms, as though you were showing a visitor around your workplace or workroom.
- On a rough sketch of your office layout, make a note of any negative feelings where the pendulum swings counterclockwise or of a blockage where it stops.
- Continue walking around the office until you have covered the whole premises. If you have a back door, leave that way.

The above example is how one can most easily identify the flow of energy. Having done that, you need to recognize any difficult areas and find a way of rectifying them.

Identifying and Righting Problems

The most powerful source of chi comes from living sources. Plants, which represent both the wood and earth elements, can be used to right all feng shui problems both indoors and out, to deflect sharp corners, to add energy to a dead area, and to get the energies flowing gently. Hanging plants will help create the right level of flow and are good if you need just a subtle adjustment. They are regarded as natural health enrichers anywhere in the workplace, but doubly so in the feng shui tradition.

To identify and right the problems in your workplace:

- Note where the blockages are by checking the energy flow. If the pendulum stops or hardly moves, the air is sluggish there. Is there a cluttered area that is slowing down the flow so much that the pendulum hardly moves?

- A dead area may need a wind chime, some greenery, or a fish tank to get the chi flowing. If an area feels stagnant, incense or oils can also offer an instant boost. A gently moving water feature brings together wind and water. If you are in a hurry, ripple your fingers—or feet—through a bowl of crystals.

- Does a door or window open onto a blank wall (dead energy) or the corner of another building (*sha*)? In either case, a mirror facing outward will reflect the unproductive energies out again.

- Is there a long corridor? Break up long corridors along which *sha* can rush with banners, bamboo flutes at 45-degree angles hung from the ceiling, and mobiles. A long room or corridor can be decorated with hanging pictures of raffia or silk. Red ribbons tied to overhead beams will also break up the negative energies that run along them. Break up straight paths through an open-plan office or walk-through reception area with plants, seating with rounded edges, fresh flowers, and wind chimes where necessary.

- If your pendulum swings clockwise but the movement becomes fast and fierce, you are moving through an area of too much intense chi activity. To slow down the chi, place a still object like a statue, rock, or piece of pottery in the area. Don't use an object that is hollow or the chi will disappear down the hole. If using a vase or similar object, fill it with flowers to keep the chi in the room.

A statue of Kwan Yin, the ancient mother goddess, is ideal for slowing chi and also attracts abundance and keeps away harm. Rugs, especially round ones, are good for slowing chi as are silk drapes or a bushy plant. Large plants can slow down chi in a hall or vestibule in a larger building or area such as a through lounge.

- Put pictures of beautiful scenes along unbroken stretches of walls to encourage a healthy flow of the life force.

Experiment room by room; move furniture. In the areas of blockage or negativity, add a wind chime, a mirror, a prism, or some greenery. Then retest the flow with your pendulum. Though there are countless books on feng shui, if you trust your own feelings, you will know if an area feels dead and if people seem consistently lethargic when sitting or working there. Then you can add wind chimes, plants, or mobiles one by one and note any improvements. Equally if visitors as well as colleagues get hot and bothered in a certain place, the energies are flowing too fast, and statues, rugs, and flowers need to be placed there to slow things down. Sensing the energies will become spontaneous with practice, and you will know at once after a few days' break if someone has rearranged things and upset the balance in your workplace in your absence.

Feng Shui and Workplace Prosperity

According to more formal feng shui practice, a building or room is divided into eight areas. You can use an ordinary compass to identify each area or a traditional octagonal *bagua*, which depicts the pattern of the eight areas, and lay one over a plan of your workplace or home if you work from there. You can buy a *bagua* with instructions from Oriental and New Age stores.

Each of the eight areas is associated with an element, a direction, and an attribute. The area with the attribute of wealth and money will always be in the southeast section of a building or room. Formal feng shui also identifies other areas that are significant for business, such as fame and success in the south and creativity in the north or west.

You can find out about these areas and about using a *bagua* or a Chinese compass in books on feng shui listed under Useful Reading and on numerous feng shui–related websites. However, here are some guidelines relating to the uses of the compass. Traditional practitioners always stand in a south-facing entrance facing south in order to read a room, using a Chinese compass or laying the *bagua* over the room from that viewpoint. If you are using an ordinary compass, stand in the center of the building and face north. The directions are the same whichever way you face. However, if you are using a traditional Chinese compass where south is marked at the top (many Chinese houses have the front door facing south), southeast—the wealth and money region—would be at your top left, rather than top right.

This has caused much confusion with users of popular feng shui. If in doubt, get out your compass or face a place you know is southeast of your house. Southeast is southeast is southeast even if you stand on your head. It's just that you have to be consistent in always facing south or north when identifying it.

You should choose the southeast area or room for doing accounts. This is where you should place a cash register or a computer on which you take orders and send invoices, and make your money-related phone calls here.

Adapting Feng Shui to What You've Got

It may not be possible to use the southeast area of your workplace for generating money. Don't despair of making your first million. There are lots of ways you can still generate business with traditional Chinese wealth symbols, wherever in a room or building you have to work to attract your wealth.

To adapt feng shui to your particular work location:

- Hang three Chinese divinatory coins with holes in the center with red ribbon or string on the inside of the door handle to activate wealth within the room.
- Bury nine coins in the soil of a potted plant in the room or corner you use for money making.
- Red and green are good for attracting wealth, so you might like to have something red and green in the main money area of your workplace.

- Place a three-legged lunar toad, traditionally depicted with a coin in his mouth, in the place you use for generating money (or in the entrance of the building facing inward). The toad also likes sitting under your desk.
- Goldfish in a tank in the money room, near a cash register, or in a corner attract good fortune.
- The laughing Chinese Buddha is doubly lucky. Rub his tummy and wish for money or rub his right ear and you'll receive good news.

There are a number of overall tips to ensure general good fortune in the workplace. I have found the following to be very useful.

To ensure good fortune:

- Wherever your work space, sit with a wall, not a window, behind you for support and authority. If possible, face or have a good view of the door.
- Avoid facing stairs or a bathroom that could drain away your energy and good fortune too fast.
- If you have to sit with your back to a window, put a plant on the window ledge as a shield.
- Do not have sharp or spiky plants (like a cactus) or a paper shredder or cutter near the main door as these are bad for harmonious relations.
- A clear crystal sphere (called "the essence of the dragon" in Asia) near a telephone or on top of a computer or fax machine brings in advantageous business calls.
- Because the most beneficial chi enters through the front of a building, the door and entrance areas to a workplace are especially important. They should be light, bright, well-lit, and with mirrors, wind chimes, and a picture of whatever guardian you favor (a powerful animal such as a tiger, horse, or dragon), especially if the stairs are straight ahead of the door.
- Set fierce Chinese china or stone dogs on either side of the entrance or, if you want to be very grand, place stone dragons or lions to turn away all negative people and to guard the premises at night.

- If you want promotion, hang a wind chime over your desk to keep the energies flowing.
- Keep clocks in working order and accurate in order to avoid time wasting and time wasters.
- Lintels over windows can block chi but can be cleared by hanging small vines, wind chimes, ribbons, or even a combination of all three in an airless room. They can also be used over the lintel of a front door that opens on to a staircase.
- You can also hang strings of bells in or near the entrance to your workroom to encourage good fortune energies to enter your work space, as the wind stirs the air with the melodic sounds.
- Flowing water is another dual sound and movement remedy, and it encourages abundance to flow. There are many small indoor fountains and water features available commercially.
- Plants in your office absorb harsh electrical impulses from computers, faxes, and so on, and on the window ledge they will stop pylon or phone mast pollution entering.
- Bathrooms, a workplace kitchen or food preparation area, or utility areas need to have their doors kept closed and any water exits covered when not in use so chi, and with it prosperity, does not vanish down the nearest watercourse.
- A tall upward-flowing plant in any bathroom area gives energy to the room and directs the flow of chi upward and onward.
- Above all, overflowing and cluttered drawers and work spaces, dirty coffee cups, unread advertisements, and broken gadgets block free-flowing chi in your office. Regular decluttering not only helps the energies flow feng shui style, but in any system it is a psychological boost to efficiency.
- If you want to introduce the five elements for extra harmony, wood can be represented by a living bushy plant in the southwest. Fire can be a lamp with a red shade in the south. For metal use anything brass, gold, or silver that is

very round, like a Kwan Yin mother goddess figure in the west or northwest. Earth, often something yellow, can be a rock in soil or a clay statue, perhaps the lucky Chinese three-legged toad with a coin in his mouth in the center or the northwest of the building. Water can be a fountain or aquarium in the north, if possible containing black and blue fish.

Following the above recommendations, or some of them where most applicable, provides a general sense of well-being. However, there is also the additional need to attract money and good fortune to your workplace, without which even the most altruistic business aim cannot survive. We will work more on these issues in chapter 11.

The whole concept of energy balancing is intuitive; the tools and methods I have described in this chapter are effective for creating a successful work environment and for calming down hyped-up colleagues. Combine the Eastern and Western methods according to what works for you. All of these systems are ultimately only guides; some parts will seem more relevant to you than others.

In time you will feel instinctively whether you need to inject a little extra elemental energy to break up your office stagnation. Before long you will know what is wrong with a layout upon entering a business premises—you might even set up a second career as a business energy expert.

In the next chapter we will consider planning forward, psychic style, so you can be at least two steps ahead of your competitors and make sure you are never without the necessary information for everyday decision making.

CHAPTER 7

Divining the Future: Planning Forward

In the introduction, I described how the most successful stockbrokers have their fingers on the speed dial or computer send key seconds before the relevant information is transmitted to them from a conventional source and they consciously process it. The key to fashion, publishing, sales, or indeed any creative industry is to be able to instinctively anticipate the mood and needs of the public months in advance. Of course, a rock star or movie idol endorsing the product is a huge bonus, but it is not the whole story of trendsetting. The British record company who didn't sign the Beatles or the publishers who sent back J. K. Rowling's first Harry Potter novel, unread with a polite printed rejection, lacked foresight in a major way.

But ordinary people also possess what is often called the sixth sense. Mothers and sometimes fathers routinely wake in the night seconds or minutes before their babies do, even if the infant is in another part of the house and has no regular waking pattern. Adoptive parents are just as psychically tuned in to their children.

Most adults can recall an instance when they suddenly decided to phone their mothers only to find the phone engaged. Spontaneously, she had decided to phone her offspring, maybe hundreds of miles away, at the same moment. Usually there is a good reason for the activation of such telepathic connection. I have hundreds of attested cases on file.

We have already worked with the pendulum as a way of accessing information not yet available to our conscious mind. It is quite possible with practice to fine-tune this intuitive power into full blown clairvoyance or *clear seeing*, becoming able to peer over the horizon of time. This ability to gaze into the future may at first be only a fleeting impression, but in time we can fine-tune the power to gain detailed and accurate information. In this section we will experiment with ways of developing what are innate but often underutilized psychic skills to make predictions about business matters or creative opportunities.

Experiencing the Future

Time is not fixed. On a very superficial level, when I phone my publisher in California at 6:00 P.M. United Kingdom time, she is getting ready for a busy morning ahead. When the Gregorian calendar replaced the older Roman or Julian calendar in Europe in 1582, eleven days vanished from the calendar and Christmas Day changed from January 6 to December 25. However, the new calendar was not adopted in Protestant England until 1752. During the intervening period England was in its own time frame.

Time is a useful method of measurement, not an absolute, and since all matter is moving energy, potentials not yet manifest already exist in this fluid form. Therefore it is possible to tap into these potentialities. With practice you can become aware of the options most likely to occur in your immediate future given the mix of people, circumstances, and prevailing energies that are interacting with your natural mind-set and preferences. You can then make informed decisions about the path you would like to follow and become more in control of your destiny.

Of course there is always the random joker in the pack, the unexpected factor; otherwise, the stock exchange and lotteries would be entirely dominated by clairvoyants or those who paid them (there are more clairvoyants in the stock exchange already than one might imagine).

How to Tune into Foreknowledge

Successfully planning forward is a question of recognizing intuitively the nuggets of gold out of all the garbage that floats into our mind, especially when we are relaxed or sleeping. It involves tuning in during waking hours to the psychic kick in the butt that alerts us to the need for urgent action, warns of a pitfall, or indicates by an inner sparkle and fizz a surefire winner.

Even in small ways foreknowledge can be useful; for example, if you get a feeling late one evening that a normally reliable babysitter will call sick early the next morning, you can forewarn a friend or relative you might need them to cover (just in case). You might experience a strong intuition that you should turn up at airport arrivals an hour before the plane of a new important client lands and then see him or her walking through the gate an hour early. Maybe he or she took an earlier flight because of some unexpected last-minute change of schedule and are delighted not to have to hang around waiting for you. You might have a sudden instinct that a regular supplier is not going to turn up with vital components and have ready an alternative source that can bike the goods within the hour if necessary.

Start by making a prediction every working day about someone or some event you could not have known about by conventional means. However, you may not want to start with predictions on which large amounts of money are dependent, as that could make you anxious, or results you will have to wait for months to confirm.

Name the area in your working life on which you are going to focus each day to give you a framework for your predictions. Then, just before you make your assessment, let your mind go blank, as if it were a blackboard over which you were drawing an eraser and wiping out words written on it in white chalk— your previous thoughts. Now let a picture form quite spontaneously in your mind. It may be of a matter entirely separate from the area on which you were focusing. Go with the new prediction as it obviously is of importance, and imagine that you are adjusting the viewfinder dial on an imaginary camera. Draw the image in your mind closer so details become clearer;

you may hear words or get a more subtle impression of what is going to happen. You can vary the time of day you make the prediction, the mood you are in, and whether you are alone, traveling, or with particular people

Record your results, noting under which conditions and mode you operate best. Assess in detail how you felt when you received a prediction, perhaps jittery for an exciting opportunity, calm when you realized something was going to turn out well, or nauseous if you detected untrustworthiness in your prediction. These are the feelings that will alert you in your everyday decision making in spontaneous situations when you are getting a warning or conversely when a particular unlikely project will be a success. You can also discover the best time for you to make more important forecasts as your confidence increases.

During your working day make mini-predictions, for example, what an expected but unknown visitor will look like or be wearing; who your first external email or phone call of the day will be from; or in which area your next customer service caller lives. If you follow the money markets even casually, predict, without assessing what you know, the approximate overnight rises and falls against other currencies.

Try to imagine where the leader in your newspaper or breaking story on the morning television news will transpire. Practice multiple predictions whenever you have the chance. When you have a spare hour with access to a television, switch on CNN, an overseas news channel, or any satellite current affairs channel and guess the topic the presenters will be discussing. If it is an advertising break, guess the next product.

Practice when you travel, predicting who among your fellow passengers will get off at the next train stop, which passengers at the local airport are going to which location (the guy in floral shorts and sunglasses may be going to Frankfurt rather than Barbados, so go with your gut not with external appearances).

Out of a destination board of flight numbers and locations with similar departure times, predict which departure will be called first and to which gate. Which one will be seriously delayed? If you are on a large station, guess the train platforms for different destinations (often switched) and train delays. Predict the area of the car park where you will find a space straight away even at a busy time.

When you are more confident, begin to make long-term predictions about things that don't necessarily have supporting facts, such as that a new timid employee will turn out to be on a fast track to the top or that a particular product in spite of all the hype and projective sales figures is going to flop.

When you are asked to make an assessment or snap judgment at work, repeat either aloud or by writing them down the known pros and cons. Then create a dark space in your mind, and as a picture or impression appears, speak slowly and deliberately without doubt. But however tempting or under whatever pressure, do listen to this inner wisdom. Unless it really is life or death (it rarely is in ordinary work matters except as hype), don't be rushed into making a decision until it feels right.

If nothing is coming, still your mind. If necessary go to the bathroom and splash water on your pulse points or walk in the fresh air for five minutes and then re-create the dark space in your mind. Then if you are still feeling nothing, the decision should if at all possible wait a few hours. At other times an answer will be instantaneous. In time, even skeptics will accept your predictions.

Psychic Brainstorming with Automatic Writing

The technique of automatic writing was once believed to be one way that spirits (or angels) communicated with humans. In a more modern interpretation, by allowing our hand to use a pen without consciously formulating the words, we can tap into the stream of unconscious wisdom. This collective pool of wisdom, called by the psychotherapist Carl Gustav Jung the collective unconscious, is, he hypothesized, made up of the accumulated experiences of humans. These experiences are linked by our very distant collective heritage and are constantly enriched by the very different experiences of ongoing human experience. It is not limited by time and space.

In my view and that of many other psychic researchers, automatic writing is a good way of dipping into this collective pool, and by the principle of psychokinesis you will usually draw up some relevant knowledge that was previously unknown to you.

Automatic writing is therefore an excellent method for brainstorming both ideas and solutions. You can work alone, especially if colleagues would think you were one of the witches of Salem if you deviated from the strictly facts and figures spectrum. Even if people do not buy the collective unconscious theory, most accept that the mind is like an iceberg. People block ideas by trying too hard, especially if they are faced with a blank piece of paper or computer screen. For scriptwriters, would-be novelists, and advertising moguls, automatic writing kick-starts imagination and cures even a bad dose of writer's block.

The technique is similar whether you work alone or with others and operates better with old-fashioned pen and paper than with a keyboard or dictation machine. The pen seems to make a circuit between the psychic energy points in the hand, the unconscious mind, and the paper.

To practice automatic writing:

1. Take a sheet of white or cream paper (with spare sheets) and a pen you keep just for brainstorming. Even if you have been going around and around an issue and have partial solutions or half-formed ideas, start by formulating the basic questions or concepts of what you want to achieve (the ideas may reemerge in a different or more developed way).

2. Define the area of importance for your brainstorming session or a particular question. Consider carefully before you begin what you want to know, write the question at the head of the sheet of paper, and then switch to automatic pilot.

3. Let your mind go blank, using one of the techniques for stilling the mind, for example, visualizing a sky full of stars with each setting slowly one by one, leaving velvety darkness.

4. When you are relaxed, start writing. Some people experience a slight tingling in the fingers as their unconscious

mind moves into the driving seat. You may produce a few lines or draw symbols or dash off two or three pages.

5. Usually only one question, the consciously formulated one, will be answered, but sometimes the unconscious will cast up another related issue. When your pen stops, wait a minute or two and see whether another question or area comes spontaneously into your mind.

6. If there is one, write your second question, and when your unconscious is ready the pen will begin writing again. There may even be a third question and answer. You can use a new sheet of paper for each question or just continue on one page making sure there is a clear separation between questions.

Only when you have finished should you read what you have written. The answer may be straightforward or it may be in story form. However, the information may be more cryptic, such as some words of verse recalled from college days, a Biblical quotation, or symbols. If the answer does not make immediate sense, take five or ten minutes to go for a walk or carry out a routine task. Then read the words again. If the matter is of long-term significance, the ideas may be expanded in your dreams that night (see later in this chapter). Automatic writing is well worth practicing as it does seem to bypass blockages to creativity. Allowing your pen the freedom to write without your conscious direction can also allow you to access information and ideas that your unconscious mind absorbed without realizing it. The steps above are a good way of getting into this way of thinking; as you become experienced the process will become second nature. If you are naturally a logical person, automatic writing can free up your mind and allow the inspired side to come through, so giving you the best of both worlds in your working life.

Collective Brainstorming Using Automatic Writing

You can extend what I described above into a group activity. For such collective brainstorming, make sure everyone present around the table has at least one sheet of paper and a pen. Have spares of both in the center of the table.

As a group (you can work with up to seven or eight others), formulate the question, limiting discussion to five minutes. Then one of you should speak the finalized question out loud and ask those present to write it at the top of their paper. If you are leading the exercise, you can describe floating clouds or any other calming visual. Ask those present to let their minds go blank and then to start writing when they feel ready. If anyone does not want to write, that is fine. When the last person has finished writing, collect the papers and mix them up, handing them around randomly and asking each person to read aloud the contribution in front of them without commenting.

Then open up the forum. The smart colleague who writes something totally stupid or uses the exercise for scoring points may be a hazard the first time around. This person is probably on some ego trip or feels the need to dominate the meeting. Treat this contribution as seriously as the others and like the class joker at high school, once the craving for shock factor is withdrawn, it may be that his or her garbage contains a nugget of pure gold.

Collective brainstorming can expand upon what one individual's psychic brainstorming can achieve, as everyone will have their own niche of knowledge and information that contributes to the situation.

Coffee-Ground Readings

Coffee ground readings are another easy way of accessing future information. If matters are not adding up after logical assessment, a coffee-ground reading may help your unconscious mind to integrate the necessary information and come up with an inspired or at least sensible solution.

The advantage of coffee-ground readings for business decisions is that by the time you have made and drunk the coffee, your own intuition has done an awful lot of background research and your conscious mind has slipped out of overload to a more psychically receptive mode. What is more, if fur was flying or claws were being sharpened, the emotional heat has been taken out of the situation by the coffee interlude. Most psychic work is also sound psychologically.

Of course this unconscious wisdom has to be interpreted, for the unconscious does not just hand over secrets in chart form and certainly not in business jargon. It speaks mainly in symbols. Visual symbols have a whole lot of attached meanings built up from personal experience, what we have read from fairy stories or mythology, history, and our particular culture, both our immediate culture and our root ancestry. Our dreams use precisely the same symbols that we discover in such divinatory forms as coffee-ground reading.

Reading Coffee Grounds the Easy Way

Without realizing it, you may already be a coffee-ground reader. If you are a regular cappuccino drinker, you may occasionally sit staring into the residue, maybe thinking you'd like another coffee before getting back to work but haven't got time or should have a water or juice instead. As you gaze into the almost empty cup, you may half-consciously have noticed pictures in it. Interpreted intuitively these images will open your mind to a wider range of possibilities and information that is not accessible through more conventional means. You really need no more than your cappuccino machine or plastic cup from your local takeaway bar to try the instant method of reading coffee grounds.

To read coffee grounds instantly:

1. Scoop up a small spoon of the damp residual coffee grounds in the bottom of a coffee mug or from a filter in a conventional machine after coffee making.
2. Scatter these on a white plate or flat white dish and blow the grains on the dish while tilting it to create symbols and patterns. If the grounds are too sticky, microwave them for a few seconds on the plate.
3. Half-closing your eyes, ask a question and allow the grains to form either a scene or separate images against

the white background. In practice, if you relax you will instinctively interpret the significance of the symbol in light of your question. A plane taking off might reassure you that you would be included in the overseas trade fair team or alternatively that the promotion for which you had applied would launch your career in the new direction you anticipated.

Spanish and Mexican metal coffee makers—the more modern ones being electric, with separate compartments for coffee and water—make good instant divinatory coffee ground collectors.

For more detailed readings, first begin by choosing the all-important cup. Do not buy one of those specially marked divinatory cups, as they operate within a more restrictive fortune-telling method. Ideally use an ordinary large, shallow white coffee cup made for western coffee. You can also read with a white unadorned mug, but the shallower cup makes a reading clearer. Any light-colored cup can be used. Cups made of heat-proof glass have the advantage of letting you see the images from both sides. Turkish coffee cups tend to be small, but again choose unadorned white.

For coffee ground or syrup readings, proceed as follows:

- The secret of any coffee-ground reading is to half-close your eyes, hold the cup between your cupped hands (rather than by the handle), slowly revolve it clockwise, and, most important, keep talking. A tape recorder can be good if you are working alone. Say what you see without analysis or modification as this first interpretation is free from conscious blocks that will try to tidy up your thoughts.

- You are not looking for a perfectly formed flower, but as with the psychological Rorschach inkblot test, for a shape that suggests a flower, for example. The image is often just an entry point, and a flower image may suggest a whole garden or your ideas slowly blossoming if you persevere and nurture them. But you need to be patient and allow the flower to blossom according to its own blueprint.

- Single images may evoke words or impressions in your mind, and this holistic approach is far more helpful than just analyzing the meaning of an individual flower image (though that is a good starting point).
- Read the clearest image first. You will find more than a hundred traditional work-related symbols in appendix II that you may encounter in your dreams and in coffee-ground reading. But trust your own interpretations most of all; add to or alter my list, and keep your own symbol system in your journal.

With divination of any kind, if you define the area of concern—work, love, home—then the reading will refer to that. The exception is if a major problem is overshadowing every aspect of your life, such as someone's illness or a love breakup, in which case that needs to be dealt with before your psyche can focus happily again on office interactions.

Don't worry about trying to divide up the cup into different areas and assigning them significance, though you can read about systems that do and try them if you wish. For decision making, use the whole cup as your canvas.

You can also interpret a colleague's coffee grounds. Make sure he or she also interprets the reading, as the questioner will see the pattern of grains or white marks in syrup in a unique way that comes from deep in their psyche. Together you can tease out their meaning. If you are reading each other's cups and collaborate closely at work, there may well be a similar message about a question that concerns you both.

Western-Style Coffee-Ground Readings

You may prefer to make ground coffee and then read from the bottom of the cup. The pain of the odd floating ground is more than compensated for by the intensely intimate experience of colleagues making and sharing hand-brewed coffee, then peering into one another's empty cups, maybe to solve a joint work problem. Think of Doris Day in gingham under the stars on the prairies while a gorgeous singing cowboy brewed his coffee in a filthy pot over the camp fire.

You can use ordinary ground coffee made by the jug method (see below), decaffeinated ground coffee or herbal tea, or coffee bags split in the bottom of the cup and water added. If you hate coffee, tip the coffee away and just focus on the dregs.

To make ground coffee for divination:

1. Add a small spoon of ground coffee to a cup, add boiling or near boiling water, stir well, leave until the grounds settle in the bottom, and then drink. It is not the world's greatest cup of coffee, but it is drinkable and it's excellent for divination.

2. For more than one person, measure ground coffee into a heat-proof coffeepot or jug, about one tablespoon of ground coffee to six fluid ounces of cold water. Bring the coffee to a boil, then turn down the heat and allow the coffee to simmer for a minute. Alternatively use a vacuum or heat-retaining jug and add boiling water, then stir and cover. Do not filter the coffee grounds as you pour the coffee into your cup.

3. If you add milk to the cup soon after the water and stir, grounds will form images on top as they settle. These moving images will often create a scene that can reveal information about the context of the issue you did not know.

4. Once you get near the bottom of the cup and the grounds start to float, making the coffee too grainy to drink, invert the cup on a saucer or plate to drain off the liquid. (If there are not enough leaves for the reading from a pot, you can add a small spoonful from the residue in the pot.)

5. Pour the excess liquid from the side of the cup or mug handle to avoid spilling it everywhere. Grains may stick to the sides of the cup as well as the bottom. If any grains transfer to the saucer you can read those too. Traditionally, a cup is turned three times counterclockwise with the receptive hand, the one you do not write with, while steadying the saucer with the other.

Traditional Middle Eastern Methods

If you really want to go traditional, try Middle Eastern coffee-ground readings. The Middle Eastern Bedouin people originally heated their coffee in pots on the hot desert sand. Coffee-ground reading originated there, and if you have a Turkish or Greek takeaway near your office you can easily indulge in this ancient form of divination.

While I was in Egypt, a family of Bedouin origin taught me the art of coffee reading, using the thick syrupy Middle Eastern coffee. Their method has been around from about the sixth century CE. It is slightly different from the conventional coffee grounds method.

The beauty of this method is that because the coffee is so thick and syrupy, the residue will stick to the sides as well as the bottom of the cup. You can drain off any excess liquid in a saucer by inverting the cup, but what you actually read is, according to my Egyptian source, the white of the cup that shows through the dark syrupy residue. The images are very clear and static and startlingly accurate, in effect a dark canvas though which white lines and shapes shine through.

Initially try this method with coffee in a café that sells Turkish, Greek, or Middle Eastern coffee so you get an idea of the consistency needed. If you go to a traditional cafe you may find an old grandmother from the local community—who often gather there along with the city suits and artists—who will read for you.

Some readers do drain the cup completely until there is only residue in the bottom, more like traditional coffee grounds, and read with this. However, the whole-cup method, when the residue is still quite damp and coats the inside of the cup, is by far the best and most authentic. The art is called *kafemandeia* in Greek.

To make Middle Eastern coffee for divination:

1. Buy a traditional long-handled *briki* or *cezve*. (This is a traditional, slightly cone-shaped coffee-making vessel found in any tourist or handicraft outlet. The base is wider than the open top and you can buy special sets with the pot, small cups, and usually a pack of coffee.)

2. Put two or three teaspoons of sugar for each person in the bottom of the pot. Adding cardamom or figs or various spices to the coffee will lessen your need for sugar. Experiment until you get the right brew for you.

3. Fill the pot with water to where it narrows and fill the rest of the space, up to the very rim, with the coffee.

4. Heat over a very low light until the coffee begins to foam upward. Remove from the heat, stir till the foam goes down, put back on the heat where it will bubble up again, remove, and stir a second and third time. The coffee is now ready.

5. Stir the coffee well as you pour it into individual cups. The coffee has grounds in it that will sink to the bottom as you pour.

6. Drink it black. It is already syrupy so you won't need extra sugar in your cup.

7. Traditionally, the cup is then inverted onto a saucer before a reading, but experiment so the coffee is still thickly coated on the sides of the cup.

This surely adds further dimension to the traditional coffee break in all circumstances.

Joint Decision Making with Coffee

You can introduce coffee-ground readings to a group or team of people of up to about ten in number (four or five is best). Coffee inspiration after a hard, perhaps confrontational session will get people laughing and talking and exchanging tales of their great grannies back in Greece or Chile who treat the coffee cup as gospel.

Though some initially will be very skeptical about bringing mumbo jumbo into serious discussions, within a few minutes they will be fiercely debating the interpretation of the symbols, insisting that the image really is a dolphin in the bottom of the cup and so the Florida option just has to be the one. If your colleagues are coffee haters, you only need one coffee cup with grounds for the reading. But the more cups, the more diverse and enlightening the answers.

When I was young we used to have a central bowl, in pre-tea bag days, so the dregs of the empty cups could be tipped away for a fresh refill. One of my aunties used to read these collective dregs for family matters.

To do joint coffee-ground readings:

1. Choose one person to be the scribe, and define a question or area in which you jointly seek solutions.
2. Have everyone sit around a table, and pass the cup or cups one at a time around the group.
3. Beginning with the scribe, ask each person to describe any one image he or she sees and quite spontaneously explain what the image means to him or her. Do not analyze their responses. Do not worry either if people are interpreting the same group of grounds. One person may see a butterfly, another a bird or plane. All answers are equally valid and represent different facets of the issue.

Afterward the scribe can read out all the images and suggested meanings, and the group can put the ideas together. In the ensuing discussion a solution or choice about the original issue will naturally emerge.

Sample Reading

Jennifer is in her thirties and divorced with two teenagers who live with her and whom she supports, as her husband moved overseas and has a new wife and family. She runs a small advertising agency from a unit in a local industrial area, employing three local women for secretarial and graphic design. Jennifer also has a housekeeper to care for her children, as she has to travel all over the world, often at short notice. Recently Jennifer has become worried that so much of her profits seem to be disappearing in overhead and that when she is away working, productivity seems to dip dramatically. She always feels rushed and stressed and fears that her boys are growing up without her as well as without their father.

One option is to downsize and go back to being a one-woman concern, working from home. Jennifer has seen an ideal property with a barn at the back that could convert into an office in the countryside where she lived as a child and where she still has family and a number of friends who would help with childcare. However, this would mean working for other firms rather than being her own boss. Can she take a backward step? Jennifer wasn't going to change her whole life on the strength of a coffee-ground reading, but she was uncertain what was best to do, even having made costings and taken advice from her accountant. So using the dregs from the small filter coffee machine she kept for her personal use, Jennifer tipped them on to a white plate, blew on them to scatter them, and quite spontaneously decided to leave them in the sunshine to dry for an hour. She could remember her Brazilian great-grandma drying coffee grains naturally in sunlight before reading them and letting the patterns form.

Later, Jennifer sat in the sunshine looking down at the symbols on the plate and saw a galloping horse. Horses are a symbol of fertility, travel, and harmony, none of which Jennifer had experienced recently as the work was secure and lucrative but not exciting. In her present small company, she did not have the resources to take risks or attract big clients. Looking through half-closed eyes, Jennifer recalled riding through the countryside as a child with the wind in her hair and a sense of freedom. Now she traveled from hotel to airport to meeting and back again.

The second image seemed strange, a hydrant lying on its side, a huge hole and what seemed to be drops of water falling down it. Jennifer understood instantly; it was her resources draining away, the boys' teenage years rushing past, and her own enthusiasm declining as she lay awake balancing books and trying to keep to impossible deadlines.

The third image was of a rock, tall and pointed. Jennifer was puzzled. Was this an obstacle; did this mean her new plans would hit the rocks? That did not feel right, so Jennifer looked at the rock again and deliberately cleared her mind. Then she made the connection. *The Rock* was the logo of the firm she had worked for as a freelancer until her divorce when she set up her own company.

On sheer impulse Jennifer phoned her old boss, Neil, who was delighted to hear from her. With the installation of an interactive communications system, he had changed the nature of his business so a team of independent managers worked mainly from home, coming to London for meetings once a month and liaising with clients mainly by satellite phone or mail. Neil had been looking for new managers to work on their own initiative as his company was doing so well, with the view that each would in time set up his and her own cells of undermanagers.

Neil had not thought Jennifer would be interested. Without her overhead, Jennifer realized she would be financially better off working for Neil, and in fact the opportunities were far greater than her solo efforts. Jennifer did downsize, and her family now cares for the boys when she needs to visit clients.

I'll See You in My Dreams

Dreams are a powerful way our unconscious mind processes information that is not available consciously. They may spontaneously provide the answer to problems that are troubling us or act as a store of creative potential from the collective pool of universal wisdom.

Friedrich A. Kekulé, a German professor of chemistry in Ghent, Belgium, in the 1890s, was involved in research to discover the question of the structure of the benzene ring molecule, but without success. One evening he fell asleep in a chair and had a dream in which long rows of atoms began to twist themselves into a snake-like formation. One of the snakes caught its own tail and began to spin round in a circle. Kekulé woke and, using the closed-ring model seen in his dream, revolutionized organic chemistry.

In 1844, the American Elias Howe, who patented the first sewing machine, overcame the problem of threading the needle when in a dream he saw that the head of the spears held by attackers who were trying to execute him had eye-shaped holes in the top of their spears.

In both these dreams the information came in the form of symbols that the dreamer quite easily interpreted. The main problem comes in recalling the information from a dream, which can rapidly fade. I have often written an inspired chapter or two in my sleep or overcome a major structural problem in a book only to find by the time I had got the children ready for school that the information had faded.

Now I use dream recall so when I have a spare moment, I can access all the hard work I did in my sleep. I certainly don't advocate going to bed worrying about or even thinking about work, but if you do have a work-related issue on your mind, it will naturally form part of your dream, and the result of the dream may be helpful in resolving the daytime issue.

Practicing Dream Recall

It is no use having the most creative or prophetic dreams in the world if you do not remember them. Even if you have technicolor dreams pulsating with vivid detail, it is all too easy once the day kicks in for those elusive answers and meaningful words to slip away, especially as the logical mind starts to tidy up our thoughts after the night.

A vivid dream usually wakes us. At that point you have two options. If it was reaching an interesting stage, you can go back into it by visualizing the scene in detail from the moment you left the dream, hooking onto something specific, such as an unusual object in a room, an unfinished conversation, or the face of someone you had not encountered for years coming toward you. Focus just on that small segment in graphic detail—colors, textures, emotions, sounds—and then expand the frame so you are part of the dream scene again. If this is difficult, allow your imagination to continue the scene as though watching a film, while relaxing your body so you can return to the place where the dream ended and merge into it.

Alternatively, if you feel the dream has reached a satisfactory conclusion, the other option is to write down every detail you can remember, including symbols you do not understand, phrases spoken, impressions, fragrances, and above all your feelings during the most significant parts. Keep a pen and notebook by your bed, as all dreams have some significance and work-related dreams are no different in essence from more general ones. If the dream is work-related go into work a little early and sit quietly rereading the words you wrote.

A dream's meaning may be instantly clear, but if not, write down or draw a key symbol and draw lines radiating out from it to associated thoughts. Then see if those associations can be linked to create a web of meaning.

Often one or two dream symbols that are not necessarily the focus of the dream, but which arouse emotions in you, will hold the key. You can look through the meanings in appendix II to trigger your own ideas for dream interpretation.

Understanding Your Dreams

Paul was worried about a job interview to join the police department the following week. He dreamed that he had lost his shoes and had to go to the interview barefoot. But that created a bad impression, and he was rejected. Surprisingly, in the dream Paul was not at all sorry, rather he was relieved. His dead grandma was waiting outside and said, "Now you don't get to ride in the truck like your brother." At that moment Paul's father arrived in a shiny new pickup truck that turned into a police car with sirens, and Paul's older brother got in. They whizzed off, leaving Paul on his own.

Paul wrote down the word "police" and joined it to "father, brother, grandfather, bravery, admiration, inclusion, and truck ride." All Paul's male relatives had been in the police, and now Paul was set to follow the proud family tradition.

Then separately he wrote "lost shoes," and radiating from that he wrote "avoidance, exclusion, disapproving grandma, birds, contentment, and right path."

He realized that the shoes represented alternative paths. Paul suddenly recalled how when he was young, he had always enjoyed playing in the yard on his own and caring for his aviary of birds. When his uncles, all police officers, came over to take his father, retired grandfather, Paul, and his brother out shooting in a shiny pickup truck borrowed from the local police office.

Paul would sometimes pretend he couldn't find his shoes. The men would become impatient and leave without him. His late grandma, who brought up the boys after their mother died, would tell him he'd never be a real man like the others and would waste his life. Paul had done well at high school, but he chose to join an animal welfare shelter, rescuing abandoned and trapped animals.

But his family insisted that was not proper work, so Paul had agreed to apply for the police. The dream made Paul realize he did not want to go for the interview; he wanted to take up a job offer to go help maltreated animals in the Middle East. He could not live his family's way just to earn their approval.

Sometimes what we think is not a work-related dream, but is about childhood or school, can offer all kinds of clues about career matters. This is especially true when we are still carrying about attitudes ingrained in us years before about what is the right course to take.

As with coffee-ground symbols, the dream symbols in appendix II are just a guide to possible meanings. Create your own dream and symbol dictionary on a computer or in a loose leaf folder so you can rearrange your symbols alphabetically in your journal. Though dream and divinatory symbols do have universal meanings, they also have personal significance, often rooted in childhood, such as Paul's lost shoes telling him that police work was a path he did not wish to walk and the pickup truck representing acceptance by his family.

Note vivid dreams in your journal, using the notes you made when you woke, especially those that shed light on future endeavors. You can check back on how many of your predictions came true. The accuracy will increase the more you work with dream recall and interpretation. If a warning in a dream stays with you all day, remember that it is symbolic but try to understand what your unconscious is telling you. A car crash does not mean you will crash your car on the way to work (though maybe your automatic radar noticed the tire pressures need checking, which your conscious mind had not picked up on). But the dream may be telling you to proceed cautiously at work in any project you are pushing ahead with or steering without checking all the implications or whether it is taking the right route to success.

Our unconscious mind does have advantages over the conscious mind in decision making because, as I have suggested, it draws on information not accessible to logical thought processes. What is more, it is not bound by clock time, which is excellent for catching trains and planes and keeping appointments, but is restricted to time zones and other largely artificial measurements. Sometimes when you do use intuition to plan forward, you may discover that what you thought you wanted or needed are blind alleys or dead ends. When you have a wider picture, you can choose between options and plan both your immediate and long-term future using all possible information available.

In the next two chapters we will work with more formal divinatory systems: bibliomancy, the I Ching, and numerology.

CHAPTER 8

Decision Making with the *I Ching* and Bibliomancy

Though the use of formal divination in business was and still is mainly practiced in the Far East, increasingly it is becoming recognized in other parts of the world that counsel from sacred or established sources of wisdom and can offer insight into work decisions and relationships, as well as into more personal aspects of life. However, formal does not mean instant or straightforward, like a chart being instantly organized and analyzed the minute we press the appropriate command on a keyboard.

The Roman sibyl, the cave-dwelling prophetess who lived at Cumae, would sometimes write her prophecies on leaves and then scatter them to the winds so seekers had to chase them and piece the different parts together. I know people who work sibylline style, writing different options or answers to a work-related matter on various pieces of paper, marking a spot on the floor, and then switching on an electric fan on their desk. They hold each option in the airstream to see which is carried nearest the designated spot (try it for a decision in a hurry).

In this chapter I have concentrated on two traditional and less physically arduous methods than leaf or paper chasing that are very effective for work-related questions: use of the *I Ching* and Bibliomancy. If you do choose to learn the I *Ching* in detail, I have suggested suitable titles and versions (in the Useful Reading section at the end of the book). As you study, your whole intuitive awareness will expand. But for work purposes (and indeed most everyday needs), the basic introduction below will be quite adequate even for the most complex decisions.

Bibliomancy

The art of Bibliomancy goes back to the first written volumes, more than two thousand years before printing was invented. It is the process of selecting a passage from the Bible, or an otherwise sacred book, seemingly at random, to answer a particular question. The Bible, especially the St. James's Version, which is frequently consulted as a source of spontaneous inspiration, has given its name to the art, though "stichomancy" is the purist word for consulting nonbiblical texts.

Sacred sources can include, according to one's religious or cultural background or intuitive sense, the Hindu Rig Veda, the Koran, the written and very extensive I *Ching* volume, the Hebrew *Tananch*, the works of Shakespeare (or a large volume of Shakespeare quotations), volumes of famous quotations, or anthologies of poetry through the ages. One guy used the *Lord of the Rings* trilogy. The choice is yours.

The exercise can be used by one person or a number of colleagues who can each read aloud a randomly chosen passage from their personal source of wisdom to contribute to a collective decision-making or brainstorming session.

If you are working alone, choose your volume. You may choose to always use a particular favorite collection of wisdom that you keep at work. Equally you might possess a whole number of different inspirational works at home that you rotate. Paperback editions of great works are very cheap, and there really is no limit to your choice. I even heard of a guy (probably an urban myth) who worked in a huge sex goods supermarket who relied on the *Kama Sutra* to select his special offer for the day.

To practice bibliomancy:

1. Hold the closed volume in your hands, and ask your question aloud (or, if it is a daily reading, focus on the day ahead and name any challenges or opportunities you are expecting during the coming day; the chosen passage may reveal unexpected ones too).

2. Close your eyes and, repeating the question or again focusing on the day ahead, open the volume to where it feels right. Take your time and let your fingertips guide you.

3. Open your eyes and begin reading from the top left of the left-hand page (or top right-hand page if the book is in a language or script that conforms to the right-to-left sequence of text pages).

4. If the selected passage is the end of a quotation from the previous page, flip back as the information will lead into the quote on your chosen page and provide valuable information. Continue reading until the section has natural closure or, in the case of a poem, to the end of the relevant verse or if short the whole poem. Sometimes you will instinctively want to read on, but on other occasions a few lines will suffice.

5. The significance arrives in two waves, an initial pointer and then over the following hours a slow release of deeper symbolism and relevance as your imagination and intuition get to work, weaving options and solutions.

6. Note in your journal the source of the passage read and conclusions drawn so you can refer to it again if necessary and can monitor how subsequent events relate to the passage you read.

For a group, which can be any manageable number, either supply a variety of texts to distribute at random or ask participants to bring along their favorite work. Allow plenty of time for discussing or working on ideas that the readings inspire.

To practice bibliomancy as a group:

1. Formulate the purpose of the divination or the areas in which ideas are needed, for example, new ideas for publicity. Have everyone take a turn doing a reading, one at a time.

2. The first person should close his or her eyes and open his or her chosen book anywhere that feels right. This person then begins reading from the top of the left-hand page or the bottom of the previous one if linked for two or three paragraphs or verses. Discuss the reading's relevance.

3. Move on to the second person and have him or her choose a passage, continuing until each person has added a random reading. The earlier passages can be reread if necessary as the picture builds up.

Joint readings can also be a nonconfrontational way of smoothing out personality misalignments or tensions if the passages are used for extracting general principles of better workplace practices rather than for finger pointing or blaming.

Uncovering Underlying Daily Trends

As well as doing readings for yourself when you have a major question to answer, you can select a passage from a sacred work or make an I Ching trigram (a three-line formation) in the morning before leaving for work. While traveling I have sometimes used the Gideon Bible, found in every hotel drawer, as my divinatory source of inspiration and reassurance in an unfamiliar location.

A passage from a book or an I Ching formation will capture the prevailing energies of the day ahead and/or give guidance to a particular event or issue that you know will arise during the course of the day. Note any early morning (or evening if you are on night shift) readings in your journal, and you may see a pattern emerging, especially with the I Ching. The significance of an early-morning reading may unfold during your journey to work or during your first coffee of the day if you work at home. It does not matter which method you choose. Even with Bibliomancy, though the passages chosen at random will probably be different each day, a similar message may repeat over a period of time.

Let me give you an example. Phil was a senior computer operative in his late forties with a large software company, a job he had held for many years. However, over the past two months he had become increasingly unhappy, as he was having a major personality clash with his new and very talented section leader, Judy. Judy, twenty years younger than Phil, constantly found fault with the way Phil worked, saying he was slow, and she criticized him to colleagues and managers alike.

On the advice of his wife, Pat, Phil did not resign since it was a job he loved. Nor did he want to make an official complaint as he hated confrontation. He picked a passage at random from the Bible each morning, though he was not particularly religious. Though the quotations were different, each counseled that he be patient and endure with cheerfulness and all would be resolved in the fullness of time.

After two weeks of similar messages from his early-morning readings, Phil was offered the chance to work as a computer troubleshooter (he was always solving problems other people had with their computers) and to teach newcomers how the firm's computer network worked. Ironically Judy had drawn attention to this quiet patient guy so his talents were at last noticed. His tolerance and maturity in handling Judy, who had upset a number of other workers in her short time with the company, had impressed the senior management. Not long afterward Judy was moved also so she could work solo and use her own talents in a more constructive way.

The Origins of the *I Ching*

The most popular divinatory tool for business decision making is the I *Ching*. The I *Ching* has been described as a map and guidebook to life's change points. The basis of its philosophy is that nothing is static, and by forming three- or six-line formations of two different symbols, *yang* and *yin* (see page 159), seemingly at random, you can tap into your personal destiny map at any point. These three- and six-line vertical formations are common to every method of the I *Ching* and are called trigrams (three-liners) or hexagrams (six-liners), respectively. Originally, trigrams and hexagrams were formed by reading the cracks on the back of a heated tortoise shell (our method is more tortoise friendly).

The I *Ching* will help us to tune into the prevailing energies at the moment of the reading and those that are rapidly approaching. In this way we can anticipate and ride the crest of the wave rather than being submerged by it or paddling too long in the shallows and missing the creative surge.

There are two root components of the I *Ching*, which means "Book of Changes" or "Work of Changes." Whichever method you adopt, *yang*, the original sun concept of light, power, masculinity, assertiveness, logic, and action is depicted as
━━━━yang,
and *yin*, the moon aspect of darkness, receptivity, femininity, intuition, acceptance, and inaction is depicted as
━━ ━━ yin.

Each of the I *Ching* trigrams (the three liners) and hexagrams (the six liners) you create to answer your questions are made up of different proportions of yang and yin. Both forces are equally important energies in the workplace as in life in general. Indeed, one of the principles of Taoism, the philosophy that underpins much of the I *Ching*, states that when one energy (yin or yang) reaches an extreme, it changes into the other in a constantly changing and balancing system.

By combining yang and yin lines in a trigram or hexagram, you can identify current and approaching trends and forces that suggest the best kind of action (or sometimes that it is a time for inaction).

Making Trigrams

The basic three-line yang and yin formations are valuable for giving yourself a morning reading to tune into the prevailing energies of the day. They can also be interpreted in the office whenever you need to anticipate the best response, perhaps before a phone call or meeting, to prioritize or to make a decision about the best approach to a project or problem.

Would an earth wait and let matters mature approach be best? Should the gentle persistence of wind prevail or is it a time for embracing major change with thunder? The trigram you cast reflects the future immediately ahead of where you are now, the crest of the wave just too far out to sea to identify.

There are a number of ways of making a trigram at a time when you need an answer, for example, by throwing coins or manipulating yarrow stalks. If you are interested in learning more about this ancient device, you have plenty of time, and are good at mathematics, I have listed books describing these methods under Useful Reading.

However, with my own extensive research working with individuals both on career as well as personal decisions, I have found that making I *Ching* pebbles and casting them are much closer to the intuitive early pre-Confucian methods and seem to trigger images easily and rapidly.

Hexagrams are just six lines instead of three, and I have described them more fully later in this chapter. We will start by working with trigrams. But before we go any further, we need to make our basic tools, the I *Ching* stones.

I *Ching* stones are very portable. You can carry your stones in a small pouch and use them anywhere, without worrying about calculating coin value or recording the different number values you obtain. I *Ching* stones made from small flat jade crystals are especially powerful as a divinatory tool, but you can make them from ordinary white stones collected from a beach, river bank, or any place that has positive associations for you.

You will need six small stones of similar size and shape (plus one or two for spares as they are easily dropped). The stones should be about the size of a large coin and flat on both sides so you can mark on them. On one side of each of the six stones mark a yang, an unbroken line, with indelible pen or acrylic paint and a fine brush. For a clear effect on the stones (not crystals), etch out the yang signs with a sharp metal object such as a screwdriver and then paint the indented shape.

▬▬▬ yang

On the other side of each of the six stones, mark a yin, which is a broken line.

▬▬ ▬▬ yin

Your six I *Ching* stones are now ready for use. When you have marked them, keep them in a drawstring bag or purse. The more you use them, the more potent they will become.

Casting the Stones to Make a Trigram

Casting or throwing the stones is far simpler than the more common method of shuffling stones or adding up the values of coins you have cast heads or tails. Casting or throwing is one way that the conscious mind is bypassed and the unconscious mind allowed to direct the throw so it can answer the question using all the available information.

Casting will involve throwing three stones for a trigram (or six stones for a hexagram) one at a time and determining whether a yang or yin falls uppermost for each throw. In this way you can build up your vertical row of yangs and yins that when interpreted will answer your question. If you keep your stones in a purse or small bag, you can draw each one out slowly and throw it on a table in front of you.

To make a trigram:

1. Hold your bag of marked stones between your hands and ask aloud the question you want answered or if in the morning, ask what will be the most helpful strategy for the day ahead.

2. With your power hand, the one you write with, pick a stone from your bag and cast it on to a table or any flat surface.

3. Place the stone you cast nearest to you, with the side that fell uppermost, yang or yin, at the base of a column that you will build upward. This is the first line of your trigram. Both trigrams and hexagrams are created and read vertically, from bottom to top. The top line is the last stone you put down and read.

4. Pick in turn and cast two more pebbles, adding them to your column, until you have a vertical row of three patterns to create a trigram.

Interpreting the Trigrams

The trigrams, or three lines composed of different mixes of yang and yin, divide the energies into more finely tuned ideal reactions to challenges or opportunities. As you read them you may identify your own character with one of the forces, though we carry within us qualities of all eight of the forces associated with the eight trigrams; at different times the other seven strengths will come to the fore.

I have listed each possible trigram next, along with a number of their attributes and images. Focus your imagination on some of these images as you read. Pictures will build up spontaneously in your mind that will illustrate the meaning of the trigram and its manifestation in different types of people and activities and in nature.

These images will help you when you are using the I *Ching* to answer questions and to relate a chosen trigram more specifically to the area under consideration.

Chi'en, Heaven or Sky

☰

This is pure yang, the trigram of undiluted power and energy, of acknowledging and asserting what it is you want and then going all out to achieve that aim.

In business terms, Chi'en augurs the success of creative ventures and ambitious schemes. It suggests immediate focused action and says that you should aim high, seizing any opportunities to expand business and to develop potentially promising markets or projects with an all-out effort.

As a personal omen, it augurs promotion, leadership opportunities, results beyond those you hoped for, and the emergence or expression of a talent that will produce tangible material results in the future for you. If you are planning on setting up in your own business, Chi'en indicates that now is an opportune time to strike out alone.

The only hazards can be if the desired end result is used to justify ruthlessness or if Chi'en energy is dissipated on empire building or creating rival factions within the workplace.

Attributes: strength, focused energy, creativity, logic, courage
Animal: horse, tiger, lion
Body: head, mind, skull
Family position: father

Roles: sage, military commander, philosopher, elderly men

Associated images: outer garments, cold and ice

Direction: northwest

Season: the approach of winter

Color: white or gold

Plants: chrysanthemum, all herbs

Trees: fruit trees

K'un, Earth

This trigram is pure yin and represents total acceptance of people and situations as they are, not as you would like them to be. K'un says ideas can only be manifest within space and time, and you must allow for plans, projects, and potential to take root and incubate at their own optimum speed.

In business terms, K'un augurs waiting patiently for the right moment to invest or initiate change and accumulating the necessary resources and consensus to carry a project through before surging ahead. It talks of the necessity of acknowledging different viewpoints and perspectives and the importance of investment in personnel in terms of welfare, training, and nurturing embryo talents if a company is to thrive.

As a personal pointer, K'un advocates that you do not make any rash moves or enter confrontations even if a situation is less than satisfactory.

Not a good trigram for job moves or promotion, K'un suggests you work on developing your own areas of expertise and wait patiently for the right moment to make an upward move or move on.

The only hazard of K'un can be if compromise becomes inertia and indecision and if trying to accommodate everyone's opinions goes against economic good sense.

Attributes: tolerance, receptivity, intuition, nurturing, patience

Animal: ox, cow, mare, ant

Body: stomach, abdomen, womb, the unconscious mind

Family position: mother

Roles: wise woman, old women, ordinary people especially in crowds

Associated images: a seamless cloak that envelopes all things without question, an old cart that carries everything

Direction: southwest

Season: the approach of autumn

Color: black or dark brown

Plants: Potatoes, all bulbs

Trees: tree trunks of all kinds

L'i, Fire

This is the trigram of illumination and inspiration and of the necessary link between the fire energy and what fuels it; without fuel the fire would cease to burn and without fire the fuel would be lifeless. Hence one of its attributes is clinging. L'i also cleanses what was imperfect or no longer needed.

In business terms, L'i advises that plans or ideas be shaped by a definite strategy and time scale for achievement. Clear communication is important both to persuade others of the viability of a course and to avoid misunderstandings that could lead to resentment or negativity. L'i also counsels that if a project is going nowhere or a particular market appears to be drying up, this may be a good time to divert resources and energies or cut losses.

On a personal level, L'i offers a chance to take on a more active, creative role at work and to diverge energies into exciting and profitable areas. It is excellent for recognizing artistic or creative talents, such as writing or maybe an opening into the public marketplace for your work.

The only hazard of fire is if the destructive deck-clearing phase is not followed by immediate new creative input or if projects are abandoned at the first sign of a problem.

Attributes: clarity, illumination, cleansing, communication, inspiration, clinging

Animal: pheasant, sacred turtle, goldfish

Body: eye, the blood, speech, heart

Family position: middle daughter

Roles: artists, young women, generous people, craftsmen

Associated images: the sun, lightning, objects with holes such as shells and armor

Direction: south

Season: summer

Color: orange

Plants: tomatoes, red and yellow peppers

Trees: dry trees, hollows

K'an Water or the Abyss

K'an refers to fast-flowing water and sudden steep descents, such as waterfalls or a rocky cliff. It is the trigram of fluidity, of flowing with events and situations, risk taking, and exciting opportunity. However, as with navigating boats on fast-flowing rivers or white-water rafting, it is important to be aware of sudden possible changes in direction and be able instantly to adjust to the new situation or needs.

In business terms, K'an is a very exciting trigram, demanding constant monitoring or intuitive awareness of trends and changes in mood, whether of the public or employers, employees, or colleagues. It advocates accepting unexpected opportunities while looking out for sudden hazards (those rocks that may appear suddenly in the water threatening to hole the boat), whether in a meeting or when making career plans.

On a personal level, K'an is good for all speculation or for moving beyond your conventional area of expertise. It says you should listen to your instincts as to whether a person or offer is trustworthy and to open yourself to possibilities and try new things even if you don't immediately succeed.

The only hazard of water is if you try to swim against the tide (or the overall prevailing mood) or if you become too reckless in risking other people's money or resources.

Attributes: desire, emotion, instinct, fearlessness, danger, hardship

Animal: pig, rat, wild boar, bat

Body: ear, kidneys

Family position: second son

Roles: young men, the sick and troublemakers, fishermen

Associated images: wells, moon, the deep, rain and rivers, floods

Direction: north

Season: winter

Color: blue

Plants: reeds, water lilies, lotuses

Trees: willow, alder

Chen, Thunder

This is the trigram of natural renewal. In Chinese mythology the thunder comes out of K'un the earth (his mother's womb) in the spring, scattering the seeds of new life and new beginnings. The sudden dramatic thunderstorm, seen as dragons fighting, helps to bring rain to a parched land and to remove stagnant energies. But storms can also be destructive and so this trigram contains energies that need to be handled with care.

In business terms, Chen represents creative brainstorming sessions and positive changes, whether in personal or corporate working practices, which bring fresh perspectives and ideas. Therefore it suggests that if an impasse or stagnation exists, an alternative approach should be considered, perhaps seeking new markets, maybe overseas, even something as simple as adjusting working hours or trying a new supplier.

In a personal sense, Chen may indicate you have been smiling outwardly while seething inwardly about an injustice, an oversight, or lack of cooperation at work. It may be time to quietly but firmly set your personal and professional boundaries and reasonable limits. Chen is an excellent omen if you are planning a trip abroad or a career change or move.

The only problem with Chen comes if you lose your normal self-control and yell or cry, so putting yourself in a weak position even though right is on your side.

Attributes: arousal, renewal, surprise, spontaneity, initiative, male or animus potency

Animal: dragon, eagle, swallow

Body: voice, foot

Family position: eldest son

Roles: men up to middle age, princes, inventors, musicians

Associated images: thunderstorms, hurricanes, volcanoes

Direction: east

Season: spring

Color: yellow

Plants: all blossoming flowers

Trees: evergreens, blossom trees, bamboo

Sun, Wind and Wood

Sun (the Chinese word, not the sun that shines in the sky) is the trigram of gentle but persistent movement, such as the slow but enduring upward growth of a tree. It also signifies the gentle pervading breeze that stirs up still waters, so kites can fly, boats can sail, and garbage can be blown away.

In business terms, Sun represents the power to achieve goals, not by force but by persistence and perseverance. It augurs the growth of small businesses and true equality in the workplace, such as an end to unspoken prejudices, unfair privileges, secret locker room deals, or favoritism.

In the personal sphere, Sun says that you will succeed no matter how daunting the opposition, whether officialdom or the IRS is causing problems for your small firm or if you are going for promotion or admission to an official body and have to overcome hidden bias or a weighting of candidates.

The only drawback to Sun comes if you lose your positive focus and end up complaining about a bad situation and being ignored or giving up halfway and settling for second best.

Attributes: gentle but determined penetration, adaptability, flexibility, endurance, justice

Animal: cockerel, snake, tiger

Body: thigh, legs, lungs, the nervous system

Family position: eldest daughter

Roles: women up to middle age, teachers, travelers, people engaged in business

Associated images: trees, fragrances, clouds, ropes, webs

Direction: southeast

Season: the approach of summer

Color: green

Plants: grass, poppies, lilies

Trees: incense-giving trees and peach trees (these were believed to be life-giving manifestations of the mother goddess), all tall and high trees

Ken, Mountain

This is the trigram of stillness and a desire to rise above material and limiting daily concerns. There are nine sacred mountains in China, and according to Taoist belief, mountains are the medium through which by ascending them humans might communicate with the immortals.

In business terms, the mountain represents ideals and integrity and also taking the long-term and more global perspective, rather than looking for fast profit. It also signifies a time of calm productive work, without external crises or dissension within the workplace, good therefore for any pay talks or group enterprises.

On a personal level, Ken indicates you should avoid being drawn into company gossip or factions and rise above any pettiness and attempts to undermine your confidence, ensuring that you are not led to compromise your personal integrity.

The only drawback with Ken is you can spend so much time seeking perfection and setting yourself such a high standard that you never get anything finished.

ALCHEMY AT WORK

Attributes: stillness, withdrawal, silence, meditation, spiritual aspiration

Animal: dog, bull, leopard, mouse

Body: hand, back

Family position: youngest son

Roles: boys under sixteen, prisoners, the faithful and sincere, priests and monks

Associated images: door, opening, narrow path, walls, watchmen and watchtowers

Direction: northeast

Season: the approach of spring

Color: purple

Plants: all mountain plants

Trees: nut trees, gnarled trees

Tui, Lake or Marsh

This is the trigram of the inner world, of psychic insights, spreading joy, listening to dreams, and peacemaking. Lakes and marshland were regarded as misty, mysterious places so this is the trigram of secrets and what is yet to be revealed.

In business terms, on the surface an unlikely business trigram, Tui indicates that all the facts about a matter are not known or at least not revealed. This is not a time for memos or formal meetings, but rather for informal discussions on a one-to-one basis and for networking and behind-the-scenes efforts. It is an excellent time for workplaces and projects where imagination is crucial and to resist takeovers from larger companies.

On a personal level, go with your instincts and your intuition. Try to mediate between colleagues and keep any confidences you are entrusted with. Pay extra attention to detail.

The only drawback with Tui is that you can end up becoming the office cheerleader and losing your own inner harmony if you worry too much about others' problems.

Attributes: pleasure, joy, inner tranquility, healing, magic

Animal: sheep, birds, deer

Body: mouth, lips that smile

Family position: youngest daughter

Roles: women under sixteen, daughters, concubines, sorceresses

Associated images: valleys, mist, the harvest, low-lying land

Direction: west

Season: autumn

Color: red

Plants: magnolias, gardenias, all lake plants, spices

Trees: trees bleached with salt

The basic meaning of the trigrams as listed above may answer your question. But if you want any more information, use some of the images I suggested for each trigram and allow a picture to emerge spontaneously in your mind. Focus not only on what you see but also on the feelings and impressions the images invoke. These will shed light on the issue under consideration and possible outcomes of action or inaction.

Make a note in your journal with the date and time of the reading and the pictures your mind created. You can scribble a sketch or you may be inspired to write a great deal, as information floods from the depths of your unconscious wisdom and through that from the cosmic bank of future possibilities. Next time you throw the same trigram, different images will appear to reflect subtle differences in the question and context. Have a page in your journal for each trigram, for as you work you will discern different images in addition to those listed above, especially concerning the trigram that resonates most closely with your personality. The I Ching formal system was created over thousands of years ago by different people, but it is still essentially a living and growing form of divination.

Sample Reading

Let me explain more clearly how trigram interpretation works with an example of Maria, who is senior nurse in a busy emergency room in a large city hospital. Maria has noticed that work generally has been suffering because of constant gossip and a bad atmosphere since a young intern suddenly stopped dating one of the ER nurses in favor of a new very glamorous radiographer. The situation came to a head when a confrontation between the intern's present and former lovers upset a patient needing an urgent X-ray. Since the ER nurse involved was basically a good worker, Maria did not want to instigate formal disciplinary procedures.

Maria cast her *I Ching* crystals. She made the *Ken* or mountain trigram. Though Maria understood that she needed to rise above the pettiness of department gossip, the answer was not entirely helpful. As senior nurse she needed to resolve the situation, not stand aside.

Maria started to work with some of the associations of the mountain energies in her mind. She instinctively chose priests and monks, a narrow path between spiky plants growing on a mountain, and a watchtower high above everything.

In her mental picture she followed chanting monks who were in an ordered line walking along the narrow path between the spiky plants. At last they reached the watchtower. Spring was coming although it was still quite cold.

In her reverie Maria asked advice from one of the monks who had led the others and now climbed to the top of the tower. He put his hands to his lips to indicate silence and then drew a line in the air in front of him, which Maria took to mean the end of the matter.

At last Maria understood what the images were telling her. She was walking a narrow path between very difficult situations. It was nevertheless her job to keep an overview (climbing to the top of the tower) and ensure that the priority was dedication to the patients. As the leader it was her function to ensure the others were likewise focused on the path of idealism and integrity, walking in ordered rows (behaving profession-ally at all times). Maria so far had kept out of matters, fearing she would make them worse.

Maria called a meeting of all the nurses on the day roster and insisted that whatever the rights and wrongs of the situation, there could be no more personal vendettas and no more gossip on work time. They had all taken a job that demanded total devotion to the patients, and one unhappy patient was one too many. To Maria's surprise there were no mutterings and the staff settled back to work, relieved to have an imposed line drawn under the matter. Maria explained the situation to the head of radiography, who had likewise been reluctant to intervene. The intern moved on to another conquest and matters settled again.

Making and Interpreting Hexagrams

You can if you wish continue to use the trigrams, which with the pictorial method (the pre-Confucian system whereby you create pictures in your mind according to the trigram you form) can reveal a great deal of information about work-related or indeed any aspects of your life. However, for more complex matters, those with long-term implications, and for any collective decisions, try making a hexagram, which is simply two trigrams on top of each other. Now that you are familiar with the basic building blocks of the eight trigrams, you can create your own pictures in your mind of how the forces combine to answer your question according to the order you threw the yangs and yins.

So, for example, you might have made a trigram of the mountain first and then one of fire. Spend some time combining these different forces in different ways. For example, you might see a beacon of fire on top of a mountain guiding your way, suggesting you seek guidance from someone who is in authority or very wise (high up like the mountain), or you might see the fire as the sun rising over the mountain indicating tomorrow is another day. Of course, as you imagine the scene, the fire over the mountain might seem like a sunset, in which case the message is to let go of what did not work out today, but to welcome what you did learn or gain and let it rest in your mind.

The interpretation would depend on how your mind saw the images at a particular time. If you think of them as though on a painting in your mind or in a natural scene, your wise unconscious mind will create the illustration for you. The secret is to relax and to trust yourself to interpret your inner picture. If, of course, the fire trigram was formed first and afterward you put the mountain trigram on top of it in your vertical row, then you might have a volcanic fire raging inside you, indicating you are ready to erupt over an injustice and therefore need to control the fire so it does not destroy everything in its path as well as the offender. But on another occasion you might feel that this means your own creative force is buried under a mountain of responsibility and so you need time away from worries. It really is that fluid, according to the question you ask. You make the pictures, aided by your wise unconscious; you interpret them using the best tool of all—your imagination. As you tell stories about your pictures, you will continue to discern a whole lot of hidden meaning behind the combination of two simple images. I have given more suggestions on reading hexagrams later in this section.

To make a hexagram:

1. Use all six of your stones, again asking a question as you hold the bag.
2. One at a time, cast the stones as for a trigram.
3. Seeing whether the yang or yin aspect is uppermost, build a vertical line of six stones (two trigrams on top of each other), extending away from where you are sitting or standing.
4. Read the trigrams separately, starting with the bottom one and moving upward to the top one, to see what each is saying to you. Use the associated images of each trigram to help you with the reading.
5. Now, working on the valuable Gestalt psychological principle that the whole is different from and, many believe, greater than the sum of its parts, combine the two natural forces of the separate trigrams in a joint image. Visualize the hexagram exactly as it is created, as if you were looking at a picture of the natural forces represented by the hexagram, mingling and reacting with each other.
6. Again, note these in your journal with date, time, and any insights you received.

The hexagram I have illustrated below is called hexagram 16 Yu or enthusiasm. Earth is on the bottom and thunder is on top.

☰☰ Thunder, Chen

☰☰ Earth, K'un

To interpret this hexagram, I might picture thunder bursting from the earth in the spring (this hexagram is associated with March), scattering the seeds of new life that fall into the plowed soil, ready for me to begin growing. Perhaps you did not see that image, but rather an equally valid vision of thunder and lightning flashing over a still plain. You would still get a feeling of movement and energy, like that wonderful moment when after a hot airless day the stagnation is suddenly broken by a storm and rain pours down on the baked earth.

Allow your mind to create pictures, and scribble down the impressions, feelings, ideas, words, and maybe even sketches of what the two forces together are telling you about the question you asked.

If you made this hexagram it would be the right time for breaking an impasse by speaking out, for changing the status quo or work practices if the firm has hit a flat or unproductive period, for launching a new venture, standing out against injustice or obstacles, and for maybe clearing the air of underlying tensions or mutterings by a direct challenge to a bully or persistent dissenter. Maybe you are the dissenter standing up to a bully or defending a weaker colleague who is being badly treated.

The idea of spring carries with it new beginnings and an awakening of the earth so you can be sure that your efforts initiated now will continue to grow over the coming months. It would also be a good omen if you wanted a baby. The hexagram is not predicting what will happen, but suggesting the best course of action or possibilities coming into your sphere. If you were to consult an I *Ching* translation (see Useful Reading), you might find something like this for the judgment or overall significance for this hexagram.

There are fierce debates as to whether Confucius himself wrote many of the judgments or explanations commonly found in I *Ching* texts or whether they were added by his followers. A judgment is a careful consideration of how the energies inherent in a hexagram might apply to life or at least the lifestyle when the judgments were written.

But of course you don't need to consult a written I *Ching* unless you wish, and for workplace decisions it is often better to cast your stones in situ and then scribble down a picture or words that come to you in answer to your question. Even if you do refer to an I *Ching* translation (see Useful Reading), make and work with your own interpretation first.

As with trigrams, in your journal have a separate page for each hexagram and note down any special phrases or images, as well as specific readings, with their date and time. You can check back on any possibilities to see whether you followed them through, three or six months after the reading.

Sample Reading

Helena is the only woman in a lawyers' office in Stockholm. A number of the men are related. Though they are all experts in Sweden's comprehensive equality laws and keep them to the letter, Helena is aware that a lot of major decision making takes place at weekends on the golf course or at a sailing club. Though Helena plays golf well, the one time she went along to the club she felt so uncomfortable that the experience was never repeated. She has been wondering about moving to another firm, but she does generate a lot of business (and so personal bonuses), and the firm's facilities and resources are excellent.

A particularly annoying incident occurred when she discovered that a case for which she was the most qualified had been offered over a sailing weekend to one of the older men who was far less experienced in tax law than she was. The reason given was that the director of the company they were due to represent was a member of the same sailing club as the senior lawyer at her firm, and the client wanted to work with someone he already knew and trusted. Helena was furious but knew that shouting or crying would be a sign of female hormones.

Helena cast her *I Ching* during a lunch break and made the thunder over the earth hexagram. How could she effectively and forcefully make the others take her grievances seriously? The image she visualized was of two dragons fighting and creating a storm that a crowd of people on earth was watching. Spontaneously in her imagined scene, a pearl (dragon's treasure) fell from the sky and she caught it.

Then she got it. She was a major generator of the firm's profit because a lot of businesswomen liked dealing with her and she won almost every one of her cases. The pearl was what she gave to the firm. If she walked, a lot of valuable clients would follow her. Therefore she called a meeting and, to the surprise of the others, she coolly announced that as a partner (albeit a junior one) under the constitution of the firm she was required to be consulted on all major decisions and on the distribution of cases. Therefore the other members of the firm could either confine finalizing business deals to the morning meetings or they could sponsor her for both the golf and sailing clubs, so they would have no excuse not to include her in any meetings there. If neither condition was met, she would leave, along with her client base.

After a lot of uproar and muttering, the men agreed that before finalizing any 19th-hole deals they would discuss the matter for her approval during working hours. Helena has noticed that they are now like chastened schoolboys asking her opinion on everything.

The I *Ching* is far more than just an individual divination system, and once you have gotten used to it you can apply the principles to your workplace as a whole. Even if you can't totally change the overall rationale, you can see how the yang and yin currents are flowing in your workplace. Then by using different methods from this book (for example, in the chapter on creating an oasis of calm), you can slow down an excess of yang so the general feeling is calmer and more genuinely productive.

Some businesses are far too yang, with the emphasis constantly on proactive approaches and responses so workers suffer burnout or a sense of depersonalization (more of this in chapter 9 on working with the seasons, the sun, and the moon).

In contrast, the early hunters, the first food-producing industry, like their modern counterparts who live by hunting, had long yin periods, the time of waiting in the thicket, relaxed but alert for the animals to come. They had finely tuned intuitive antennae that alerted them to the approaching game animals; in this way their energies were not dissipated by sitting for hours with bow drawn. When the moment of kill came, their thrusting edge or yang energy could be activated instantly.

Too many hunters of industry do suffer burnout. If your every working day is pure undiluted yang—constant yelling, hyping of the workforce, and maximum sales pressure 24/7—then there is no light and shade as with the hunters in the forest, and the impetus to strike has been worn away before the real opportunity or crisis occurs.

You can do readings for colleagues to guide them and for yourself to see how you should approach a particular person or situation that you know is going to lead to overload. That way you can ride the pressure wave or discover ways not to be sucked into the general panic. You may sometimes work for long times with your trigram or hexagram picture, maybe drawing and coloring it or writing a story or poem. At other times your reading need only take a few minutes, and you can get a quick image to respond to an urgent need. They are your stones, and your imagination and inspiration and will soon become like a wise best friend.

In the next chapter we will work with natural timings, based on solar, lunar, and seasonal energies. If recognized and incorporated into your working life, these can assist you in anticipating and riding the crest of the wave of good fortune or promising circumstances.

CHAPTER 9

Getting the Timing Right: Day, Night, and the Seasons

As I was writing this chapter, a vast area of the eastern United States and Canada was suddenly totally without power for twenty-four hours, affecting tens of millions of people. Commuters in New York were trapped for hours in subway trains in soaring temperatures. As darkness fell, city workers and tourists alike ended up like their early ancestors (but rather less prepared), sleeping on the streets. Those who had run out of cash were unable to buy even staples, whose prices soared, as cash machines failed. As I was revising this chapter later that month, news came in of a similar blackout in London.

If we work and live in cities, it is easy to forget the power of natural phenomena unless we experience a major blackout, an earthquake, a hurricane, a tornado, exceptionally prolonged blizzards, or floods. Unless there is six feet of snow blocking the drive of our house or the freeway starts to melt, we can remain cocooned in an artificially heated and artificially lit insulated world, losing touch with our innate connection with the natural surges and ebbs of energy to which our bodies, minds, and psyches are connected.

Does it matter? Yes. The sun, the moon, and the seasons do offer powerful optimal energy currents at certain times that can be harnessed for achievement; at such peaks you can fill your sails with the wind and move forward swiftly and effortlessly. That is why, if we push relentlessly ahead when there is prevailing energy dip or wane, it can feel like battling against a cosmic headwind. It has been shown in surveys that people working overtime regularly don't necessarily achieve any more or better results than those who work fewer hours but do so during maximal energy peaks. There is something intrinsic that ties us to a natural daily sequence of light and dark.

The Solar Clock

Our personal inner sun clock is tuned to the time zone and region in which we live and revolves around four peak times in any twenty-four hour period: dawn, noon, dusk, and midnight. Each time period has a tide that lasts until the beginning of the next time peak. The same concepts apply wherever you live in the world.

Since dawn and dusk vary according to the time of year, the time interval between them will likewise change. You can't get out your bedroll in the office at sundown at 4.30 P.M. on a dreary November day (unless you are stuck in a major power failure) or work all night every night in the summer in the far north when it barely ever gets dark. But you can, by connecting with natural light cycles, plug into these natural daily transition points and allow your body and mind to subtly shift gear so you can take advantage of fresh energies before, during, and after your working day and thus avoid system overload due to never varying your pace.

If you are a regular night worker, dawn may come near the end of a shift; you can tap into it to give you a final lift of energy and enthusiasm after a hard night. Equally at midnight, a time of rest and pushing away what gives you pain or is no longer needed, on a night shift you can center your energies if you are working, pushing away tiredness and the doubts that can overwhelm us in the middle of the night.

In practice, aligning yourself with the external light patterns helps shift workers to adjust more easily not only to working outside the natural light and dark patterns but also to returning to the mainstream time frame on rest days and vacations. It can also minimize the worst effects of jet lag.

Whatever else we may feel about our modern technological world and a twenty-four-hour society, we remain tied to the age-old cycle of night and day, even if it is hidden deep within us.

Dawn

Even in the center of a city, early morning brings renewal and freshness when the garbage trucks or overnight rain has carried away the stagnation of the previous day. Wherever you are, you should try to stop and quietly and gently breathe in the early morning promise.

Dawn tide energies last from the varying true dawn to noon, though from about 11.30 A.M. you start to move toward the noon tide influences. In the winter months this energy band is quite narrow and so should be maximized.

Within dawn energies you can initiate projects, spend time planning forward, send emails or faxes before the system gets clogged up, capitalize on all those brilliant ideas you carried over in your subconscious from sleep, and generally launch yourself on the first tide of the day.

The earlier part of the morning is naturally a better time for communal meetings and brainstorming sessions than the customary 11:00 to 11.30 A.M. start. It is also a better time for briefings and trawling for new business, as people are open, fresh, and optimistic and have not started to growl with hunger. If you remember these aspects of dawn and relate them to the tasks in hand, it can prove to be a very beneficial time of day in terms of work rates and overall creativity.

To absorb the energies of dawn:

1. At least two or three times a week if possible, either when you rise or before starting work, focus on the sunrise glow or, if dawn is late, on the lightest area on the horizon. Try to be outdoors if possible.

2. Gently breathe in and out through your nose, picturing the light flowing into you as warm liquid gold as it flows through your psychic and mental pathways. Should the day be gloomy or you are working indoors, hold a clear quartz crystal or sparkling yellow citrine in each hand and picture their crystalline energies flowing up your arms into your body as you activate your dawn light body, your inner spiritual power house. Use crystals too if you had a late or disturbed night.

3. Recite in your mind or aloud as a continuous whispered breath mantra: "I am pure light. I am gold, golden bright, and the light is intensified within me. I am energy."

4. When you feel as though you are filled with power, shake your fingers and picture the light spiraling around you, surrounding you. If you look in a mirror you may detect a faint radiance as your aura is filled with light.

5. Before you start work (again) fill a crystal or sparkling glass with filtered or bottled spring water and add two tiny clear quartz crystals or citrine. Cover the glass and leave it in sunlight or by a window. We will be using this water at noon.

Now you are prepared for whatever the day might bring.

Noon

The time of the mighty hunter, noontide energies operate from about 12:00 P.M. to 4:00 P.M., though in winter you may start to feel the dusk energies drawing in from early afternoon. Noon itself is recognized as the most powerful solar marker, though the day may get hotter and with it the energies move into overdrive. Even in midwinter in lands where it barely gets light, you can tap into the maximum power of this period by using lots of light sparkling crystals and, if necessary, fiberoptic lamps that diffuse light.

Lunchtime deadlines are far more likely to be met than those set for dusk or going-home times. They take advantage of natural energy highs and inspirational peaks.

Use the 12:00 to 1:00 P.M. upswing for making the metaphor-
ical kill. This may involve putting the morning's efforts into
a coherent package, making important phone calls, pushing
through a sales thrust while people are mentally hungry, following up morning meeting queries with initial facts and projec-
tions, drafting vague proposals into workable form, clarifying
aims for a business lunch, or enjoying a burst of creativity that
helps you put everything in place for the afternoon finalizations
and fine-tuning.

Feeding is an essential part of this period when you fuel
yourself physically and mentally as well as fueling the metaphor-
ical prey with which you will be lunching. The connection
between business lunches and clinching deals or impressing
new clients is a throwback to the conclusion of the successful
hunt while the animals relaxed in the midday sun.

Unless you are committed to a business lunch, try to get
away from your workplace after the main mental hunger peak,
about 1:00 P.M., for a short period. If it is a hot day find a place
with greenery and water to eat your lunch and to cool and
refresh your psychic energy in order to maximize the afternoon's opportunities.

If possible after you have eaten, fit in the now popular
twenty-minute power nap (or sit quietly with your eyes closed
for a few minutes, visualizing the stars going out one by one or
use one of the other stilling exercises in chapter 2).

In Mediterranean lands, the cultural rhythm is slightly different and the noontide flurry is often followed by a siesta in
the heat of the day, after which business people awake ready for
their next stage in the early evening. There is a thriving trade of
lunchtime hotel bookings of a room for an hour or so in cities
such as Madrid.

After lunch our mental and physical hunger is replaced by a
sustained energy peak. Use your afternoon fed-and-watered
contentment for finalizing contracts and sales deals, preparing
relevant paperwork and follow-up letters and emails from
lunchtime agreements, and pursuing new leads acquired during
your lunchtime trawl or ideas that floated into your mind during your power nap.

However you spend your noon period, be sure to splash your crystal sun water on your pulse points and drink the rest, which is excellent if you really cannot stop for longer.

Dusk

This is a good period that gets even better as the mighty hunter flows toward the calming dusk energies. In the summer when the sun sets late, this transition period can be quite long and is excellent for all people matters, negotiations, networking, sorting out future deadlines, imaginative enterprises, delegating, and more persuasive or reconciliatory phone calls to sort out problems while there is still some zest but the assertive edge has gone dull.

While still at work, winter darkness brings a softness for realistic and nonconfrontational assessment, personal or with other workers, of what has been achieved and for sharing disappointments or worries rather than taking them home. Winter or summer, dusk is an excellent time if you are in a supervisory position for thanking workers for efforts made, pointing out what has been achieved.

As energies slow toward going-home time, what needs to catch the post does while other less pressing matters are consigned to tomorrow's dawn. Ending the day on a positive relaxed tide with clear objectives for the next day makes for relaxed workers who will sleep well and return with enthusiasm.

If you can see dusk from a window, take a minute or two to breathe in the sunset colors (as you did for sunrise colors at dawn). If dusk is late, about 5:00 P.M., focus on an amethyst or pink rose quartz for just two or three minutes, breathing in the sunset light and exhaling as sighs during your in breath any tension, regrets, and annoyances from the day so you end on a positive and gently creative note.

If you work from home, this period is doubly important. Be sure to end on a calming note so you don't end as I often do making a transatlantic phone call while cooking dinner or scrabbling one-handed through the wash pile for number two son's clean shirt for his all important social whirl.

Midnight

The midnight period covers any dark or after-work time until dawn, though from 10:00 P.M. to midnight healing energies are especially strong. No matter how late you get home, try to mark closure under the main working day even if you really have to bring work home or, as I do, burn the midnight oil after the kids are asleep.

If you have time for a shower or bath, use lavender or rose products for natural tranquility, and as the water drains away, repeat an adaptation of one of the age-old water cleansing chants, such as "Stress and worry flow from me, from the rivers to the sea, leaving only harmony."

If you are going out straight from work, sprinkle a few drops of clear water around your head, your hairline, and on your wrists and shake like a dog to cleanse off the pollution of the day. You will need another closure before you go to bed. If you work from home, have worked late, or have brought work home, this shutting down is especially essential, likewise if you have been rushing around before bed, getting ready for the next day.

Try the following to close down your energy centers. You can repeat it over and over until you fall asleep when lying in bed if thoughts of the coming day or unfinished business whirl around and around and you have an early start the next day.

To close down your energy centers:

1. Sit by the light of a small white candle or lamp.
2. Picture a glowing white sphere in the center of your hairline and then see it gently fading, as it closes for the night. Say good night to your inner managing director.
3. Next picture a purple jewel-like sphere in the center of your brow and then see the light slowly fading. Say good night to your inner planner or forecaster.
4. Then see a rich sky-blue sphere close to the center of your throat and then this light also gradually disappearing. Say good night to your inner communicator.
5. Next visualize a rich green sphere in the center of your chest and then see this also gradually merging with the night. Wish your inner counselor good night.

6. Now focus on a glowing golden sphere in the center of your body, midway between your navel and heart level. Close this sphere slowly, saying good night to your inner salesperson or initiator.

7. Move downward to the rich orange sphere just below your navel, and allow this also to disappear gradually, saying good night to your inner negotiator.

8. Finally picture ruby red light centered on the small of your back, and as it fades see security locking up your inner office for the night.

9. Switch off your light or blow out your candle and drift into sleep.

Now you can effect a restful end to any stressful day.

Working with Other Time Zones

If the initiative is on you to sell a product or attract overseas customers, you will need to operate within their time zones and visualize yourself in morning mode if it is 9:00 A.M. in their country even if it is 6:00 P.M. where you are and people are putting on their coats around you.

Picture your customer or client in morning or noon mode and hold a crystal to help you make the transition to the broader time zones: citrine for the dawn to noon energies, clear quartz crystal for the noon to dusk period, amethyst or rose quartz for the dusk to midnight period, and smoky quartz or Apache tear for midnight to dawn. When broadcasting to overseas radio stations for a morning show when it is 1:00 A.M. my time, I use a kick-start of a drink of citrine-infused water to make me perky for coffee-time listeners on the other side of the world. You may have ready-prepared waters in which the relevant crystals have soaked for eight hours to splash on your pulse points and drink them as needed. These are good for jet lag if, for example, you arrive at noon but your body says it's bedtime. Drench yourself with clear quartz water, and you'll bounce through lunch.

Working with the Moon

It is not just night workers who are affected by the moon, for lunar energies pervade the day and night. What is more, as a waxing or increasing phase develops, the moon is often visible in the sky on clear days, and during the later waning period you may see the previous night's moon clearly during the morning.

The movement of the moon has traditionally strongly influenced people's moods and behavior. This is perhaps not surprising since lunar variations affect the tides so dramatically and our bodies do contain a high proportion of water. If you live close to the ocean or a tidal river, you will have noticed that tides are much more extreme during the weeks of the new and the full moon each month. At the time of the full moon, according to worldwide statistics, road traffic accidents increase, as do crimes of violence and admissions to psychiatric units.

More positively, during the full moon, astrologically when the sun and moon are in opposition, people are at their most passionate and open to change. When women's menstrual cycles were routinely in harmony with the moon, women were at their most fertile on the night of the full moon. Women at college, like nuns, tend to have menstrual cycles that move into synch, and among those peoples who do not have artificial lighting, women still menstruate along with the moon.

An office full of women with PMS? Male readers might be tempted to retreat to an all-male seminary at the thought. But lunar harmony has the opposite effect. When all people and not just women are in harmony with natural lunar rhythms, bodies and minds flow harmoniously and the workplace is more happily and naturally productive.

Let's first look at the moon's three main cycles and their energies, and then we can fine-tune the specific moon path through the month. Moon energies can harmonize beautifully with the more focused solar energy waves.The moon is slower and more gradual in its power than the sun, but you can combine lunar and solar energies. For example, noon on the day that the moon becomes full will give you a huge boost of power for a major change or for seizing an opportunity.

You can find out the current moon phase at any time either by looking in the sky if the weather is clear or by consulting the weather page in a newspaper, an almanac such as *Llewellyn*, *Old Moore*, or *Farmers'*, or a calendar that gives moon phases for each day.

The moon has eight astronomical phases, but for the most effective energy we will work with three broader energy bands: waxing, full, and waning.

The Waxing Moon

During the waxing or increasing energy phase, the light of the moon increases in size from right to left (a crescent moon has light on the right and points on the left).

Count this phase from when you see the crescent moon in the sky (two-and-a-half days after the true new moon, which is invisible at the beginning of the cycle) until the night of the full moon.

Use waxing energies that become more intense the larger the moon becomes for initiating and developing new ideas that may take a month or a moon to come to fruition. It is also a good period for making new connections, especially overseas, and for trying alternative markets or outlets. The waxing moon favors all matters concerning children and young people, training new staff, learning languages, or introducing new equipment or methods. It is also a good time for travel and for gradually changing and improving work practices or conditions.

But it can be difficult to focus on one area or task and so keep your work varied, and if necessary rotate staff.

The Full Moon

If you want to be a real purist, the moon is full at the second it rises, and thereafter wanes, on the full moon day. But in practice, full moon energies are from moonrise to set on that day, and the hours and its energies are manifest in animal and human lives for two days around each full moon appearance.

Because the energies are unstable and emotionally charged, it is a good time for personal changes in career, as long as the motivation existed before the full moon day and is not just a reflection of the general lunar instability, for launching a new business, especially one involving people or creativity, for solving a long-term problem by a sudden flash of inspiration, for decision making when you need to rely on a hunch, or for taking a chance.

However, this period should be avoided for confrontations, demands for better conditions, or bringing personality clashes to a head, as tempers may run high.

The Waning Moon

After the night of the full moon, which appears in the sky around sunset, the light and energies thereafter decrease also from right to left until the final crescent on the left that points right disappears, marking the end of the waning phase.

The waning energies are not at all negative, and they are excellent for bringing tasks to fruition, for understanding the point of view and problems of others, for domestic markets and working with known contacts and outlets, for fine-tuning projects, for letting go of what is not working well, and for closing unprofitable doors in the business world. The waning period is also good for work connected with older people and for work with conventional or traditional rather than innovative approaches.

The key to the wane is to pace yourself and staff steadily, avoiding panic or too many deadlines (use the wax or full period then) and to avoid irritability and careless mistakes.

About two-and-a-half days later, the crescent moon appears again on the right, and your cycle starts anew.

The Zodiac and the Moon

The moon travels around the Earth every twenty-nine and a half days. In its orbit it passes through each of the sun, or zodiac, signs (the same as the birth signs) for about two and a half days. Check the sun sign through which the moon is currently passing; you will find this information in horoscope sections of national and local newspapers and also in calendars.

Keep notes in your journal of your own moods and those of others as the moon passes through each of the twelve signs during the month and for two or three subsequent months. You may find that patterns emerge when the moon is in the different signs.

You may discover you are most affected by the moon when it enters your own birth sign each month and most strongly during your birth sign period once a year. There will be common factors in the mood of colleagues at different times of the month. Some people will be more strongly affected than others by the lunar movements, especially those born under watery signs like Pisces, Scorpio, and Cancer, the Cancerian most strongly of all as they are ruled by the moon. Because the moon is so tied up with emotions, you may find that on certain moon days even placid people may react more forcefully than usual.

Here are the key moon locations with respect to the zodiac:

Moon in Aries A time when people—especially those born under fire signs, Aries, Leo, and Sagittarius—will feel restless and eager for action, so it is an excellent time for gathering information or increasing sales or outlets.

Guard against inexplicable bad temper, toddler tantrums over trivia, irritability if frustrated by slow-moving events, and office flirtations.

Moon in Taurus A very relaxed work period that is surprisingly productive and when profits rise—especially among the office earth signs, Taurus, Virgo, and Capricorn. People will be very patient and so office tensions will be low. A good time for creating anything of beauty or of lasting worth.

Beware stubbornness and make sure that the work environment caters for creature comforts at this time (bring in extra nice soap for the bathroom).

Moon in Gemini If the workplace were a farmyard, it would be filled with howls and yowls and roars. Communication goes into overload—especially among the air signs, Gemini, Libra, and Aquarius—and innovation is the order of the day. The phone bill will soar; computers become red hot with internal mails, and hopefully so will the results.

Watch out for too much gossip and temporary factions.

Moon in Cancer Suddenly everyone—but most notably the water signs, Cancer, Scorpio, and Pisces—are typing secret passwords in their computer and working on private projects. However, apart from the squirreling instinct, it is a harmonious period when new members of staff, especially trainees, will be welcomed and helped to settle in. It is a time when intuitive decisions and hunches are likely to be accurate and customer relations especially are favored.

However, people are also incredibly sensitive, so keep the tone soft, avoid criticism, and watch out for false rumors of takeovers or imminent financial collapse due to overactive imaginations.

Moon in Leo If you're putting on the office annual pantomime, success is assured; a fabulous period—especially for the fire signs—or all sales initiatives, sales conferences (no shortage of star turns), and presentations to those you want to impress. A time also for creating sales brochures and for advertising pushes.

If you are boss, watch out for an empire builder further down the food chain; this is a time when everyone wants to lead, so followers and backstage workers may be in short supply.

Moon in Virgo Make sure the bathrooms and food-preparing areas are spotless and desks are tidy. Anything less than pristine will attract adverse comment—especially from Earth signs— even among those whose workspace generally resembles a garage sale. A good time for detailed work, stocktaking, accounting, sorting computer files and filing cabinets, and chasing up late payers (your accounts department will be like hawks).

Definitely not a time for major alterations in routine.

Moon in Libra Another harmonious period—especially for the air signs—for negotiations, for righting matters that seem unjust or resolving inequality issues amicably, for setting up committees, and for a general lack of panic even when deadlines are close or work piles up.

However, decision making may take an age, as everyone considers everyone else's point of view ten times over. Beware also of accepting a deal or new person on surface charm, as it is a period when flattery and fine words are all too plausible.

Moon in Scorpio Fortunately the moon only turns up in Scorpio once a month. Suddenly everyone—but most intensely the water signs—seems able to read your thoughts and twist your words. Old rivalries and vendettas rear their ugly heads, and every point of practice or principle is fought to the death. A time when inappropriate passions can ruffle the calm of a normally business-like atmosphere.

Often blamed (by men) for female PMS, the moon in Scorpio does at least produce intense focus on work and usually extra hours put in to get ahead.

Moon in Sagittarius Quite the nicest of the fire signs during its turn with the moon in residence, this period is excellent for publishers, anyone involved in the media, or travel industries; it is auspicious for business travel or making new overseas connections and following up existing ones. Now is the time for training days or learning seminars and for introducing new equipment, as long as sessions are broken into short segments as attention can wander.

Staff may apply for new jobs and you may be tempted into a different field (wait and see if you feel the same when the moon has moved on); it is an encouraging time, however, for starting self-employment or moving premises.

Moon in Capricorn The period when bankers sigh with relief as employees—especially earth-rooted signs—focus on figures and balance sheets with an enthusiasm seen only in potential World Bank presidents—and at this time of the month.

In any workplace the cautious will become more cautious, and even the normally creative will be more meticulous then usual. Habitual latecomers turn up early, and career becomes a priority even for social butterflies.

Not a time to collect money for birthdays or plan office outings as purses and wallets have a temporary lock.

Moon in Aquarius Definitely the period when the wheel was invented—for air signs especially—people become quirkily creative and may be found scribbling diagrams, modifying their computer key functions, and crawling down shafts to discover why the air conditioning blows hot in summer. Good for the self-employed and home workers, especially solitary ones; personal space may become a major issue.

Odd habits become more pronounced and lateral thinkers move off the clock. It's not worth sending offenders to the works' counselor as relative normality will soon be restored.

Moon in Pisces Time for the drama kings and queens to emerge from the woodwork for their monthly outing—especially among the water signs. Treading on eggshells is the phrase to sum up this moon phase, for normally even-tempered souls may burst into tears or retreat in hurt silence over a well-intentioned joke or remark.

Changeability is the keynote so use the time for exploring alternatives, using the acute psychic sensitivity for assessing future trends and for creating imaginative and finely tuned adverts or press releases; but forget definite decisions and common sense until the moon moves on.

Void-of-Course Moon Even those who dismiss astrology as quackery are often unable to explain away the effects of a void-of-course moon when every venture, phone call, or fax meets with a brick wall or a permanently unavailable signal.

Recently my British editor, Robin, emailed me to tell me about his awful day. On the way to an important meeting some eight miles away, his car developed a puncture near home that ripped through the tire. His normal garage came out and was uncharacteristically totally out of his brand of tires, and his spare had also inexplicably developed a hole. His other transport attempts left him frustrated, and after several hours he was not much nearer his destination. Eventually hot, tired, and enervated he went home.

He asked me what was wrong. Looking in my almanac, I saw that the moon was void of course starting about the time he set out and lasting until he got home.

The definition of a void-of-course moon is the period between the time when the moon makes its last major aspect (or angle) to another planet as it is leaving one sun sign and the time when it changes to the next sun sign. The void-of-course period may only last a few minutes, in which case it is not a problem. But sometimes it can last for hours or at the most extreme (not that often, fortunately) up to two days, depending on the positions of the planets.

You can find out when the moon is due to go void of course by looking for the symbols "VOC" in a moon calendar or any almanac or on an on-line daily astrology site. Monitor a brief void-of-course period, and you will notice how many cups of coffee get spilled, emails don't get through, or clients decline offers more than usual. Such annoyances are invariably minor, and sometimes a void-of-course moon just means nothing at all is happening.

So if you can, wait to send off some precious typescript, ask for a salary increase, or go for an interview (a VOC interview board will generally make a totally inappropriate choice). However, it is an excellent window for getting rid of what you do not want or making duty arrangements that you will be glad do not come to fruition.

Seasonal Energies

Our forebears had regular reality checks to keep them in touch with their seasonal mood and energy swings. If it was the height of summer, they might work in the fields for seventeen hours during the long hours of sunlight. When winter froze the land and the nights were long, they would tend the animals in the barns in the dim light and, like the animals, huddle close in their homes for warmth (late summer was not surprisingly baby boom time in the human world after all that huddling).

We can still respond to these natural energy ebbs and flows twenty floors up in a centrally heated apartment block. And while we may not be able to make our autumnal nest against the winter snows under our desk, if we can recognize these seasonal calls, we can regulate our natural innate body rhythms and understand the behavior of those we work with.

The four main seasons of the year are marked by the three monthly divisions by the astronomical equinoxes and solstices. In the southern hemisphere the traditional associations move around six months. In Australia, the height of summer is marked by the midsummer solstice or the longest day when solar influences are at their greatest, coming around December

21 rather than June 21, the northern hemisphere midsummer. Because the solstices and equinoxes are astronomical markers, the date may vary by a day or two depending on the movement in the skies, but animals and birds and some people living close to the land pick up the changing seasonal energies at least a week before they occur. The most intense effects are manifest around the actual solstice or equinox.

Spring: The Time of Sowing

March 21-June 20 (for the northern hemisphere), from the spring equinox to the summer solstice

This is the time when people suddenly lighten up and start buying spring flowers on the way to work and taking lunch in the park. The more macho guys in the office may start to get territorial, and the female biological clock goes into temporary overdrive.

This is good news for the undomesticated, as piles of pecan pies and home-baked cookies are stockpiled in the office after frantic Sunday-morning baking sessions (the equivalent of hen-feather ripping to make a nest for the chicks).

Office romances may begin to bud, aftershave fills the air, and drawers are decluttered, workspaces cleared, and targets set, as the phone lines buzz purposefully.

Whether male or female, old or young, spring energies are good for personal career plans and moves, for thinking about setting up your own business or sideline, for training or retraining, for updating skills and equipment, or for downsizing and leaving town. Anything is possible, and positive competition can be a great incentive for defining and striving to attain personal goals.

Summer: The Time of Creativity

June 21-September 21 (for the northern hemisphere), from the summer solstice to the autumn equinox

Now the target charts really are filling up, and rumors abound of mergers, takeovers, and management buyouts. Newcomers or office sleepers suddenly become front runners in the scramble for recognition and promotion. People are jogging or cycling to work, and the first flurry of vacation photographs, after-work barbecues, and home do-it-yourself projects are emerging along with picnic lunches covered in gingham cloths.

This is a peak time of energy and strength when ambitions can be achieved, horizons widened, and the spring plans for moves or upward steps within the company become firm offers. Opportunities can with courage be seized, and advantages can be maximized.

As the *I Ching* says: "Be as the Sun at midday" and make every moment count.

Fall: The Time of Harvest

September 22–December 20, from the autumn equinox to the midwinter solstice

Now you are scrunching leaves in the park, and your colleagues are squirreling away papers in their drawers that will not see the light of day until next spring. People are feverishly ordering extra stationery like it was going out of fashion and anxiously watching other people doing the same.

Personally, autumn is a time for balancing gain and loss, realistically assessing what is possible in the coming months, determining what projects need more input and perseverance to get off the ground, and abandoning what is not going to bear fruit. It may also mean liberating the ritually rewritten novel first dated September 1986 either to the scrutiny of an agent or to consignment on the unlit back burner until we are cushioned by the profits from our fifteenth reprint of the less soul-stirring effort, "How to pay your tax on time."

Folks are getting into work a bit later each day, and flasks of homemade soup are appearing even if temperatures are still mild.

Winter: The Time of Darkness

December 21–March 20, from the midwinter solstice or shortest day to the spring equinox

Some people may go into mini-hibernation mode, becoming anxious if the office biscuit tin gets more than half empty and making contingency plans for every imaginable disaster or privation, buying backup batteries for laptop computers and chains for their car wheels.

Even people in relatively warm winter climes such as California may have a throwback gene to distant ancestors in Russia or Scotland and drag in security rugs or buy coats with huge collars in case the power fails.

Winter is a wonderful work time, when energies are not distracted by the sun outside, jobs are done thoroughly, checked and double-checked, and people skills are especially strong as we go into cave mode.

Job security and a happy workplace become more important than competition or change, and Thanksgiving through to Hanukkah and Christmas creates a sense of anticipation and camaraderie that make cooperation at its peak. Then the days get slowly lighter through to spring

Personally, there is a strong sense of commitment and loyalty, whether to a workplace or a personal project if we work alone. Patience and perseverance support the dreams we incubate in winter and sustain us until the first spring flowers.

Once we move away from relying entirely on clock time, a wider source of energy becomes available to us. You can ride high on the full power of noon, understand why people are less willing to share ideas when the moon is in Cancer, and avoid forcing the pace for change when your ancestors would have been snuggling down against the winter snows. The modern business world knows all about the conscious mind, but an awareness that even the most hardheaded businessperson may be unconsciously affected by older, slower forces can enable you to anticipate when it would be a good time to try to strike a deal or to offer a tidbit of praise, knowing that if the moon is void of course you might as well take the morning off.

We will work more with instinctive energies in the next chapter when we consider ways of calculating your best times of day and lucky dates using numerology.

CHAPTER 10

Crunching the Psychic Numbers: Numerology at Work

Numerology is one of the simplest and most accurate ways of discovering your optimal personal moments. Numerology is an ancient psychic art dating from ancient Greek Pythagorean practices (Pythagoras was the mathematical genius whose theorems are still recited in schools today).

Under Pythagoras's system, each letter of the alphabet represents a digit from 1 to 9. For example, the letters A, J, and S all equal 1; the letters B, K, and T equal 2; and so on (see the chart below to save you working out each correspondence). The Hebrews also developed a numerological system thousands of years ago, but for practical use the more straightforward Greek one is used most in the modern world.

Whether you use an electronic organizer or a desk calendar, you may find that an ancient Greek numerological database helps you to gain maximum advantage from your appointments. Of course if you have a flight definitely booked for 9:00 A.M. on Friday or a meeting that has to take place at 2:00 P.M., you can't make excuses about inauspicious times and the state of the stars.

But when you do have some flexibility in arrangements, there are special times of day and night when our personal success vibes are particularly focused and responsive, whether for an important meeting, a presentation, or a business lunch. At other times we'd be better off working quietly, traveling on a routine journey, or just slowing down. Auspicious numerological times are more finely tuned and individualized than the broader sweeps of solar and lunar energies I wrote about in the previous chapter.

How the Method Works

Using the chart below, you can see what numerological value is attributed to the various times of day and night. The chart (set in military format so, for example, 10:45 P.M. is written as 2245) sections time into fifteen-minute slots. You can then look at the chart to see the numerological number for each time slot. Numerology is the study of the numbers one through nine, so the final numerological value for a numerical subject, such as a time or a date, or a word, such as a name, will be a single digit. To determine the numerological value of a number, the digits are added up. If the resultant number, however, is more than one digit, you would then add these digits. For example, with 2145 (9:45 P.M.) you would add 2+1+4+5 and get a value of 12; then you would add 1+2 (the digits that make up 12) to get 3, the value attributed to 2145.

Optimal Times of the Twenty-Four-Hour Clock

0015 6	0030 3	0045 9	0100 1	0115 7	0130 4	0145 1
0200 2	0215 8	0230 5	0245 2	0300 3	0315 9	0330 6
0345 3	0400 4	0415 1	0430 7	0445 4	0500 5	0515 2
0530 8	0545 5	0600 6	0615 3	0630 9	0645 6	0700 7
0715 4	0730 1	0745 7	0800 8	0815 5	0830 2	0845 8
0900 9	0915 6	0930 3	0945 9	1000 1	1015 7	1030 4
1045 1	1100 2	1115 8	1130 5	1145 2	1200 3	1215 9
1230 6	1245 3	1300 4	1315 1	1330 7	1345 4	1400 5
1415 2	1430 8	1445 5	1500 6	1515 3	1530 9	1545 6
1600 7	1615 4	1630 1	1645 7	1700 8	1715 5	1730 2
1745 8	1800 9	1815 6	1830 3	1845 9	1900 1	1915 7
1930 4	1945 1	2000 2	2015 8	2030 5	2045 2	2100 3
2115 9	2130 6	2145 3	2200 4	2215 1	2230 7	2245 4
2300 5	2315 2	2330 8	2345 5			

Midnight (2400) is a free time when anything is possible, and it does not appear on the time chart. You can either use 2359, which gives you 19, which gives you 1 (1+9 is 10, and 1+0 is 1); or 0001, which gives you the same value of 1. Alternatively you can take a chance on 0000, excellent for a step into the unknown.

Though I have presented fifteen-minute intervals in the time chart, you can add up any time. For example 0831 would give you 12, which reduces to 3, though a minute earlier (0830) would give an entirely different number (2) if split-second timing were essential (yes, you can even add in seconds if you are a number devotee).

For most matters the broader fifteen-minute window that gives you the ruling energy of a time frame is quite sufficient, but if every minute counts you can break down the individual subenergies.

The value of a number can guide you when scheduling your day. A meeting or appointment may span several fifteen-minute time segments. You can choose a block of time where, for example, your entrepreneurial skills (number 8) kick in after the first half hour when you have relaxed a client and perhaps enjoyed a social chat and a soft sales pitch (a number 6). Later in this chapter I present the meanings of the nine numbers. Optimal personal periods are important at night as well as during the day, not only if you work nights or late shifts but also if you cross time zones on business or deal with overseas clients in distant time zones.

If you want to determine the best date for an event, just add those numbers in the same way, reducing the final number to a single digit, so August 8, 2004, would be 08082004, which would equal 22=4. You can also check on the best day of the week; for example, Monday would be 4+6+5+4+1+7 (see the values of letters below), and you would add that in as well to the grand total.

You can also use peak opportunity windows of time when you want to be especially alert for planning or working on a difficult project.

Because number synchronicity is symbolic, you don't have to adjust for seasonal differences such as daylight saving time.

Deal with the time as it is in your time zone. If talking across zones on the phone, stick with the time you are currently in, being aware that you need to choose the best time window out of the options you have (there are several in any twenty-four-hour period) to suit your client. You might pick your 3:00 A.M. peak so the overseas person is midmorning and not grumpy about being woken. You can supplement yourself with lots of coffee until you get really successful and overseas clients have to fit in with your schedule.

Maximizing Your Skills

If you work in sales you can determine which windows of time will be the most fruitful periods for doing business. In addition, you can get information as to the best strategy to adopt in your time windows as the number associated with each of your best times identifies the particular strengths that you can utilize to add to your natural abilities.

For example, 4 is the number of the realist so honesty about the advantages and limitations of what you are offering will create the most favorable impression at a meeting during a 4 time window rather than sexed-up sales talk.

Should you know the name of the person you are meeting or phoning and the way you plan to address them (in emails @ is counted as *at*), you can add their name to the one you will be using to get a joint optimal window. If emailing use your email address as it appears on your email heading, including the service provider. If there are numbers in your email address simply add those into the calculation.

As you know, the timing of an email can be crucial.

How to Calculate Your Number

To calculate the number of your name, first add up the numbers of the various letters in your name, using the chart below. For example, if your name is Becky, add 2+5+3+2+7 to get 19, then add 1+9=10, and 1+0=1.

1	2	3	4	5	6	7	8	9
A	B	C	D	E	F	G	H	I
J	K	L	M	N	O	P	Q	R
S	T	U	V	W	X	Y	Z	

For personal calculations, which you will use most of the time, add all the numbers together of the name you will be using (including Ms., Doctor, or Dr.), plus any qualification initials you may have written after your name (such as on an official program).

You can determine which number harmonizes with the precise name you are going by on a particular occasion. Our business names can vary according to how well we know the people we are meeting or corresponding with and the formality of the occasion. I know that when Bill, my bank manager, calls me "Mrs. Eason" when booking a financial review, he wants to talk about my monetary *outgoings* and how the money fairy didn't turn up as promised.

Once you know which times of day synchronize with the business name you will be using, you can arrange your calendar so an appointment or a crucial segment of an appointment occurs when your energies and creativity are at their peak. So I need a good Mrs. Eason window to start twenty minutes into the bank interview when the list of what I had promised I was going to pay off comes out.

You can also calculate the numbers of the various people you are working with on a project. If you are meeting with a number of people or mailing them concerning the same matter, you can use a calculator to add up any number of names to find a time slot when all the separate energies will mesh.

Numerological Meanings

Each of the nine digits represents particular energies. I have given each one a title. Though in this book the numbers predominantly refer to work, they can also be applied to your social or home life.

One, the Innovator One times are excellent for new beginnings and exploring unfamiliar markets or for initiating contacts, for energy (helpful if you are working with jet lag), for introducing changes, for brainstorming and all creative ventures and projects, for finding an original solution to an old problem, and for getting things moving after a period of stagnation.

Two, the Integrator Two times are excellent for one-to-one meetings, for two-way phone calls, for setting up or developing partnerships at any level, for integrating two different strands or balancing two conflicting priorities, and for business lunches and socializing no matter how many are present and where there are people or organizations who need to be brought together in a common cause in spite of major differences.

Three, the Achiever Three times are for exchanging contracts or finalizing deals, for encouraging optimism and confidence in the future, for three-way meetings and phone calls, for producing results and setting deadlines for others, for meeting personal deadlines, for introducing a newcomer to a tightly knit team, for drawing up positive profiles of business opportunities, for having a promotion or job interview, and for working away from your home territory.

Four, the Realist Four times are helpful for operating successfully in less than ideal circumstances and with less than ideal material, for introducing constraints on plans and planners who are wildly overbudget or off course, for talking to staff about underperformance or overcoming difficult times, for setting and getting others to agree to realistic deadlines, and for selling by pointing out problems as well as advantages.

Five, the Communicator Five times are for marketing yourself or your ideas, for explaining new methods or technology to others, for giving lectures, presentations, effective sales promotions, or media interviews, for setting up effective advertising and publicity, and for persuading others to accept your point of view as part of a job interview (ideally close to a 3 window) when you have to sell yourself against fierce competition.

Six, the Counselor Six times are opportune for appealing to someone's better nature, for ironing out work tensions, for maximizing your personal charisma when you are not on particularly strong ground, for dealing with drama kings and queens, emperors and empresses, and the frankly neurotic as you get them to see or at least do things your way, for dealing with major customer complaints, for a soft sales pitch based on building up empathy, and for teaching staff how to deal with the public more effectively (run the 6 time into a 2 where possible).

Seven, the Magician Seven times really are the wing and the prayer, for creating a degree of confidence you do not feel inside when you are not sure of your facts or have not had time to prepare, for pulling the magical rabbit out of the hat when the odds are against you, for holding sessions to plan forward, for asking the right questions, for meeting people about whom you know nothing except their name, and for powerfully accessing your intuition.

Eight, the Entrepreneur Eight times are beneficial for all financial and real estate dealings, for sorting out tangled finances or administration, for expanding sales territories and marketing opportunities so they will prove lucrative, for meetings with bank managers, IRS representatives, potential investors, shareholders, and accountants (run into a 5 and 2 time if anticipating problems), for taking out loans, and for developing seemingly unpromising leads or outlets.

Nine, Action Man/Woman Nine times are good for troubleshooting, for dealing with critics and doubters, for sorting out matters involving justice, the law, or the state, for campaigning for equality for self or others, for outfacing autocrats and bullies, and for traveling, especially overseas ventures and meetings (a good window to finalize travel plans or to book a flight that will depart during a 9 time—delays don't affect the viability of the original time).

Power Names

The ancient Egyptian deities were said to have five secret names of power, and magicians adopted the same idea. In the modern world, witches and Druids and Druidesses have a power name, known only to people within their magical society.

It can be an amazing boost of confidence to think of yourself as the holder of a name that signifies power and control, so you can say to yourself at times when you are feeling distinctly wobbly to yourself "I am Sekhmet" (my own favorite lion-headed goddess and protectress of businesswomen). By speaking your name in your mind and writing it down, you can endow yourself with courage and confidence. After all, would you refuse Sekhmet an increased overdraft limit?

By choosing a name that has the numerological qualities you desire you can empower yourself further. For example, Sekhmet is 1+5+2+8+4+5+2, which equals 27, which makes her a 9 (2+7), an Action woman. If you added an A on the end, creating Sekhmeta, that would equal 28, which translates into 1 (8+2), an Initiator.

Creating a Power Name

To the ancient Egyptians the *ren*, or the name, was part of a person's soul and often reflected particularly desirable qualities. For example, Tutankhamen was named after Thoth, the God of wisdom (Tut is a shortened form of Thoth). Ankh is the name of the hieroglyph that means immortal, and Amen was the creator god.

Writing or saying a name invoked power into the person, whereas to wipe the name of an enemy from a statue was to destroy the spirit. Felicity E. Clark uses several versions of her name at work. Each forms a different aspect of her character as well as telling her different peak times in the leader role that she performs monthly at a local business college.

F E L I C I T Y E. C L A R K becomes 6+5+3+9+3+9+2+7 + 5 + 3+3+1+9+2, which equals 67, which equals 13, which equals 4, the number of the Realist.

Felicity's honest and practical approach certainly won her many friends at the college. But she feels real success has eluded her in this area, which she loves and hoped to develop. If Felicity were to drop that E, something she had included because many successful businesspeople did use a middle initial we have the following.

F E L I C I T Y C L A R K becomes 6+5+3+9+3+9+2+7 + 3+3+1+9+2, which equals 62, which equals 8, the number of the Entrepreneur.

That's more authoritative and geared toward inspiring her audience (and the senior college staff). But if she really wants to make an impact (there is a major conference she would like to be asked to lecture at) she could change her seminar work name even further.

F E L I C I A C L A R K becomes 6+5+3+9+3+9+1 + 3+3+1+9+2, which equals 54, which equals 9, the number of the Action woman.

Or F E L I C I A E. C L A R K becomes 6+5+3+9+3+9+1 + 5 + 3+3+1+9+2, which adds up to 59, which equals 5, the Communicator. Or she could use her middle name.

E L L E N C L A R K becomes 5+3+3+5+5 + 3+3+1+9+2, which equals 39, which equals 12, which gives 3, the Achiever.

It is surprising how adding or taking away a letter or substituting a middle name or initial can create the image you need to let your talents shine through.

Cell Phone Power

Add up the numbers on your cell phone or work phone and extension. Match that number to the same number time chart, and you can discover the best times to make calls. You can also add the number of the person you intend to call to your phone number, getting a new number to look up on the time chart for mutually harmonious talk time.

However you may decide that you want your cell phone to share the number of the name with which you answer the phone for business calls (or your secret power name). In this case it may be possible to change your number by a digit to get the number you require numerologically.

If you use the phone mainly for sales, you could select a number that added up to 8, the number of the Entrepreneur, or if you mainly arrange press releases and such, 5, the number of the Communicator would be ideal.

You can adapt your email accordingly, matching the overall strength you wish to convey. Thus if you are very creative in your work, regularly set up new projects, or look for new business, it would make sense for your email address to add up to 1, the Initiator.

Long-Term Planning

As well as calculating beneficial times, you can work with dates. If you want to know whether a special day would be auspicious for sending a typescript to a publisher or for running a training day, you can add up the day, month, and year of possible dates and find out which resonates best with the number of your name as you would be using it on that date. For example, the name on an airline ticket is generally a formal one, such as Ms. Anne French (check your old airline receipts). If in doubt, use your business card name in full. Best of all is when your name number is the same as the time, day, month, and year of an interaction.

Sample Reading

> As I said, your name, and so your optimal times for various activities, will change according to the way you are titled in particular situations. Take the example of Felicity, who works for a large computer store. She is referred to as Flick during informal meetings with other managers to brainstorm, as Felicity E. Clark on a recent seminar leader list, and usually as Felicity Clark such as when she phones the head office or introduces herself to people who already know her job description. While walking around the store Felicity wears her name badge—Felicity Clark, Customer Services Manager—and for phone calls or face-to face-meetings with people with complaints, she will say; "I'm Felicity Clark, Customer Services Manager."

In the latter situation her full title and job description become part of her numerological calculation.

How she will be addressed or call herself in any encounter, from an email to a one-to-one with the head of the company, will give her different numbers and thus different optimal times, say for answering a complaint. Felicity has three peak obligations today. The first is the customary morning meeting with the other managers, which she always enjoys. The second she is not looking forward to, a meeting with a dissatisfied customer who is threatening legal action because he was wrongly advised by a Customer Services Adviser about ordering several thousand dollars of software for his company that was not compatible with the machines he installed, a mistake that resulted in lost orders. Third is her favorite, a training session for new staff members.

The chart for calculating a name's number is repeated below so you can follow my calculations.

1	2	3	4	5	6	7	8	9
A	B	C	D	E	F	G	H	I
J	K	L	M	N	O	P	Q	R
S	T	U	V	W	X	Y	Z	

This is how it works out for her.

The Managers' Meeting

Constraints: It must be during the morning.

In this informal gathering, which generally takes place whenever everyone is free or in the first coffee break, Felicity is referred to as Flick.

F L I C K becomes 6+3+9+3+2, which equals 23, which equals 5.

Therefore, since it is to be a morning meeting, the ideal Felicity times are 0815 or 1130 (5 times), the latter probably a little late for acting on overnight information.

Since the store opens at 9:00 A.M. but the managers get in earlier, it might make sense to schedule a regular meeting before work begins in earnest rather than trying to find a time in a hectic morning. Flick is at peak power and enthusiasm at 0815, and as the number of the Communicator that time would seem ideal.

If combined with a late coffee break, 1130 might give managers a chance to liaise with Felicity informally over any communication difficulties with their own teams that may result in unenthusiastic staff customer relations. If Felicity were overall manager she might decide to arrange an ideal time based on adding together the names of everyone present.

The Dissatisfied Customer

Constraints: The customer can come any time before 3:00 P.M., but prefers early afternoon.

Felicity is wearing her official hat and wants the meeting when she is at her peak, as the customer has been very verbally abusive to staff. So for this encounter she is, as per name badge, Felicity Clark, Customer Services Manager.

FELICITY CLARK, CUSTOMER SERVICES MANAGER becomes 6+5+3+9+3+9+2+7 + 3+3+1+9+2 + 3+3+1+2+6+4+5+9 + 1+5+9+4+9+3+5+1 + 4+1+5+1+7+5+9, which equals 164, which equals 2.

Therefore 1145 and 1415 are possible times that would work well for her. Felicity would get a clear morning and please the customer who preferred early afternoon if they met at 1415. By synchronicity the number is 2, the number of the Negotiator, which is ideal for Felicity's job and for a particularly difficult, in this case, justifiably angry customer.

At 1145, another peak time for negotiation, Felicity can work privately on strategies for any similar major complaints to prevent them from escalating.

Felicity's Training Session

Constraints: This is best done in the late morning, before the lunch hour rush or in the late afternoon when there is a sales dip and Felicity and the sales staff can best be spared. Felicity has found that short regular sessions fit in better with the store's demands and also focus concentration.

Though wearing her name badge, Felicity encourages informality and so the new recruits call her Felicity.

F E L I C I T Y becomes 6+5+3+9+3+9+2+7, which equals 44, which equals 8.

Therefore the suggested times are 0845, 1115, and 1700. For practical purposes Felicity chooses 1115, when the recruits are fresh. Since the title of the session is how to improve sales by giving customers what they want; the number of the Entrepreneur is particularly apt.

Since Felicity is using her store name that staff uses, she also has 0845 available, straight after the morning meeting, to fire up staff enthusiasm for the day by visiting the different departments. This tips over into a 9 time that, while not her own number, is an Action Woman phase. She can use 1700 for another quick tour to make sure that going-home lethargy does not encourage less than enthusiastic service to the general public by the day staff, to inspire the evening shift, and to hand over to a supervisor before she herself goes home. The next slot, 5, the number of the Communicator, at 1715 will ensure everyone goes home happy.

Numbers are therefore everywhere in our working lives but can be used to our advantage, as long as we understand their significance and then how to apply the results.

In the next chapter we will work with ways of improving good fortune by the use of charms and amulets.

CHAPTER 11

Making Good Fortune: Luck, Wishes, and Mojos

According to Dr. Richard Wiseman—a British scientist who studied the lives of four hundred volunteers who considered themselves either naturally lucky or unlucky—for several years, we make our own luck. He concluded that people who were consistently lucky had high expectations of good fortune that became self-fulfilling prophecies, or as a popular British TV game show host Michael Miles used to say: "Think lucky and you'll be lucky."

Dr. Wiseman also concluded from his studies that lucky people took advantage of opportunities that came their way and tended to persevere when things weren't going so well, turning disadvantage into opportunity by their own efforts. That's the psychology of good luck and a sound business principle.

Psychic Good Fortune

Psychological good fortune and prosperity can be enhanced psychically by using empowered lucky charms. These act like a psychic magnet, attracting opportunity or at least alerting us intuitively to those times when success is most likely.

Like a rolling snowball, the charm accumulates the positive

success energies that you activate whenever you carry or wear your particular luck bringer. Just by holding or carrying the charm, good fortune vibes will fill you, assuring more success and making you even more confident, and so further endowing the charm at each successful use with power to activate even more power next time. Have a couple of identical lucky charms you wear alternately so if you lose one it's not the end of the world.

The concept of using charms and empowerments to attract good fortune is found in almost every society. For prosperity, businesspeople of Irish descent often have kelp or seaweed soaking in a sealed glass jar of finest Irish whisky on their office window ledge to attract wealth (the Scots use their beloved Scotch whisky). If you live far from the ocean, dried kelp from any health store will serve as well, but there is no substitute for the finest malt whisky.

Until recently it was the custom to keep handsel, the first dollar earned in trade, in a glass case over the door. The first takings of the Chinese New Year are likewise preserved.

In this chapter we will look at various ways of bringing good luck and prosperity into your career and your workplace, using traditional methods that carry with them the accumulated power of successful use over hundreds or sometimes even thousands of years.

Wish Boxes

I first saw a wish box, or prayer pot as they are also called, in the home of Rachel and Vincentia, who live on the Isle of Wight. Theirs was based on a miniature ancient Egyptian gold jar, and the lid was a representation of the head of their patroness, Isis, the mother goddess of magic and the moon. I have since seen similar jars with carvings of ancestral heads from West Africa.

You may find an Isis pot like Vincentia's to hold your wishes for good luck or prosperity. Isis is a good focus for fortune as she is very loving and giving. Anubis boxes and jars are also common. He was the protective jackal-headed god in ancient Egypt, effective for guarding your pot from the overcurious.

On searching the Internet I discovered two different kinds of wish boxes for sale, one from Abyssinia and the other from China. There are also numerous sites with miniature jars with a deity head for the lid or you can pick one up quite easily from a gift store. The Chinese wish box looks like a miniature temple and is called Li Yuan or House of Money.

According to legend, thousands of years ago a group of holy men are said to have discovered the original Li Yuan. By writing a request for abundance on a small piece of folded paper and putting it through the doorway, a wish would be granted within twenty-four hours. I have provided a mail address if you would like to buy one of these (see Resources).

But you can easily use any small square box with a slit (like a miniature ornamental mailbox), a wooden box with a lid, or a ceramic or metal lidded pot. A wooden or metal box that has some personal significance, perhaps a family treasure that great-grandma used to keep her love letters in, can be especially effective.

However, with wish pots and boxes you need to remain realistic. With the most elaborate or expensive box in the world, though the power of the wish as promised by Li Yuan may begin to work within twenty-four hours of your symbolically posting your request to the cosmic goodie store, you have to help fulfillment along. That means extra earthly efforts and renewed enthusiasm or determination fueled by writing and posting your request (psychology and the psychic are intimate bedfellows).

You can have a small wish box for your private use either at home or in a desk or workstation drawer. If you have like-minded colleagues, introduce a communal box in which affirmations about the success of joint projects, the prosperity of the firm, or the improved health of a sick colleague can be placed. As with the office suggestion box, notes need not be signed.

There are two rules, whether you have an individual or a collective wish box. All wishes and affirmations must be positive (not, I wish Sarah would leave because she is such a misery), and wishes are not to be read by anyone after being placed in the box.

To add a wish to a wish box:

1. Start with the hardest part, defining what good fortune you need in order to get things rolling. Would it be a job interview, an invitation to work on the sales stall at a prestigious trade fair, or a customer paying you a large amount he or she owes you in time to pay your tax bill? One wish only, so use it wisely. Be as specific as possible and work in manageable steps. It's no good wanting to be the Sydney rep if you've only been at a firm two days, but if it's what you really want you'll get there eventually.

2. Write your wish, fold the paper, and put it in the box, reciting your wish three times in rapid succession (in your mind if others are around).

3. After posting it, push the wish to the back of your mind. Focus your efforts on practical steps to furthering your wish.

4. Only use this method once a month and remember the cosmic balance sheet; do something nice for someone who is mean to you or offer help to a rival who is struggling.

5. If you have a collective box, get all the people involved in a joint need—maybe that the business will get a specific order or that the shareholders will resist a takeover—writing and inserting their wishes within the same hour. Individuals should recite their wishes three times silently and not discuss them even with those involved. You can work with just two or three close colleagues. Keep the box in the workplace, and if necessary place it out of sight and lock it.

6. The next month you can post another wish, either relating to the same matter or a separate issue.

7. When the wish box is full, take out the pile of wishes, tie them with red cord in three knots, and burn them on a bonfire or in a fire bucket with sand in the bottom. Bury the ashes under a fruit tree.

Burning wishes is a traditional way of releasing the energies of the wish into the cosmos. Its origin may be found in the practice of burning offerings on fires to deities, and it may be found in the customs of many societies and religions. Burning the contents of a wish box is a symbolic gesture of activating your own powers to make the wishes come true.

Wish boxes are symbolic ways of formulating wishes and then doing something about them, in this case placing them in a box and so setting the process of wish fulfillment into motion.

By leaving your wishes in a box and not rereading them, you are creating a space for your unconscious mind to come up with ways of getting the wish moving—and of allowing all the cosmic and natural forces to amplify your personal efforts. Then when you release your wishes by burning them when the box is full, you are symbolically generating a lot of energy to move your wishes toward fruition. In ways I can't explain, the act of posting a wish does seem to bring all kinds of unexpected opportunities into your life. Try it.

Mojo or Charm Bag

In the United Kingdom right through until the nineteenth century in country places, following a custom dating back to the Vikings, people would fill red fabric charm bags with a coin, some coal, and other symbols of abundance. These would be kept in homes and workshops to attract prosperity. Today some people carry a small drawstring bag around their necks, holding their special luck and abundance symbols that they collected at significant moments during their life. For example Penny, who is a firewoman, wears a tiny dark purple velvet charm bag around her neck containing a tiny blood agate for courage, her lucky silver coin that she was given in childhood, and a feather to symbolize swift escape from a blaze if necessary.

In America, similar bags, containing items collected for a specific luck-bringing or protective purpose, are called mojos. Originating in hoodoo, a form of folk magic still popular in the United States today, the mojo, like hoodoo itself, draws upon an African tradition but has also incorporated Native North American and European magic.

Though in recent years hoodoo has adopted elaborate incenses, powders, oils, and candles, much of its lore is based on an earlier tradition of very simple luck-bringing ingredients available even to the poorest people. Mojo bags made and used by women living in the Memphis area have been given the name of "nation sacks."

The mojo bag has spread in popularity far beyond the practitioners of hoodoo and is like the Native American medicine or power bundle used by people interested in spiritual concepts who seek a traditional focus of power.

The term mojo probably comes either from a corruption of the European word magic or more likely from the West African word *mojuba*, which means a prayer of praise. Mojos are small bags containing an odd number of up to thirteen symbols. Symbols are drawn from objects in the natural and manufactured world and are combined to attract or protect from particular energies. You can buy a bag or sew one yourself, choosing a charm that appeals to you as your mojo and keep it in the bag.

Mojo Colors and Fabrics

Mojo bags are generally made of red flannel. However, more recently, especially when used as more general charms, bags are also made in different colors suited to the person's wish and in natural fabrics or even leather. You can buy or make small drawstring bags or cloth purses for your lucky items and select a color from the following list:

Green for success in any business venture and for gradual increase in fortune and money

Blue for success or prosperity in enterprises or projects that you have already started; pale shades of blue signify peace and protection

Yellow for speculation and attracting luck in uncertain times or for necessarily risky enterprises

White for anything new or for fast results

Red for absolutely any purpose, especially in the traditional red flannel

Making Your Mojo Bag

Create your mojo when you are alone at home and will be undisturbed. Have all the components ready. You can take the finished bag into work the next day.

As you put in each charm, name its purpose. Have at least one natural substance and one manufactured item for balance (see also herb amulets on page 220). You can be as inventive as you like, but it is a good idea to use items that are of significance to you and are relatively easily obtained, so the bag is in no way alien to your personal life context. Originally mojos were based on simple ingredients available to ordinary people. You can buy many mojo ingredients from some of the suppliers I have listed in Resources (and if living or visiting a city such as New Orleans, there are plenty of specialty "hoodoo style" medicine stores). Below I have listed some common mojo ingredients that you can combine in any form:

Lucky Hand root is the root of the orchid and was traditionally placed in a bag to bring luck to gamblers. It will attract fortune to all forms of speculation or risk taking, whether in a personal career gamble or a professional decision involving uncertainty and needing luck. Lucky Hand root is also helpful for finding a job, especially after a period of unemployment.

Devil's Shoestring root is good for gaining employment or promotion.

Miniature playing cards such as the nine of hearts, which is called the wish card and promises the fulfillment of hopes and dreams. The ten of diamonds is good in any mojo bag where fast results are needed. All diamonds are associated with prosperity. A very tiny complete pack is good for doing deals of any kind or for getting a contract.

A traditional silver dollar (you can buy this mail order) or other silver coin often combined with basil or dried kelp, wrapped in a green currency note, will bring money into your life and stop its outward flow. Chinese divinatory coins also bring unexpected wealth.

High John the Conqueror root will attract new business and overcome slumps. It is good for the unemployed and for those returning to paid work after a career break or layoff. Combine it with a sugar lump or twist of sugar in foil if you need to sell an idea or product to a reluctant client or your services to a firm in the face of competition.

Gold in a form such as a gold ring, earring, collar stud, or any small round gold object, will attract slow-growing but lasting prosperity and increase confidence in a firm's viability so it will attract long-term investment or orders. Gold chains symbolize successful partnerships and networking.

Broken chains and rings will remove bad luck. Add salt and rosemary to provide extra power.

Spices, such as cinnamon, saffron, or ginger will improve sales or business and overcome a period of stagnation; they are also good for a fast infusion of money or confidence.

Tiny padlocks that are fastened represent job security; unlocked padlocks or those with keys inserted open the way to new opportunities.

A small watch will help sustain effort for a long task or goal. It will also bring in work offers, especially for the self-employed. A watch works wonders for timekeeping. Add High John the Conqueror root, salt, and iron pyrites to a green bag if the odds are stacked against you. A broken watch will buy you time if there are bills you cannot pay until money comes in.

Iron nails (if you can get nails from a horseshoe, that is even better) bring protection against unfair tactics from rival firms or overcompetitive colleagues.

Salt has both protective and empowering functions and has for thousands of years been a symbol of incoming money, health, and protection against negativity or accidents. It is a useful ingredient in any bag.

Lodestones are made from magnetic iron ore and draw money and success into your work life. By keeping a lodestone and a coin in your charm bag, you will never be short of money. They also bring in new customers of all kinds (prostitutes traditionally use them in mojos to attract a steady flow of clients). A pair of lodestones, rounded for the female stone and pointed and more pitted for the male, are good for business partnerships, especially with relations, friends, or love partners.

Wealth-bringing crystals, such as tiger's eye, jade, and peridot can be combined with miniature tools, such as a tiny silver pen if you want a book published.

Expired credit cards cut diagonally are a good symbol if you need to get loans or credit from a bank or other financial organization.

Good luck charms, such as small silver horseshoes, and four-leaf clovers will turn your luck around and restore your confidence if you have been going through a bad patch.

Angelica mixed with olive leaves will stop sniping and tension in the office and are also good for preventing interruptions if you work from home. Hide a pale blue flannel bag with these and rosebuds and a blue lace agate to garner kind words.

A St. Christopher medallion in a mojo or worn on a chain guards you if you travel a lot on business. Place one in a deep blue bag with coriander seeds, basil, and sodalite crystals.

Feathers bring protection while flying and also will launch a new or uncertain career or venture and improve overseas business.

Turquoise in any form is a must in travel mojos and also in those protecting work premises, vehicles, or tools.

Coriander or cumin seeds likewise protect equipment, vehicles, premises, and luggage.

Appendix III presents a full list of protective and empowering herbs and crystals you can put in mojos or more permanent charm bags.

Empowering the Bag

If you have included any items that belonged to someone else in your mojo, purify them first with hyssop, lavender, or rosemary infusion, one teaspoon of dried herb to a cup of boiling water, left for five minutes. Strain the liquid, discard the herbs, and sprinkle it over the artifact. Alternatively waft a lighted hyssop, lavender, or rosemary incense stick or smudge counterclockwise over the object to remove the previous owner's vibes. Some practitioners also make three circles of hyssop infusion drops around any bag before closing it for protection. A few drops of liquid are sprinkled on the bag after filling to empower it, while stating the mojo's purpose. Traditionally, the liquid used is alcohol, barley wine for abundance and whiskey or cognac for prosperity. Using empowering but less aesthetically pleasing body fluids has fortunately died out and certainly is not advisable for indoor mojos. However, you can purchase special hoodoo oils with exotic names related to their strengths. You can just as effectively use essential oil (see appendix III for a full list of properties). Your choice of oil can add particular qualities or strengths that may not be reflected in the items within the bag (otherwise you would need a mojo suitcase). For example, orange essential oil favors harmonious partnerships and brings increased confidence, self-esteem, and fertility of ideas, joy, and good health. Frankincense oil promises success, especially of major ambitions, or the fulfillment of ambitious ventures, the expansion of horizons and markets, and travel opportunities.

Recite the purpose of the mojo nine times as you sprinkle two or three drops of oil or alcohol over the bag before closing it. Even with a bag with a drawstring, always secure the top with three red cords.

Keeping the Mojo

Mojos are carried, either around the neck on a cord, in a pocket, or slung around the hips on a narrow fabric belt. They are always kept out of sight. Those on work premises are hidden near the door or in a locked drawer, again unseen, as it is believed that if a mojo bag is touched by someone else, it loses its power and good fortune. Therefore each is an individual device, though you can empower a workplace one to bring success to the whole business.

Some mojos are only intended for short-term use, for example, a job interview, but others may have ongoing power. Mojo bags will if necessary last for months unless they contain perishables. If the mojo was created for an ongoing matter, such as the continuing inflow of money or orders, replace the mojo when you feel the power waning. Dispose of the old ones carefully by burying the contents, having thrown into water anything that will dissolve or naturally decay. Burn the bag.

Herb Charms

Herb charms can also be made at home, empowered to attract good fortune, and then carried with you or left in a workstation drawer or cupboard or hung from a cord at work.

You can make charm bags with dried herbs (the kind you have in jars for cooking in your kitchen), filling tiny purses or drawstring bags with luck-filled herbs. Alternatively use a small square of natural fabric to fill with herbs and tie with a natural-colored cord at the top.

These natural charms need not be hidden and can be made as gifts for colleagues who need some good luck or better health as well as for yourself. You can also create herbal charms to protect or bring good fortune to the whole office. Herbs can be used for a short- or long-term business need. Charms for ongoing success or protection will last as long as the bag's fragrance and then must be replaced.

Making Your Herb Bags

Herb charms are far less complex than mojo bags, though they should contain a mixture of different herbs in the right proportion for the purpose they were created. A health store or old-fashioned grocery store that can be usually found in older or restored parts of cities will have a wide variety of dried and powdered herbs and roots. Make herbs even finer using a coffee grinder. There are also mail order herb firms (see Resources).

Read through the herb list in appendix III and decide on a single herb or two or three to answer your needs. For example,

two parts allspice to one part ferns would supply a sudden infusion of wealth from an overseas connection or a business trip
that would get new orders. If you work in a hostile environment,
dried and chopped nettles or rosemary are good defensive herbs
to add to the bag. If you are choosing more than one kind of
herb per bag, calculate on the portions you need (either measure
in small coffee spoons or estimate) and proceed as follows.

To make an herb bag:

1. Using a small ceramic or wooden bowl and wooden
   spoon or a mortar and pestle, tip in the herbs. You can
   either enchant your herbs or empower them while mixing them. In both cases add a drop or two of essential oil
   from the list in appendix III in a different fragrance from
   the herbs you're using. For example, if you were using
   mint to increase business, you could add a drop or two
   of patchouli to ensure the new business clients be reliable payers and a long-term source of income.

2. After adding the oil, name any time scale you are seeking, for example: "May I find employment before the
   next moon is full." Or "May the book be published when
   leaves next fall."

3. To enchant your symbol, follow the method I described
   for empowering mojo bags. Keep moving your left hand
   in counterclockwise circles and at the same time your
   right hand in clockwise circles, faster and faster, as
   you chant the purpose of the sachet aloud. Instead of
   enchanting you might prefer to mix the herbs with the
   spoon clockwise. Mix faster and faster, while chanting
   your purpose with greater speed and intensity; for example: "Cloves of opportunity bring this contract now to
   me." With both methods, the herbs may seem to be
   infused with a faint green aura after a while or you will
   sense intuitively that they are fully charged. End with a
   "Bring, if right to be, success to me immediately."

4. Plunge your hands or spoon firmly into the herbs on the
   final chant. Carefully scoop the herbs into your purse or
   cloth and close or secure it.

5. Leave the herb charm in a cool, dark place until you can take it into work.

Either after the time scale you built into the charm has elapsed or when the herbs are no longer fragrant, open the bag and scatter the herbs to the winds in an open place. Dispose of the bag in an environmentally friendly way. Create a new sachet if necessary and empower it as before.

Crystal Charms

Crystal charms have great strength. Each crystal has qualities it transmits to the owner or wearer. The more you carry it or wear it as adornment, the stronger its luck- or success-bringing energies will become as the crystalline energies mingle with your own inherent potential creativity and talents.

What is more, you can empower a favorite lucky crystal for a sudden or specific need by writing over it in incense smoke the purpose and any time scale for the charm. (See appendix III for powerful luck-bringing incenses.) This directed power is only known to you and will last as long as you specify. Let me give you an example.

Sample Reading

Andrew was a wonder at illustrating children's books, but he worked for a London firm that paid him only basic flat fees, though some of his creations had featured in television cartoons and made the firm a great deal of money. The company has refused to give him a salary increase and said he is lucky to get his ideas marketed at all, especially as he was not a natural communicator.

Astrid, Andrew's Danish girlfriend, made Andrew a malachite crystal as a charm. Malachite protects against pollution from new technology, but it is also a very powerful success stone, especially in areas such as design, and it enhances clear communication and marketing skills in every field.

Over the crystal Astrid wrote in juniper incense for new beginnings: "Lead Andrew to a new job that will fulfill his potential and bring him profit within four weeks."

A week later Andrew attended an international book illustrators' conference in Germany, and Astrid insisted he carry his crystal in his jacket pocket. Surprisingly the crystal felt good, and Andrew found that if he touched it he experienced a surge of confidence and was unusually lucid in his sales talks.

At night Andrew kept the crystal with his graphics disc, in the remote hope he might sell one of the original ideas he worked on in his spare time.

On the second day Andrew met Paul, who runs a one-man graphics company in Malmo in southern Sweden, selling his cartooning ideas to media companies around the world. The two had so much in common that they met at Andrew's hotel that night. Andrew made sure the crystal was in his pocket and found he was able to explain unusually clearly a new idea for a picture-led children's television series he was developing and how it might be marketed in different countries.

A week later, Paul emailed Andrew to say he had sold the idea to a large French firm who wanted more of his ideas. Paul offered Andrew a partnership, based in Malmo, on a profit-sharing basis with no need to put money upfront. Astrid's parents lived in Copenhagen, just across the bridge from Malmo and so accommodation initially would be no problem. Andrew already spoke Danish, which is very similar to Swedish, and in both countries everyone is fluent in English.

Andrew keeps the malachite by his telephone in his new office and touches it whenever he has to sell a new concept.

Crystal Zodiac Charms

Though I do find incense-empowered crystals very effective, you may like to make yourself a set of twelve more permanent zodiac crystals that you can use as charms for releasing specific powers into your life when you need them. Your own zodiac or birth sign charm will of course be effective at any time in your working life when you need to assert your identity and core strengths and most of all during your birth sign period each year. But you can borrow the strengths and luck of any zodiacal sign by carrying the relevant zodiacal crystal whenever you need a quick boost, for example, of Arian courage, even if it is not during the specific sun sign period of Aries and you are a Pisces.

Making and Empowering Zodiac Charms

Best of all is to make your zodiacal charms using crystals that are associated with each birth sign (listed below). But you can use any crystals you already own or simple white stones. If you need to obtain crystals, you need only buy small ones.

To make your own zodiac charms:

1. Paint the appropriate glyph on each crystal with acrylic paint and a fine brush or a fine-lined permanent pen marker.

2. Pass the crystal through or around a flame three times, name the key strength of the zodiac sign you need (choose from below), and leave the crystal in front of the candle while the candle burns down. For example, you might say: "I seek the patience of Taurus to get me though tomorrow's stocktaking with my boss, who slows us down by questioning every tiny detail."

3. Keep your charms in a drawstring bag and have a tiny purse to take the one you need to work. You can make the crystal charms altogether or separately. The day of the full moon just before dusk is an especially good time for making charms. Whenever you need a particular charm's strength, you can light its own color candle or a gold one the night before you intend to take the charm to work.

♈ **Aries, the Ram (March 21–April 20)** For providing courage or assertiveness if you are being bullied or overlooked, for encouraging ambition and ambitious ventures, getting projects moving, for kick-starting or regenerating a career that has hit a plateau.

Crystal Carnelian

Candle color Red

♉ **Taurus, the Bull (April 21-May 21)** For job security, for steady increase of salary and prospects, for establishing regular work patterns and working within a routine, for patience if results are slow; for making the work environment more congenial, for aesthetically pleasing presentation of work and advertising.

Crystal Rose quartz

Candle color Pink

♊ **Gemini, the Heavenly Twins (May 22-June 21)** For encouraging versatility and adaptability, for enhancing communication skills, technological abilities, logic, and financial acumen, for establishing partnerships, for ensuring successful business trips

Crystal Citrine

Candle color Pale yellow

♋ **Cancer, the Crab (June 22-July 22)** For developing intuitive awareness, for understanding the demands of the market, for improving people skills, for keeping secrets and information confidential, for relating knowledge gained from past trends and behavior to the present situation, for improving catering and hospitality facilities.

Crystal Moonstone

Candle color Silver

♌ **Leo, the Lion (July 23-August 23)** For developing leadership abilities and getting the opportunity to use them, for increasing sales and improving marketing, for being noticed in the promotional stakes, for self-confidence, for developing hidden talents and potential, for aiming for the top in any profession, for increasing creativity.

Crystal Clear crystal quartz

Candle color Gold

♍ **Virgo, the Maiden (August 24-September 22)** For increasing efficiency, for developing accuracy and fine-tuning skills, for increasing perfection in the finished product, for teaching others especially on a one-to-one basis, for persevering in routine but necessary tasks, for enhancing skilled critical analysis.

Crystal Jade

Candle color Green or pale blue

♎︎ **Libra, the Scales (September 23-October 23)** For negotiating skills especially over working conditions and equal rights, for balancing different demands on time, for creating a harmonious workplace, for increasing personal charisma, for fighting injustice in a calm effective way, for improving customer relations and networking, for initiating or participating in successful joint or group projects.

Crystal Lapis lazuli

Candle color Blue or violet

♏︎ **Scorpio, the Scorpion (October 24-November 22)** For surviving a layoff or unfair dismissal, for fighting inequality of any kind, for establishing a second career especially one in later life, for regenerating a firm in financial trouble and turning around an unprofitable project in which a lot of time and effort has been invested, for developing imagination.

Crystal Malachite or bloodstone

Candle color Indigo or burgundy red

♐︎ **Sagittarius, the Archer (November 23-December 21)** For expanding markets and widening personal horizons and possibilities, for setting up a new business or venture, for inspiring thinking and vision, for providing travel opportunities, for planning forward effectively and overcoming obstacles in your personal path, for promoting enthusiasm and energy when others are flagging or casting doubt, for seeing the whole picture and the end result.

Crystal Turquoise

Candle color Orange

♑︎ **Capricorn, the Goat (December 22-January 20)** For using wise caution in investments, for recognizing shrewd career moves, for persisting in following a course believed to be right or a project that will bear fruit in the long term, for inspiring loyalty in others, for furthering long-term ambitions, for providing the strength to work alone or set up a company at home.

Crystal Smoky quartz

Candle color Golden brown

≈ **Aquarius, the Water Carrier (January 21–February 18)** For thinking inventively and laterally, for creating independent and original ideas, for gaining freedom from the need or the approval of others, for maintaining personal idealism and integrity even in a large corporation, for finding personal fulfillment that may mean downsizing or working where job satisfaction rather than salary is the main reward.

Crystal Aquamarine

Candle color Dark blue

♓ **Pisces, the Fish (February 19–March 20)** For beginning any new adventures in the working world, for resolving conflicts of loyalty, for developing and trusting intuitive awareness, for seeing through illusion and deception, for running two careers successfully or combining a hectic family and work life, for developing counseling skills whether formal or informal.

Crystal Any fluorite

Candle color White

Charm Divination

Put all your marked zodiacal crystals in a drawstring bag and pull one out at random on a morning when you feel you need extra luck or before an important meeting or examination. Your choice will indicate the kind of good fortune or strengths that you may not realize on a conscious level you require.

In the next chapter we will examine ways of increasing personal power and negotiating workplace politics and relationships through working with animal symbolism.

CHAPTER 12

Animal Power and Magic

The average workplace has much in common with a well-run menagerie. There's the eager beaver, diving feverishly into piles of seemingly chaotic paperwork and emerging triumphant with the missing receipt for twelve postage stamps from September 12, 1993, needed to complete the ten year-profit and loss assessment. The immaculately groomed cat, who is filing her nails, will purr the magic solution everyone has been running around like headless chickens to find, two minutes before deadline, before returning to polishing her cuticles. The office tiger is holding at bay awkward inquiries from predators higher up the food chain until you have discovered what happened to a missing order and sent replacements by Federal Express. The owl blinks sleepily, having spent all night musing over and solving a blip in the new office software, while the dove convinces the hawk that it is not good management policy to nuke her sales team because they only worked 24/6 during Thanksgiving.

Who are you and which creature would you like to be if the office really were an animal park? If you are uncertain, ask a friendly but honest colleague which animal or bird you remind them of. You may be surprised at the strengths for which you are perceived, but if you don't like the animal persona you generally manifest, there are ways of bringing more dynamic or environmentally charismatic qualities to the fore (see chapter 6).

Even if this chapter is not one with which you easily identify, try some of the ideas just for fun. You may be startled at the accurate insights you obtain into workplace dynamics when you take a walk on the wild side.

Discovering Your Inner Power Animal

The concept of having a personal power or totem animal as a wise guide is one that has existed in societies throughout the ages and across the world. According to Native North American belief, as the most recent creation, humankind has much to learn from the older and wiser forms of life.

In a number of indigenous traditions, the spirits, or if you prefer idealized essential strengths of animals and birds, can act as guardians with whom they have natural affinity, endowing those they protect with their unique strengths and wisdom. We all have one special power inner creature, our alter ego whose qualities complement and supplement our own outer and refined but sometimes diluted ideal behavior and perceived good qualities. Sometimes these two beings seem the opposite of what we are or at least of the side we show the world.

This inner power animal (maybe part of our instinctive self) represents our hidden or undeveloped qualities that can turn us instantly when the need arises from an ego-smoothing dove into a hawk who can seize a sudden opportunity, volunteer when everyone else stays silent for extra training or a difficult assignment that will bring in extra income, or accept a promotion even though it means moving two hundred miles away to a city where you know no one. If you see yourself as a mouse (or others describe you that way), your inner alter ego power animal may be a roaring lion. Because your inner power creature is in the background, you can call on these qualities when you need them, which may be once a week or once a year.

The creature may have been present in your life from childhood. Perhaps though you were timid, you always loved hawks and the way they soared upward to the sun and hovered motionless for what seemed like hours before swooping. You may have visited a bird of prey conservancy regularly and felt an affinity with a particularly magnificent creature that would become still or move close when you observed it. You would recall the soaring hawk when you were being bullied at school or had to take an examination that terrified you so much you could barely recall your name. Suddenly for a flash you were that hawk and even the bullies backed off.

But for many people their power animal only becomes prominent when they start work or move up the career ladder and need to make headway in a world where suddenly other folk seem so much more confident and knowledgeable.

If you've never thought about the idea, or thought of the idea of power creatures as New Age hype, play around with the concept, flex your muscles, and roar. Think about the kind of creature you admire most or head for first when you visit the zoo.

Your totem may be an animal or bird indigenous to your region or one from another part of the world that attracts you. If you explore your ancestry, you can often trace the roots of your fascination to a creature from an area your forebears occupied. If your special creature lives on the other side of the world, a little detective work will often reveal that your creature may have been indigenous to your home region hundreds or thousands of years earlier and you have tapped into the folk memory of the place.

Totem Animal Magic

The following creatures are those that my own research and work in the business world have shown to be especially effective power icons. I have also listed how you might identify the personalities in your workplace, just in case you need to placate the office bear with honey!

Power icons, whether traditionally male or female biased, can be used to give strength to either sex. Indeed, I have recently noticed that a number of younger women I have interviewed, especially when in highly competitive or chauvinistic workplaces, favor a personal power animal with a strong animus, such as a tiger or a bull. In contrast, guys are gradually moving toward more nurturing inner alter ego power creatures such as mother wolf or the intuition of the mystical cat.

Bear

Bears were worshipped and sacrificed by early humans. Bear shrines and bear skulls and bones have been discovered with the buried human remains of Neanderthal man. Many male and female shamans (the priest magician healers in traditional indigenous societies) claim direct descent from a bear that has been killed at a time the shaman underwent a ritual death.

Bear as a power animal The bear brings strength to overcome all obstacles and opposition. The bear endows fierce territorial instincts if your space or ideas are constantly being invaded. The bear brings a repository of wisdom and authority if you are young or uncertain. This power animal helps workers whose job pattern is affected by seasonal changes and demands.

Bear in the office The bear fills every available space, even if the human version is physically quite small. He or she may knock the contents of desks flying. Very strong and protective of younger or vulnerable staff members, the bear will always come up with a precedent or strategy that worked in the past. They usually have a store of herbal or homeopathic remedies in their drawer for anyone who is unwell. They can be very possessive of their space and belongings, especially in the late autumn before hibernation and early spring at cub time, so ask before you borrow or intrude.

Beaver

Often the clan leader, the beaver is a wise guide to Native North Americans especially in times of change and uncertainty; this is a form taken by the Great Spirit.

Beaver as a power animal The beaver brings versatility since this creature is equally at home on land or in water. The beaver is helpful if you need to get the balance right between logic and intuition or between home and work commitments (a beaver is able to switch rapidly from one to the other). The beaver also displays intense perseverance and organizational skills and brings harmony to the world in which it lives. The beaver is helpful for twilight or late-shift workers.

Beaver in the office The beaver may seem chaotic as he or she constantly rearranges an ever-growing paper mountain, but in fact can within seconds lay hands on any memo or research whether produced that morning or filed at the time of Abraham Lincoln. The person with the beaver totem is incredibly hardworking, never phased by interruptions or two demands at once, and able to switch tasks without pausing. Not at their best in the morning, avoid commenting on the untidiness of their workspace or touching their paperwork without invitation.

Blackbird

The blackbird is an especially magical bird. The blackbirds of the Goddess Rhiannon sang on the tree at the entrance to the Celtic Otherworld and acted as doorkeepers; so sweetly did they sing that none were afraid to enter and none noticed the passing of time.

Blackbird as a power animal The blackbird infuses you with optimism and self-confidence if you are uncertain about your abilities or if you work in an unfriendly environment. The blackbird's fiercely defensive nature is an asset in a very competitive business or if you work with colleagues with strong personalities, helping you to get noticed and to impress with your communicative abilities, and helping to obtain equal rights. The blackbird is good if you work early shifts.

Blackbird in the office Invariably the first to arrive, the blackbird whistles, sings, or hums his or her way through the day. Always encouraging and cheerful no matter what the crisis or how great the task, the blackbird welcomes newcomers and is very patient when training younger staff. However, the blackbird is very territorial and can become quite aggressive if others try to take over his or her tasks or sales areas. A person with the blackbird totem makes it clear there is only room for one cheerleader.

Buffalo (or Bison)

To the North American Indian nations, the buffalo was the source of everything needed for survival. Even though the buffalo herds were almost wiped out by the settlers, a recently born white buffalo calf has become a symbol of hope for the future revival of spiritual values in the world.

Buffalo as a power animal The buffalo is a strong often female power icon that will attract abundance and success into your life. The buffalo encourages generosity of spirit, if you face spite or meanness at work. The buffalo also helps you to focus on assured long-term success, especially if you have suffered a setback such as a layoff or a shortage of employment opportunities in your chosen field after leaving college. The buffalo is an excellent companion if you work in the caring professions or are responsible formally or informally for the welfare of other workers.

Buffalo in the office Whether you've a broken nail or wounded heart, the buffalo personality will be your first port of call at work. The buffalo is usually the organizer of raffles, birthday collections, and home bakes for any and every occasion; you can rely on your buffalo to do more than their fair share of the work and to help others out, usually claiming little credit. However, ingratitude or disrespect may leave you feeling distinctly trampled.

Bull

The bull is a male power symbol that appears in early Neolithic art, with the Earth Mother giving birth to a bull or horned god figure as her son and/or consort. Bull dances and bull sacrifices, the origin of the Spanish bullfight, were performed in honor of the Mother Goddess in Crete and in pre-Christian times in other Mediterranean lands such as Spain.

Bull as a power animal The bull will give potency both to your image and to the results you produce. Use the bull if people are not taking you seriously or are passing you over for promotion, for increased productivity, for the strength to withstand intense work pressures, and to make a supreme effort that will further your ambitions. Also use the bull to resist bullies and take a stand against injustice.

Bull in the office Usually but not always male in human form, the bull is often a boss or if young the thrusting newcomer eager to usurp the power of the throne. Screw down any objects that will go flying as he charges through, speaking before thinking, sweeping obstacles out of the way to meet a deadline and occasionally losing control when faced with incompetence or opposition. An incredibly hard worker, the bull invariably delivers what has been promised and is a good one to have on your side as he can be uncharacteristically gentle and kind in case of genuine need or distress. Bulls often do not realize that their customary forthrightness causes offence, so steer your bull toward a people management manual or course.

Butterfly

The butterfly is associated with the sixteenth-century mystic, St. Teresa of Avila, who likened the process of dying to a butterfly emerging from a chrysalis. The mortal Psyche, whose name is Greek for soul, who married Eros, God of Love, whom she was only permitted to meet in darkness, was transformed into a butterfly on her death, a common form according to early Greek myth for the human soul to take between incarnations.

Butterfly as a power animal The workaholic's friend, the butterfly will help you to lighten up if work has become a chore and you seem to be taking more than your fair share of responsibility. Its metamorphosis offers the ability to transform a career going nowhere or one where there have been few rewards. But the butterfly's greatest power is always to live in the present, dealing with what needs doing right now rather than worrying about the piles of work still unfinished or fretting about yesterday's mistakes and how you will cope tomorrow.

Butterfly in the office Mainly female, you'll notice her most on sunny days, brightly dressed or with innovative touches that transform a boring uniform. The butterfly is the ideal messenger or courier, delivering even bad news with the gentlest touch. Moving constantly from place to place and settling to a task for a short while but never completely still, the butterfly will be constantly reaching for a colored highlighter pen to doodle on the minutes of a meeting and opening windows to let in any sunshine. A joy, quick to laugh and see advantage in any situation, the butterfly finds her work a real pleasure, though those who have to finish her tasks may not agree. Then one day she is gone without warning to grow sunflowers in the country or to take up a multimillion dollar three-book contract she never mentioned she was writing.

Cat

Any unlucky connotations regarding cats derive from the two black cats that pulled the chariot of the Viking goddess Freyja. When Scandinavia was Christianized in the eleventh century, Freyja was downgraded to a witch and banished to the top of a mountain, and black cats shared her fate as witches' familiars. In contrast, Bastet, the Egyptian cat-headed goddess who accompanied Ra, the sun God, in his solar boat each day and protected him from the serpent Apep, gave the cat more fortunate associations.

Cat as a power animal If you are generally a practical prosaic person the mysterious mystical cat will open up the intuitive side of your nature. The cat teaches the ability to assess the right moment to speak or act. The cat also imparts a sense of independence from the need to win approval and inspired solutions, instead leaping from A to Z without needing to go add up all the intervening columns. The cat is a good icon for all who work at night.

Cat in the office The cat in your workplace will be graceful whether male or female and generally very still, speaking only when there is something worth saying. Nevertheless, even when you think your feline has fallen asleep, he or she is totally aware of everything going on and will react in seconds with the answer everyone has been taking hours to fathom. For this reason the cat generally is highly valued by senior management. While cats tend to walk alone and do not join factions, cliques, or even discussions, showing a cat appreciation and a supply of creature comforts may be rewarded by unexpected help or kindness.

Cobra

The cobra is a magical and sacred snake in both India and ancient Egypt, where Uadjet was the cobra goddess of truth and justice and protectress of the pharaohs.

Cobra as a power animal The cobra offers you protection, especially against spite and human venom, however powerful the adversary, and is an effective channel for claiming or reclaiming power after a setback. Use cobra energy when dealing with important clients, the media, or executives to sell yourself or your ideas in a way that will lead to rapid advancement and prosperity, and even a degree of fame.

Cobra in the office No ordinary serpent, the cobra seems to dance or glide across a room and take on a dozen different guises. The cobra in your office will listen intently and in a mesmeric voice persuade you quite the opposite of what you intended and silence complaints at ten feet. The cobra will never be spiteful or petty, but if angered by betrayal or disloyalty will not hold back his or her venom.

Chameleon

An amazing creature, legends of many lands regard the chameleon as a magical creation because of its ability to change color and merge with the background.

Chameleon as a power animal The chameleon is an excellent counterfoil if your work is high profile or controversial or if you spend a lot of time dealing with the general public; it helps you to keep a low profile when necessary, to become sensitive to atmospheres, moods, and environmental changes, and to work as part of a team where your own views are not necessarily those of the contractors. The chameleon is also good for recognizing the point of view of others and surviving in a hostile or unfamiliar environment.

Chameleon in the office Having a different outfit and opinion for every occasion, do not rely on the vote of your chameleon. Very adaptable and willing to work with anyone in any area of expertise, the chameleon avoids confrontations and meetings where opinions are demanded. If present at a meeting, this person will usually be the one taking the minutes, organizing the graphics, or making refreshments. The chameleon is amazingly effective at uncovering hidden information and overhearing conversations half a mile away.

Crane

The crane is a sacred bird in Japan, a symbol of health and long life. It is called the Honorable Lord Crane, and according to both Japanese and Chinese myth lives for a thousand years or more. In China, white cranes are especially sacred and live on the Islands of the Blest, the Chinese earthly paradise. A guardian of the Celtic Otherworld, the crane also represents great knowledge.

Crane as a power animal The crane is an excellent creature if you need to work alone, to keep secrets, or are on a spiritual or alternative health career path. The crane offers strength if you need improved health and increased stamina or are trying to learn a new skill or enter a new field that involves years of study. Lord or lady crane also represents standing apart from the crowd, perhaps over matters of principle or because you have a personal quest to fulfill.

Crane in the office No one can probably remember how long a crane has worked for a firm, but certainly they are legendary in their long service and inscrutability. The crane is often found in a corner of a laboratory, behind a pile of dusty files (no computers for him or her). If you ask a crane for advice you will, after a long pause, learn a great deal about yourself and your life path as well as the matter under consideration. Your secrets will be safe with the office crane.

Deer and Gazelle

In the north of Scotland and the Scottish Isles especially, there are many myths of goddesses or fairies assuming the form of deer. Deer goddesses date back to the hunter tribes who worshipped the Mother Goddess as Mistress of the Herds.

Deer as a power animal The deer offers sensitivity and responsiveness to the moods of others and so can be of value in people-related careers and when there is strong office politicking or factions that could cause divisions. The deer is good for changing your career direction, especially for choosing fulfillment over material rewards and for bringing gentleness into a competitive world or softening your own ambitions if these are conflicting with your personal happiness.

Deer in the office Easily startled, the deer will usually have a workstation shielded by greenery and finds that noise and stress bring on migraines or stress reactions. Usually female and very feminine, the deer will be very supportive in times of crisis, but gets deeply upset and will bolt for the bathroom if criticized or if an exchange of views gets out of hand. Watch for unexpected restlessness as the deer has sensitive antennae. The deer's unrest may be forewarning that, as with her, it may be a time to make yourself scarce for a while.

Dingo, Jackal, and Wild Dogs

In ancient Egypt, jackals, predatory wild dogs who came from the desert in search of prey, were often seen around the tombs in the Valley of the Kings and Queens, and their nocturnal howling was interpreted as protection of the deceased. A popular magical tradition that has been sensationalized in a recent film, *Return of the Mummy*, records that the jackal-headed warriors of Anubis, the Egyptian protector god of the Underworld and of rebirth, were sent magically against powerful enemies.

Dingo as a power animal Use the dingo or wild dog if you travel a lot on business, especially to big cities, as a protector, to inspire loyalty in others, for courage in a ruthless business environment, and to develop your own survival instincts so you know whom to trust and whether a business deal or job offer is sound. The dingo is a good power animal if you are naturally shy and sensitive.

Dingo in the office Probably male and usually on the road, barking down the telephone or studying maps and target charts, the dingo is liable to snarl if interrupted or anyone tries to encroach on his sales or business territory. Loyal to any firm, though ruthless to competitors, the dingo can be tamed with kindness and tidbits (I once used cream cakes to get a human dingo on my side).

Dolphin

Many of the goddesses take this most intelligent of creatures for their icon, including Aphrodite and Venus, the sensual Ishtar in

Babylonian mythology, and the Mother Goddess Isis in Ancient Egypt. Countless true stories recount how dolphins have rescued humans from the sea.

Dolphin as a power animal Use this wonderful mammal for heightened intuition and clairvoyant powers if you are involved in business planning or want to see your future personal direction more clearly. The dolphin brings intelligence, understanding of the whole picture, and the ability to encourage idealism and integrity in others. The dolphin can be invoked to create a more spiritual workplace; but if you adopt this creature you are committing yourself to maintaining the highest personal and professional standards.

Dolphin in the office Rare but unmistakable, the dolphin is the person with the gentle smile who never has said a bad word about anyone, who can and will mend any quarrel or coldness, and who could make money from incredibly tuned clairvoyant powers. The dolphin is often headhunted, but usually is more concerned with ethics than position. His or her inspirationally creative ideas always have an inner purpose for good as well as for profit. The dolphin will form the heart of the office and at any time of the day, people will be gathered around there to draw on the dolphin's calm and uplifting energies.

Dove

A far more powerful totem than it superficially appears, the dove features in the flood stories of the Babylonians, Hebrews, Chaldeans, and Greeks as a symbol of peace and reconciliation. The dove is also sacred to wise Athena and is the symbol of Sophia, Goddess of Wisdom. The dove bearing the olive branch back to Noah's Ark has become an international sign of peace.

Dove as a power animal Use the dove to bring peace and harmony into your life and your workplace, for reconciling conflicting priorities, for encouraging cooperative ventures, for coping with irritable or unreasonable bosses or colleagues, and for resolving personal problems that may be interfering with your concentration. Your dove will guide you safely on business trips especially by air or to places where there are internal conflicts or continuing threats of terrorism that can make journeys hazardous.

Dove in the office Generally but not by any means always female, you can identify the dove by her soft tone of voice, home-knit sweaters, and a bag or drawer filled with old-fashioned sweets we last ate as a child. The voice of moderation in meetings, pay negotiations, spats between the office cat and dog, or the sudden lunge of a predator, the dove is successful at brokering solutions in which everybody wins or at least gets second prize and at soothing bruised egos with an unexpected chocolate cake party.

Dragon

Though mythical creatures, every office has one dragon. Dragons are an ancient and universal symbol of earth energies, living in caves beneath the earth, frequently guarding fabulous treasures. Oriental dragons are much revered, responsible for bringing rain and prosperity to mortals; they live either in sea caves, deep pools, or palaces in the clouds. Western and Eastern European dragons are primarily known for being guardians of gold and for eating young virgins, especially female ones.

Dragon as a power animal If you are really timid, the dragon is the creature for you, breathing fire and devouring those who attempt to bully or browbeat you. The dragon is excellent too for releasing the hidden gold of your potential and for overcoming a stagnant or unprofitable period in your life or work.

Dragon in the office Usually female, very fierce and territorial, and called Sheila or Dorothy, the dragon will be found guarding someone or something. She is the archetypal doctor's disapproving receptionist and the senior manager's personal assistant, and was his father's personal assistant before him. Her life is to block anyone who wishes to see her treasure and to enforce the office rule book to the letter; the dragon can recite the rule book backward. Equal rights legislation was passed on her rare day off, and she will blatantly ignore it. Her invariably male boss is god, and she is his mom, and everyone else is the enemy. An institution, since dragon slayers are regrettably few and far between in Michigan or Manhattan, all dragons have a weak spot, so find it (maybe her grandkids are a route to contacting her subterranean and almost-forgotten stores of human kindness).

Eagle

The eagle, the true king of birds and a symbol of courage and power in many cultures, is central to Native North American magic. In Amerindian lore, its feathers carry the prayers of the people to the Father Sun. It was said that the eagle could fly closest to the sun and not be burned and could look into the noonday sun without flinching and not be blinded. The white-headed American eagle with wings outstretched is the emblem of the United States.

Eagle as a power animal If you want to be president, whether of the United States or a Merchant Bank, or if you are leading a single-handed crusade to bring clean water to the Third World, this icon is for you. The bird of leaders and leadership, of nobility and vision, this is a high-maintenance power icon demanding total commitment and purity of purpose.

Eagle in the office An empire builder, if not an emperor or empress already, the eagle has a regal manner, an aquiline nose, and sharp eyes that do not miss the faintest eyeblink. The eagle in your workplace will instantly follow up opportunities across the globe without going home first for a change of shirt and works with the whole picture, relying on others to fill in the details often en route. Probably already a trustee, president of the local society of businessmen or women, a member of the Rotary Club, or active in a local charity, the eagle can be quite intimidating and impatient with those who do not understand. The eagle is a natural protector of the rights of the vulnerable, is noble in defeat, and is remarkably understanding about personal problems.

Hound or Domestic Dog

The findings of three research teams, reported in November 2002 in the United Kingdom *Science* magazine, suggested that 95 percent of all dogs evolve from three founding female wolves, tamed by humans living in or near China less than fifteen thousand years ago. Even dogs in the New World have their origins in Eastern Asia. In Greek and Roman myth, Hermes/Mercury, the messenger of the gods, was accompanied by his faithful dog.

Hound as a power animal If you have a solitary job or one where you feel isolated for whatever reason, the dog is a faithful companion. The dog is also useful for gaining the trust and loyalty of colleagues and for friendly interactions within the workplace. Hounds will protect your original ideas and your own personal psychological space against unwanted intrusions on your time, especially helping to fend off gossiping or bored colleagues who want to needle you when you are trying to concentrate.

Hound in the office Always eager to please, devoted to their employers, the organization, and those they count as friends, dogs are super-responsive even to faint praise. They love errands and working out in the sales field, and they will follow up a lead or opportunity if necessary for weeks without losing enthusiasm. The pack of young male hounds who play for the works' basketball team or train at the gym together after work may occasionally become boisterous if underoccupied, and they need to know who is boss psychologically. Bitches may be aptly named and should be kept busy, separately where possible, or given young staff members of their own to care for and train.

Elephant

Pliny believed that the elephant had religious feelings and worshipped the ancient deities of the moon and stars. Aristotle credited the elephant with great wisdom and intelligence, a trait echoed in Hinduism in which elephant-headed Ganesh is God of Wisdom and is always invoked at the beginning of any journey or before any important enterprise.

Elephant as a power animal If your career or life generally is going through an unstable patch, an elephant can give you the security and solid foundation you need. The elephant is useful in getting yourself taken seriously especially if you are young and/or beautiful as well as intelligent. The elephant will provide strength and staying power to undertake a major project or course of study that may take years to complete, and this power animal is also good for enhanced memory and concentration and is a perfect alter ego for a lightweight such as the office butterfly.

Elephant in the office Steady, totally reliable, and often with quiet authority beyond his or her years, the elephant is the gentle giant or comfortably proportioned wise woman who allows people to make their own mistakes without interfering, though this person will be ready to offer support if asked. The anchorman or woman of any enterprise, stepping between predator and prey or handling it when natural competitiveness tips over into lack of cooperation, the elephant rarely gets disheartened. The office elephant knows tomorrow really is another day and the sun will shine and that there is a world outside the work premises. Proud of children and grandchildren and willing to adopt lonely colleagues, the elephant is an excellent sounding board for ideas and plans. The elephant never forgets a kindness or a put-down.

Falcon or Hawk

The bush falcon, found in Australia and New Zealand, was regarded as a messenger from the earth to the heavens and was used in establishing whether a location for a new Maori ceremonial house was favorable to the gods and ancestors. In ancient Egyptian and Native North American mythology, the hawk, like the eagle, was a bird of the sun and could also soar toward the sun and look into its brilliant face without being blinded. Sacred to Horus, Egyptian Sky God of Learning, the hawk was symbol of the return of light after darkness and so of joy after sorrow.

Hawk as a power animal Birds of prey are wonderful for bringing self-confidence and the courage to aim high if you are naturally reticent or uncertain about your life path. The hawk is helpful too for providing focus and concentration if you are a lateral or primarily an imaginative thinker. Single-mindedness and the ability to anticipate the right moment to seize advantage or an opportunity are other valuable hawk qualities. Hawks also stop you from being emotionally pressured by unreasonable demands on your time and commitment.

Hawk in the office Hawks know their target territory and can smell a potential change in the financial markets or trends in the wind. Ruthless to rivals and single-minded to the point of selfishness in achieving their goal, they are not indiscriminately unkind or aggressive to those who are not a threat. Hawks are often a necessary counterbalance to the doves who would give all the resources away to the needy and always stand back to let their competitors go first.

Heron

The heron is identified with the ancient Egyptian Benu bird, the original mythical phoenix that perched on the first mound and represented the first sunrise. Herons returned to Egypt at the time of the annual flood that fertilized the land and so became linked to rebirth. The Benu was said to be consumed by flames every five hundred years and the young bird rose, carrying the ashes of its parent that it buried beneath the sacred mound.

Heron as a power animal The heron is a wonderful symbol of freedom from restriction, for fertility of ideas, and for an eagerness for new ideas and experiences. This bird is an excellent totem if you work alone, have to generate your own business, or are rebuilding your career after a major setback. The heron will help you to break free of restrictive practices, quit a position that is draining you of energy, and follow a dream.

Heron in the office The heron will be on the road opening up new possibilities, researching, or chasing opportunities long before you arrive at work. The free thinker who fills the communal suggestion box daily, he or she is constantly suggesting new approaches or scribbling down ideas for future endeavors while the present one is still at planning stage. Don't demand long-term commitments of your heron and leave windows open for escape and the heron may settle quite happily and share its foresight with you.

Horse

The horse, which was first domesticated about 1750 BC, has always been a magical symbol of swiftness and power. In Classical mythology, Pegasus the winged horse was the flying steed of the hero Perseus. Epona was the Celtic Horse Goddess and was frequently depicted riding a mare or being a mare herself with a foal. She represented fertility, and the Romans adopted her to worship.

Horse as a power animal The horse is a source of strength and has the stamina to work hard and with consistent effort on long-term projects. The horse is known for loyalty and harmony in partnerships or as part of a team. The horse also signifies the courage to move into unknown territory, giving parents or people caring for dependents of any age the ability to combine effective care with the demands of career and offering unconditional support to a venture or firm in which you are closely involved to weather a crisis.

Horse in the office The horse is the reliable quiet, totally trustworthy, and sometimes-overlooked staff member who gets the work done while others plan and procrastinate. Usually found doing more than his or her share of extra hours or unpopular routine tasks, the horse in your office will fit into any team regardless of personalities and will defuse tension and inflamed egos. Excellent also for working on the road, doing tireless footwork, and being scrupulously honest with expenses, the horse will help anyone anytime. Some fillies can be very sensitive to noise and stress, but incredibly kind. The racehorse unlike the workhorse is constantly seeking new challenges and will finish tasks in double quick time. Show regular appreciation and do not overwork willing horses; they have a nasty kick and bite if provoked.

Jaguar or Leopard

To the Mayans, the jaguar god was very protective and guarded villages from harm. In South America it is told that the jaguar taught humans to use bows and arrows and gave them cooked meat from his own fire. But men stole the fire and killed his wife, and so the jaguar lives alone in deep forests and is now their enemy.

Jaguar as a power animal Use jaguar power for courage to overcome hostility or gossip, to travel safely especially at night, for keen sales and marketing abilities, for building up a self-employed business in a crowded field, for countering industrial espionage or plagiarism of your ideas and work, for remaining unnoticed until the moment comes to seize an opportunity, and to empower and protect night workers.

Jaguar in the office The jaguar is the woman or man who dresses mainly in dark clothes, who talks little about his or her out-of-work life, and who prefers to work alone and when possible from home. If there is not a night shift, the jaguar will instead stay late when others have gone home and may come in to work weekends or vacation periods, enjoying the quiet of the office. Though rarely forthcoming in meetings, the jaguar knows precisely what competitors are doing and will have an uncanny knack of attracting clients from rivals. Don't speculate aloud about the mysterious jaguar or try to read over his or her shoulder. The jaguar's territory is totally off limits.

Lion

In Western mythology, the lion is the king of the beasts. He represents the power of the sun and was associated with the sun gods and later with kings. Lionesses are equally powerful and protect the whole pride of lions, not just their immediate family. The lion-headed Egyptian goddess Sekhmet, a fire goddess, has become an icon of modern businesswomen.

Lion as a power animal Use the lion or lioness for developing leadership qualities, for gaining authority and attaining ambitions (bringing with them the need for the highest ideals). The lion and lioness also offer a chance to shine professionally, to create a good impression at interviews, presentations, and seminars and to establish a viable and lasting power base in whatever your chosen profession.

Lion in the office No matter what their actual position, the lion or lioness will be near the place or source of power. Less bad-tempered than the tiger, the lion is concerned with creating a good impression and will work night and day to create the illusion that some piece of work or lecture was totally spontaneous (it will always be flawless). Afraid of no one, though a little unsettled by the cat, the lion will expect tangible rewards and recognition of his or her many successes; the lioness will take a regal interest in the welfare of others. Both the lion and lioness will exude sexual charm and attract adulation, but only the finest of the herd will be acceptable as a social partner.

Monkey

In Chinese astrology, the monkey was one of the twelve animals who came to Buddha on his last New Year on earth. As a reward, he gave the monkey rulership over one of the twelve years in the Chinese astrological calendar. Monkey years are good for enterprise, speculation, finding ways around obstacles, and achieving the impossible, though they can reflect unstable business energies.

Monkey as a power animal Use the monkey for inventiveness, ingenuity in problem solving, dexterity of thought, ability to switch from one task to another and back again, openness to new ideas, experiences, and information, and for breaking free of rigid boundaries and restrictions. Monkeys bring technical wizardry, natural curiosity about the world and people, humor, and tolerance of diversity in others. A good alter ego if you are weighed down by responsibility and prohibitions, the monkey will improve persuasive skills for selling and investment work.

Monkey in the office The monkey wants to know how everything works and never refers to manuals when using new equipment or trying to mend broken objects. In spite of this, somehow he or she can fix anything. Always curious about the lives of others and trying to uncover secrets, monkeys are the greatest gossips and scandalmongers with a wicked sense of humor. However, they are so charismatic that they have many friends, and no one stays angry at them for long. The entire workplace is their territory, and the concepts of personal space and personal property are totally beyond the grasp of their quick and intelligent minds.

Mouse

Legends abound of how a tiny mouse saved a huge creature and thereafter enjoyed protection. In Aesop's fables, a mouse nibbled the cords tying down a lion. In ancient Egyptian magic, the shrew mouse was the hidden night aspect, the vital subterranean alter ego of the hawk of light, associated with the sky god Horus.

Mouse as a power animal Become a mouse when you need to keep a low profile or to be left to work in peace. The mouse is good for discovering secrets, when traveling in lonely or dangerous places, when detailed appraisal of a situation or task is essential, for unraveling confusion or the truth of conflicting facts and opinions, or for using tact when force has failed. The mouse is helpful also for starting at the bottom of a business and accumulating skills and a reputation with the workplace power source fast.

Mouse in the office Follow the biscuit crumbs to the mouse hole in some out-of-the-way corner, often behind a tall pot plant. Sometimes people are aware of the mouse only at the annual staff party, but the mouse hears and sees everything that goes on in and out of the office and often has a direct line to the top of the tree. The mouse may be working on high profile or classified material, but no one generally takes much notice, which is why he or she is such an effective spy; make sure you keep the mouse fed with tidbits so she or he keeps you ahead of the game.

Owl

The owl is called Night Eagle in Amerindian lore, being the bird who is lady of the night and moon as the eagle is lord of the day and the sun. In the classical world, the owl was the special bird of the Greek Athena and of Minerva, Roman Goddess of Wisdom. The darker connotations of the owl originated in Rome, where the deaths of several Roman emperors were foretold by an owl landing on their palace roof and hooting.

Owl as a power animal Call on the owl for wisdom and for knowledge acquired through diligence and learning, for problem-solving abilities, for keeping one's own counsel and the secrets of others, and for becoming intuitively aware of potential pitfalls and unwise allies. The owl is also good for considered thought and words. This is another power icon for night workers.

Owl in the office Not at his or her best before the afternoon, the owl will rarely join in banter or gossip and often keeps to a secluded perch surrounded by greenery. Your owl will persist with a problem long after everyone else, even the monkeys, has declared it insoluble. The office owl loves unexpected quirks or puzzles that need to be resolved; a walking encyclopedia who can recall the most obscure facts or precedents, the owl is slow to pass judgment on a situation or person, but once an opinion has been formed it is set in stone. If an owl warns against a deal or person, take the warning seriously.

Peacock

The peacock is the bird of Juno, and it is said that if a peacock spreads its tail feathers before your eyes, happiness and prosperity will follow. The peacock is a weather prophet, its dance foretelling rain and storms.

Peacock as a power animal Use the brightly plumed peacock to show others your talents and to bring joy and color into a dull world or life burdened by responsibility. The peacock will bring abundance of every kind and the opportunity to work in the public eye or to create beautiful artifacts or inspired schemes to spread happiness.

Peacock in the office Whether male or female, you will identify human peacocks by the dazzling array of different and often colorful outfits they wear each day, and by the way they are always absent on the first day of the sales with a mystery illness. Larger than life, peacocks are either spreading joy and happiness or doom and gloom, for they are very mercurial and easily offended (but equally easily placated). Valuable in bringing imagination, flair, and an instinctive awareness of the prevailing moods and trends from the wider world into the workplace, peacocks are inspirational in creating slogans and attracting publicity not only to themselves but also to their products.

Pelican

The pelican is famed for her maternal instinct. People once believed that the mother pelican, reaching in her pouch, was ripping open her breast to feed her young on her own blood. Consequently the pelican with her brood became a heraldic symbol of piety.

Pelican as a power animal The pelican is a good power creature for anyone concerned with the welfare of others and for creating a caring workplace. Use the pelican if you work at home or combine outside employment with bringing up a young family. The pelican is good for making short-term sacrifices for a long-term gain and for putting fulfillment and ideals above profit.

Pelican in the office Almost invariably female, the pelican's nest is unmistakable, with cushions and with bags overflowing with knitting or crocheting and her remedies for every ailment, for she is a bit of a hypochondriac. Concerned for the welfare of others, the pelican runs her private agony aunt consultancy from her workstation, and if the canteen closed down, she could feed the five thousand with the contents of her cake tin and cookie jar. Work is an extension of her very cozy home, and she tends to spread her nest into adjoining areas. She can be possessive about *her* surrogate family who works closely with her, but she is brilliant at defusing hostility and encourages a happy harmonious workplace.

Scorpion

Some of the very early ancient Egyptian kings took the title of Scorpion King as a sign of their mastery over enemies. The most famous scorpion icon is Serqet or Selkit, the beautiful Egyptian scorpion goddess who was fiercely protective of those she loved and who offered them protection against the scorpion stings that she administered to her enemies.

Scorpion as a power animal The scorpion is not a comfortable power icon but is valuable against attack or spite. The scorpion is good for protection while traveling and for overcoming money problems, inequality, and unfair competition. Use the power of the scorpion very sparingly and only with the highest intent as it is a double-edged sword.

Scorpion in the office Sharp-tongued, mercilessly sarcastic, and very funny, your scorpion may not be the poisonous kind, but nevertheless this person has a nasty sting. The scorpion will not be liked but is certainly respected; this person is efficient and well organized, and is effective in dealing with ruthless competitors from other firms. The scorpion will defend colleagues to the death.

Squirrel

In Viking mythology, Ratatosk the squirrel carried messages up Yggdrassil the World Tree, moving between the realm of the deities and the realm of mortals. In Native North American myth the squirrel was once huge but was so quarrelsome toward humans that the Great Spirit stroked the squirrel until he was no bigger than a human hand. But the squirrel still becomes quarrelsome when he sees humans and runs up and down trees chattering.

Squirrel as a power animal Use the squirrel for injecting spontaneity into your life or workplace, for boundless energy, for challenging the status quo no matter how low down the food chain you are, for conserving resources to allow for times when they are not so plentiful, and for pacing yourself to avoid burnout.

Squirrel in the office Usually female and rivaling the bear for autumnal forays to the stationery cupboard, the squirrel hates waste and will rifle through discarded books and papers for what is still of use. Make her the first port of call for spare parts, pins, clips, needle and thread, lost phone numbers, or order forms. Though the squirrel roams freely over everyone else's territory, beware encroaching on the squirrel's hoard without consent

Stag

The stag is the symbol of the Horned God, who was the son and/or consort of the Neolithic Earth Goddess. Found in a number of traditions, the Horned God is especially associated with the Celts where he was Lord of the Hunt, of wild animals, of winter, and of male potency.

Stag as a power animal Use the stag for fighting your way up in a competitive environment, for getting a job or promotion when there are a number of other candidates, for courage in standing up to bullies or against unfairness, for creative power and when decisive action is needed to seize an opportunity, for invincibility in uncertain times, for willingness to fight for beliefs, and for pride in personal strength and talents.

Stag in the office Oozing virility (or if a woman overt sexuality, though most human stags are male), the stag may be found in middle management, but is upwardly mobile. He rules by natural magnetism and mesmeric power that few dare or wish to question. How much the stag actually gets done is debatable, but the stag will try to dominate any encounter or meeting and often creates the impression that the world would stop turning if he or she was not around. The stag usually has a docile adoring personal assistant, an invisible partner who smoothes the domestic path so the stag can focus on hunting. The stag can be an excellent salesperson when focused on profit and not prestige. Keep well back if two macho stags in an office are fighting over the does or the best sales territory.

Swan

In India the swan laid the golden cosmic egg from which Brahma, Hindu Creator of the Universe, emerged. The black swans of Australia are in some areas considered the manifestation of the mother/sister female counterpart of Balame, the Aboriginal All-Father.

Swan as a power animal Use swan energies to bring inner stillness and outer calm to a frantic lifestyle or workplace. The swan is good for transforming image and positive life changes, for enhancing and expressing creativity and imagination, for making each day special, and for finding your own unique niche in life.

Swan in the office The swan (male or female, but more usually female) glides through the workplace in clouds of fragrance. When the swan is present, meetings become harmonious, and her workspace forms an oasis of calm no matter how noisy or chaotic the environment is around her. Very artistic and able to create beautiful things from very little material, work is only one part of the swan's world, and she may suddenly move overseas or to the countryside as the nights draw in.

Tiger

The tiger is the king of beasts in Eastern mythology. In China the tiger is given the title of Lord of the Land Animals, and the souls of tigers are said to pass into amber crystals after their death. In Japan, a tiger is believed to live for a thousand years.

Tiger as a power animal The tiger offers courage, commitment to pursuit of desires and needs, passion for life and work, and fearlessness to step into the unknown. The tiger is good for righting inequalities and empowering those against whom the current workplace ethos or balance of power is weighted.

Tiger in the office A loner rather than a leader but very successful and single-minded in pursuit of a goal, the tiger is characterized by pacing up and down while speaking or thinking (often becoming tangled in a trailing phone cord). A tiger will regard the whole workplace as his or her den. This can be uncomfortable for their natural prey, but the female tiger will defend other workers against outside attack or criticism. The tiger can be bad tempered and easily irritated by inefficiency or people who are not as committed to success as they are.

Wolf

The wolf is regarded as a particularly wise teacher in the Native American tradition. In other cultures too the wolf is revered not only for its skill in hunting but also as a pack creature with intense loyalty to its kin. Fiercely protective, a mother wolf is said to defeat even a tiger in defense of her young.

Wolf as a power animal Use your wolf power for attracting or increasing workplace loyalties, for developing talents or a power base quietly, for working as part of a team, for enhancing your instinctive awareness of danger or an opportunity, and for following your own unique calling to fulfill your chosen life path. The wolf is an excellent icon for night workers.

Wolf in the office The mature female wolf is concerned with the good of the pack, helping others who fall behind target, organizing outings, and keeping an eye on newcomers. The lone male wolf will be much more territorial, happiest when out in the field, searching for new markets. He is unwilling to pass on information, preferring to work long hours to bring a project to fruition unaided. The young male wolf is a menace, and a wolf pack regards the workplace as hunting territory. They will persist even though others are unimpressed by their unsubtle approaches, especially toward female colleagues; it's best to get a mother wolf to cuff them around the ear.

Finding Your Own Power Totem

If you don't have an immediate sense of your power totem, you may have to do some animal research using an encyclopedia. An illustrated encyclopedia, which has pictures of creatures from around the world, works best.

To find your power totem animal:

- Still your mind using the relaxation techniques discussed in chapter 2.
- Open a page of the encyclopedia at random, allowing your hand rather than your mind to guide you to an image.
- Find out all you can about your chosen creature. It may not be the one your conscious mind would have selected.
- Investigate your animal on the Internet, in books and videos, at natural history museums, and, if possible, in person at a zoo or conservation park.
- Place pictures of your animal on your bedroom wall and also keep a few near your workstation.
- Try to see the creature in the wild either on the weekend or while on vacation if it is not indigenous to your area or found in your local wildlife park.

There are excellent wildlife conservation areas and zoological gardens throughout the world. In these, animals have plenty of space, privacy to breed, good care, and where possible eventual release into the wild, often preventing a species from becoming extinct. My own favorite animal places are the San Diego Zoo in California, the Owl and Otter Sanctuary in Ashurst, Hampshire, and the Monkey Sanctuary at Wool near Wareham in Dorset, the last two in the United Kingdom. The Wool Sanctuary rescues monkeys from all over the world who have been cruelly treated or whose mothers have been shot by poachers.

If your creature is indigenous to your region, go to nature conservancies or known habitats in the early morning or just before dusk when the area is quiet and you will not be disturbed. Early and late in the season are good times also. You can also attract wildlife into your garden by leaving areas of long grass, growing wildflowers, and leaving piles of leaves in the fall. If, after all the above, the creature you chose from the encyclopedia really did not feel right and after preliminary work you are not building up any affinity with it, note this in your journal. This creature may possess strengths you are not yet ready to acknowledge or absorb. Pick another power animal, again by opening the book at random.

Getting to Know Your Power Animal

Now that you are acquainted with your own special animal, there are steps you can take to learn more about it.

To learn more about your power animal:

- Find out what your totem eats, where it sleeps, where it breeds and cares for its young, and whether it is nocturnal or hibernates.
- Buy or craft from wood or clay a small statue or model of your power creature that you can hold or place close to your bed.
- Find a small ceramic model or silver charm to place in a tiny cloth bag that you can carry with you when you need your power animal's strengths.
- Each morning and each night as you lie in bed, create the image of your animal in your imagination, moving it

closer until it fills your inner screen. With practice, the
picture will appear spontaneously whenever you need
your totem's power at work or when traveling.

- Imagine your power animal's sounds and practice them
when you are alone.

- If your power animal appears in your dreams, when you
wake hold its statue between your hands and allow
words of wisdom to flow through your mind about the
day ahead. You can be sure the dream appearance heralds
a significant time immediately ahead, and the words will
help you to adjust or prevail. Recurring dreams of your
power creature suggest you need to be extra vigilant at
work and in your life generally.

Tapping into Your Animal Power

If you grow tired of being the office mouse, being thrown the
tasks no one else can be bothered to finish, or always being
backstage while others get the credit, you can bring your inner
power creature to the fore on a daily basis (not too rapidly or
you will scare colleagues witless) and reinvent yourself.

Alternatively you may always be called upon to sort out
problems, go out and hunt for orders in the more difficult areas,
and defend your department's performance to the head office
when figures dip. It would be good once in a while to stop growl-
ing and snarling and stand back like the wise crane and make
considered assessments instead of snap judgments on the move.

It may be a time in your life when your inner and outer
creatures need to share the stage or maybe when your outer
creature needs to take the backseat more often. The balance will
soon right itself, and for every dramatic conversion of gazelle to
lion, there are a hundred people who subtly reveal their hidden
claws or roar just enough to make people sit up and take notice.
Before long, folks realize you will only whistle and sing like
the very cheerful blackbird as long as the workplace skies are
sunny, you get plenty of corn, and people show respect for your
normally optimistic persona.

If you do want to change your image either temporarily or more permanently in the workplace, have, for example, a miniature charm of your hawk or a blue hawk's eye crystal or some other power creature symbol on your desk or in your work bag. You can hold the symbol to infuse yourself with the strengths of your alter ego, though just carrying it with you may transfer the desired energies.

The following technique is easy and very effective in drawing the spiritual powers of your inner creature around you. After initial practice, it can be activated at work or when you are traveling so you can either lower your profile or give off "don't mess with me" vibes so you aren't harassed on the subway late at night or while waiting for a taxicab in the center of a city.

To make a psychic connection with your power animal:

1. Focus on your power creature, picturing it in the habitat in which you have seen it, either in actuality or on a video or picture, as though you were standing in front of a huge screen.

2. Watch the imaginary screen and make the picture three dimensional, adding the fragrances the creature would smell, feeling the cool morning air or the water lapping on its fur. Feel the motion and disturbances of leaves or wind current as the creature flies, moves stealthily through the jungle, or hides in the thicket, stilling breath and motion while a fierce predator passes.

3. The animal is facing you, looking into your eyes, and the outline of the screen disappears so you can step forward into the scene. Now fall silent, and in your mind's vision see the creature coming so close that the boundaries between you blur.

4. Take a step forward and continue to do so slowly, maintaining eye contact. If it is a tiny creature, you will nevertheless see it filling your field of vision.

5. Listen in your mind to its breathing, whether slow and deep or tiny panting breaths. If you have watched videos of your creature or listened to audio clips on the Inter-

net, you may be familiar with its breath pattern. Match the creature's breathing either aloud if you are alone or in your mind.

6. As you continue to breathe, imagine your skin touching the creature's fur and its strengths flowing into your own body, until you share one physical form.

7. You are now within the creature's space so you can see through its eyes, hear through its ears, and breathe with its rhythm. The creature may be at rest or moving fast, either hunting or hiding. Feel the ground beneath you and the throb of the energies you seek from your totem, making your heart beat and your mind pulsate.

8. When you feel filled with the animal's strength, thank your host and allow the boundaries to begin to reemerge as your animal very gently recedes. Mentally turn away, re-creating the separate boundaries between you and the creature once more and gently withdraw your own essence back into your body.

9. Continue to practice until you can step almost instantly within your animal's power and protection when you need it, just by picturing them, whether you are trying to avoid being dragged into an angry confrontation at work or conversely speaking up where normally you would be reticent.

You might like to give your power animal a name so you can call softly in your mind or aloud when you need assistance.

Sample Reading

Mark, who now very successfully works in industrial photography, loved tigers from an early age. He had pictures of them on his bedroom wall and would stand for hours watching them in a local wildlife conservancy.

When Mark started work, though he had excellent qualifications and a real eye for composition, his colleagues would leave him to do the dull routine tasks. They would pick his ideas and present them as their own at the morning meeting. Mark was increasingly unhappy and because he was doing so much background work for others, he was not developing his own portfolio.

He went home for a weekend to contemplate his future and saw his magnificent childhood Siberian tiger picture on the wall, a creature threatened with extinction. On impulse he took his collection of tiger pictures back to his new apartment and put them on his bedroom walls. Before going to sleep, he recited a rhyme he had learned as a child. "The eye of the tiger glows from the thicket; he waits until none expects and he strikes, sure. He makes his kill and leaves again unseen."

Subtly Mark's behavior changed. He stopped discussing his ideas with his colleagues. In meetings when the heads of the different departments were present, Mark waited while his colleagues boasted and procrastinated. Then he would leap in with a solution to a seemingly insoluble problem, based on one of his own original ideas or photos he had taken at weekends because he got little chance to go out taking pictures during the week.

Mark practiced his tiger roar, so he was able to speak out decisively over the meeting's uproar. Mark rapidly earned promotion and is respected for his willingness to work hard on necessary routine work, but those who have attempted to take advantage of him have seen the hidden tiger emerge occasionally from the thicket.

Animal Management in the Workplace

Why not save zoo watching for the customized safari ride at Disney Florida? We all evolved from animals and birds (some folks maybe not very fast or far). Psychologically we seem to have retained individual affinities to furry or feathered species that are reflected in our work habits, preferences, and staking-out of territories. Recognizing and matching these symbolic affinities in colleagues can help bring harmony to meetings and create effective teams so the predators don't get to regularly swallow the prey and the office mouse feels safe enough to reveal vital crumbs of information that nobody else has noticed from their more elevated perches.

You may also become more aware of invisible but very real territorial boundaries that explain bad-tempered or squirreling responses that are apparently without reason. The bear's den is not a place to bounce into for a brainstorm if he or she is tenderly nursing a new private project. Nor come November should you ask the office squirrel to borrow a highlighter pen when he or she is stockpiling supplies to last three winters of stationery famine at least.

In contrast, you will come to realize it's not a personal affront when a curious monkey is constantly touching items on your desk while talking. He or she may fix a broken piece of equipment while chattering or suggest unusual but potentially lucrative outlets if you resist the temptation to slap the monkey's hands.

Make a list of the animals and birds your colleagues, seniors and juniors remind you of, noting natural predators and prey, as well as strong but not predatory creatures that can keep the temperamental seesaw balanced. Notice the nocturnal operators who need their quiet corner and prefer to communicate by email even with key workers five yards away but who form excellent backroom production staff, allowing the showier creatures of the sun to clinch the deal.

See how, in animal terms, the dynamics work presently and how they might be improved with a few subtle shifts, patting, or petting. Draw up your own workplace profiles. This way you can work on the approaches likely to get the best response, like making sure the workhorse has plenty of emotional as well as actual sugar lumps before asking him or her to work late two nights running or to cover for you while you go to your daughter's sports day.

Look at the present workstation arrangements and adapt your personal territorial boundaries, maybe with a bank of greenery or a chair half-facing a wall for confidential phone calls. With these barriers in place, you don't get the pack of office hounds charging through baying about last night's match results when you are negotiating a loan, and the free-roaming peacocks don't preen in your territory when you have a deadline or it's just a bad hair day.

Make sure the pack creatures have communal areas to let off steam and strict time limits for nonproductive gatherings. If you fix meeting or project teams, don't match the autocratic marketing marvel lion with its natural prey, the fleet gazelle. She is vital for her ability to monitor and respond instantly to unexpected changes in direction or market flow, but the lion needs the buffer of the knowledgeable elephant, who has been with the company for years and will not back down before leonine bluster, but will direct the energy and assertiveness usefully.

Welcome your clever monkeys with lots of executive toys and gadgets and nibbles at the meeting table, but invite the stately and world-weary crane to divert his or her ingenuity into a realistic time frame and achievable goals. If your feline is to give you the benefit of her lateral thinking and mysteriously accurate future planning, ensure that she has a comfortable seat at meetings or in one-to-ones, congratulate her on getting yet another mention in the regional bulletin, and treat her words as jewels beyond price (which they usually are).

Drawing on Other Power Totems

Once you are comfortable with your inner power animal, you may find that you can spontaneously identify with other animal or bird strengths you need, either on a regular basis or to meet particular challenges in your life. If you are a regular night worker or on permanent late shifts and are having trouble adjusting or sleeping during the day, you may find that you need to call on one of the night creatures, such as the jaguar or the cat that walks at night and can sleep or relax during the daytime.

From the list of power animal descriptions, you can consciously choose the animal powers you need and draw them to you by picturing the creature walking by your side, standing guard, and encouraging you to speak or act—or to step out of the firing line. You can add other creatures to the list of animals and birds that would be especially helpful in your life, discovering their characteristics by watching the creatures to whom you are attracted and noting the impressions you receive.

Myths and legends about creatures from the Australian Aboriginal or Native American or African traditions are an excellent way of understanding the spiritual strengths of different helper creatures, and you may like to create a special power totem section in your journal as the list grows.

The Animal Oracle

If you have a new challenge, are traveling to an unfamiliar area, have to learn a new skill, or wake up with a sense that today will be special or different, you can use homemade animal cards or a set of children's animal and bird learning picture cards to help you understand the strengths you will need. If you are using commercially prepared cards, choose those that are either photographic representations or artistic impressions of the spirit of each creature. There are also commercial divinatory animal oracle sets. Look at them before buying to see if they are right, and do not feel tied to the meanings any more than I expect you to stick rigidly to mine.

To make and use your own set of animal oracle cards:

1. Cut out white cards about the size of playing or Tarot cards. On each one glue or draw the image of a different animal or bird that resonates with you. Alternatively write the name in black pen of the different creatures you feel attracted to. You can also download photos or representations from the Internet or use your own photos or digicam images from a visit to a conservation park.

2. There is no limit to the number of cards you can devise. If you cut out extra blank cards, you can add to your oracle set at any time. Substitute other creatures that seem more relevant or make yourself a set based wholly on indigenous creatures living in your own country or state.

3. Laminate the finished cards to make them more durable.

4. When you need guidance or in the morning before a potentially challenging day, shuffle the pack and, without looking at the images, place the cards face down in a circle.

5. Select one card at random or use your pendulum and see over which card it pulls down (see chapter 1).

6. Turn the card over. It will indicate the special protection or power you will need. The creature may complement your inner totem or on occasion may be totally different from the strengths of your usual power creature (like calling in the FBI if the local police department doesn't have the expertise to fix an unusual situation).

7. Trace the image or the name of the totem on the card with your index finger onto the palm of your power hand and recite the animal's name nine times, saying: "When I trace this image, the power of—" will enter me. Feel the power rising up your arm into your body. When you need the strength at work or on a journey, you can touch the palm of your power hand and visualize the image as a painted outline or formed in tiny lights.

8. If a creature appears regularly you may need to adopt it as a subsidiary power creature. If life is very hectic or stressful, your totem may need long-term reinforcements.

9. Note in your journal how the new creature was helpful, and you may find that even without using the cards, you can sense the nature of the extra energy you need.

Tigers in the office; mice in the photocopier? As you explore these ideas you may discover unexpected facets of yourself and those with whom you work. Once you understand the territorial divisions in your workplace and recognize hidden strengths or quirks in yourself, life will run more smoothly and people (or should I say creatures) at work will become more amenable when you approach them in the right way. In time you can transform even the fiercest or most chaotic office jungle into a well-run conservation park.

Conclusion

Our work defines the way we make our mark upon the world. It enables us to express our talents and creativity in tangible ways, whether we are growing vegetables, advising people on the best way to fix a broken roof at the local do-it-yourself store, generating ideas, or sending millions of dollars no one has ever seen to and fro across the world.

Paid work or indeed work at all is not, however, the sum of what we are. You know folks whose first question to anyone they meet socially is always, "So what do you do for a living?" followed without pause for breath by explaining what they do that makes them such a great person that you are grateful they stopped to speak to you at all.

Living is not about what we do, nor primarily about what we earn, but about the kind of person we are, our relationships, dreams, and emotions—not just the roles we occupy in our business life. Yet people do define us by the label we are currently wearing unless we point out, if necessary a thousand times, we are not just our perceived status, the numbers on our salary check, or the job title on an official form, but a whole person of infinite and unique worth.

Even if you bought your doctorate over the Internet in the history of the knitting needle, people will address you in hushed tones when you use your new title of doctor and ask you about their painful knees or if they should take more zinc in their diet. Of course, it works the other way too.

When I was pregnant with my first child, Tom, even before the bump showed, physicians, nurses, and health workers started referring to and calling me Mom, though I was a graduate psychologist and head of a teaching department in a London school and thought of myself as pretty essential to the daily turning of the world. Thereafter my brain power and competence were regarded in the maternity department as being in inverse proportion to the increasing size of my womb. One eminent consultant leaned across me to speak to my husband and said, "When she goes into labor she must come to the hospital." At least I was invited to share the big event.

Twenty-five years on and fifty-two published books under my belt, when I go with my younger teenage kids to the local health clinic or to see their teachers at school, the key workers say, "Hi Mom" or more personally, "Hi Bill and Miranda's mom." They then tell me exactly what my children have done wrong or have wrong with them and why it's my fault either for staying at home and being boring or going out to work and leaving the children to fend for themselves (or in my case both).

I've no problem with being the mom of Tom, Jade, Jack, Miranda, and Bill (except three times a day when the dishes are still unwashed). But I'm so much more than what I deliver of monetary value or am perceived to do in my job as author, broadcaster, lecturer, family chauffeur, first aid expert, mom, housecleaner (we still call them housewives in England!), and veterinarian to the local wildlife population.

I am also a Druidess and a Quaker and very very occasionally a seer, a nature and animal lover, someone who is passionate about old places, and someone who enjoys collecting statues of goddesses, spending time in my trailer by the sea, reading, gardening, traveling to new places in my ongoing search for folk lore and legends, taking incredibly slow walks in the countryside or along the shore, and spending time as a total devotee of retail therapy.

When we go into work we don't stop being a mother, father, daughter, brother, friend, member of the local swimming team, a lover of small furry creatures, or a campaigner against world poverty. Rather the whole person that we are including all our experiences, good and bad, enrich what we bring to the workplace.

Workplace alchemy can be truly magical if we believe in ourselves and love ourselves enough. Whether we had the best start in life or had to struggle to make our way on to the first steps of the ladder, anything is possible if we want it enough and focus our minds, willpower, intuition, and that indefinable sparkling extra ingredient we last saw in childhood when we still believed in fairies and saw angels whenever we wanted.

But that potential for fulfillment we all carry has to be what *we* want, not what our moms or dads, teachers or college professors wanted for us or even what other people count as success and achievement. If you want to grow tomatoes instead of running for Congress, make sure they are the best tomatoes you can possibly grow and infuse them with enthusiasm and pride. Equally, if you do make it to the White House Oval Office, remember that the responsibilities at least match the privileges—and you won't ever get it wrong.

For our work is our gift to others and to the cosmos, not just a way of earning money or getting personal recognition. My late mother, who was not at all successful in the world's terms, used to say, "You've got to be able to look at yourself in the mirror when you wash off the dust of the day."

The sky has grown dark while I have been working, and it is time to draw a line under the day and this book. I think inexplicably of great-great-great-grandma Anne getting up from her workbench when the light was no longer clear enough to see the fine metal rods she worked on. Maybe like me she walked for a few minutes in the garden in the cool of the evening before making dinner, as the crickets and frogs croaked and chorused. Was Anne's mind still full of the day and unfinished orders like mine, with worries about how to pay the rent or in my case seeing my youngest through school and getting the eldest to pedal his own bike through life and not get so many parking fines on the way? Did Anne's children like mine call her as she dreamed in those precious minutes back to their world and their needs?

In these pages I have shared with you my knowledge and my ideas. Now like the alchemists of old, my words go back into the melting pot to be refined and improved by your own talents, insights, and experiences, so you are inspired to make tomorrow the best day of all.

Crystals

These are crystals I have found helpful in working life and during business travel or commuting. Some, such as jade, amethyst, or clear quartz, have many purposes, and you may settle with a core set of perhaps ten or twelve stones that will form your workplace crystal set.

*Those crystals marked with an asterisk are good core crystals.

Amazonite

Colors: Blue green or turquoise to darker greens with white lines, opaque.

Amazonite reduces free-floating anger and irritability when there is a heavy workload. It improves concentration and will open doors of opportunity. It is good for combating any form of inequality.

Amber*

Colors: Translucent, yellow or golden orange, sometimes brown, often containing fossilized insects or tiny plants. Occasionally black, violet, green, or blue.

Amber attracts gradual prosperity and success. It melts rigid or confrontational attitudes in others and is excellent if a workplace is fiercely competitive. It's good for older employees, for worries about retirement, and for taking a long-term view. Amber will reduce technological pollution and is a good traveling companion especially in cities. It builds self-esteem and confidence and prevents panic in crises; it encourages creative solutions. Amber is good against negative earth energies.

Amethyst*

Colors: Pale lilac and lavender to deep purple, translucent (reflects light), semitransparent and transparent according to kind, also purple and white banded.

267

Amethysts defuse tense situations and so are good if you have to deal with difficult customers whether directly, on the telephone, or by mail; they soothe impatience, irritability, and obsessive traits. They are helpful also for calming anxieties about deadlines and unfinished tasks so you do not waste energy fretting; amethysts are excellent for slowing down workaholics and perfectionists. This is the best crystal for clearing negative earth energies.

Angelite

Colors: Medium blue with white veins, opaque.

Angelite softens the attitudes of abrasive or perpetually angry people in the workplace. It deflects sarcasm, counters prejudice of any kind, and promotes tolerance of different points of view. Angelite is supportive of anyone who has a disability.

Aventurine

Colors: Light to darker green, especially a soft mid-green, blue, also red and peach, opaque, sometimes with a metallic glint.

Aventurine guards against accidents due to haste or carelessness. Increases self-confidence and faith in your own abilities and protects your personal space against intrusion.

Bloodstone or Heliotrope

Colors: Dark green with red or orange spots and sometimes white marks, opaque.

Bloodstone offers protection against psychological bullying at work. It is a supportive stone if you have demanding family responsibilities you must balance with your career; it is good for long-term fulfillment of goals, especially those with a socially useful or altruistic function.

Blue Lace Agate*

Colors: Pale blue, sometimes with white lace threads, opaque.

The stone of peace, blue lace agate water softens critical words and sarcasm. Make drinks with water in which blue lace agate has soaked for eight hours to minimize aggression, especially when controversial topics are under consideration. Blue lace agate enhances communication abilities when you need to address a meeting or explain a proposal; it should be kept by the telephone, like rose quartz, to encourage positive calm interactions. The crystal encourages tact and patience with difficult people.

Calcite

Colors: Many shades, but especially useful in green, orange, and pink in the workplace.

All calcites ease the tensions in a small workplace or space. Green calcite reduces stress and protects against accidents and combats workaholic tendencies. Orange calcite creates a warm welcoming atmosphere in reception areas, helping newcomers to integrate (set one on your workstation when starting a new job). Pink calcite will lower pressure at times of stress and is good in crises of any kind; it is excellent after theft or damage of personal equipment, vehicle, or tools to overcome shock and feelings of violation.

Carnelian*

Colors: Orange to red, also occasionally yellow or brown, translucent.

Carnelian attracts prosperity and new orders to a company and brings abundance in every way. It aids decision making and will encourage free and profitable interchange in all forms of buying and selling. Carnelian is good for courage and for those who work in the building trade or do-it-yourself stores to guard against accidents.

Citrine*

Colors: Yellow from pale to golden yellow, honey or dark orange.

Citrine will clear negative earth energies. Keep a citrine inclusion (tiny crystals in rock, see geodes in chapter 9) in a room that seems dark, cold, or unfriendly. Citrine encourages optimism and joy in the workplace and is an instant energizer as sun water (water with tiny citrines in it left from dawn to noon, especially on the morning of the summer solstice, around June 21 in the northern hemisphere and December 21 in the southern hemisphere). It is excellent for workers in the media and the arts and technology.

Clear quartz crystal*

Colors: Clear, glassy, sparkles in the sun.

Clear crystal clusters in the center of a room help people to work together harmoniously, especially in an open plan office. Clear quartz brings instant energy, optimism, clear purpose, and openness to innovation. This crystal is an excellent antidote to harsh lighting at work or in a room that seems always dark for whatever reason; clear crystal water will offer instant energy. Clear crystal spheres attract good fortune, success, and prosperity and will absorb negativity and transform it into light. Place your hands around a sphere to center yourself and fill yourself with its light. Use a crystal ball placed in direct sunlight so the internal reflections and refractions create rainbows inside it for instant optimism and confidence.

Fluorite*

Colors: Green, colorless, lavender and purple, also transparent or semitransparent and usually very gentle in its shades.

Green fluorite absorbs workplace stress. Good for improving concentration, green fluorite attracts the gradual inflow of money and success into your career and workplace. It focuses a group of people on joint projects. Lavender fluorite lowers tension and clears panic. Darker purple fluorite will make writing proposals, training materials, and presentations easier; it is good for interviews or progress assessments. Clear fluorite helps to develop firm time scales and definite programs from good ideas.

Garnet

Colors: Burgundy and other deeper or lighter shades of red, varying from transparent to deep and translucent, also green.

Garnet is protective against those who steal, whether possessions, ideas, or credit for work. It overcomes writer's block and lack of inspiration in any field; it protects travelers from all kinds of harm and especially attack; and it traditionally guards against vampires and so forms a shield against people who drain you of energy.

Hematite

Colors: Brilliant silvery black, steel gray metallic, also dark red or reddish brown.

Known as the lawyer's stone, hematite will help with all disputes and their resolution, legal matters, and injustices and will mark out your personal space. It also banishes irrational fears and helps you to avoid becoming too emotionally involved with the problems of others. Hematite overcomes fears of flying and reduces jet lag.

Iron Pyrites or Fool's Gold

Colors: Silvery or dark gray, black with golden glints as chunky cubes, scattered through a cluster or polished as dull golden crystal nuggets.

Not at all foolish in spite of its name, you can use pyrites for brainstorming sessions and for all creative thinking. Shiny gold pyrites in your workspace will attract good luck, draw increased money, maybe a salary rise, and will repel hostility.

Jade*

Colors: From a pale to a dark green; transparent to opaque.

Jade brings good luck and money to its owner. At work have jade in your pocket or on your desk when you are negotiating or trying to attract new business. Jade is also good for keeping you alert, especially if you are working overtime or late to finish a project. It heals quarrels and coldness with others and encourages kind words and tactful communication.

Jasper*

Colors: Red, yellow, green, and brown, single colors and patterned, opaque.

Red jasper provides instant energy, especially on cold days or when you feel unwell; it brings optimism, focus, and determination. Yellow jasper protects against spite and jealously. Place it in your workspace to stop others gossiping about you; leave it on your desk close to where you sit when you have a day off to extend this protection in your absence. Brown jasper encourages perseverance and accuracy in routine detailed tasks and prevents mistakes creeping in when you are tired; it ensures the continuing steady performance of established businesses.

Jet

Colors: Black or occasionally very dark brown, opaque but glassy.

Jet is naturally protective and will stabilize finances; it is good for overcoming debts especially with sole traders. Set jet in your workspace to keep negative people and vibes at bay.

Kunzite

Colors: Pink to lilac or pinky violet, streaked with white, semi-transparent.

When traveling by car, either commuting or on long journeys, keep jet in your glove box or as part of a vehicle charm or mojo bag to counter road rage in others and against accidents. Set one also in your workspace to counter noise and harsh lighting or inefficient air conditioning.

Lapis Lazuli

Colors: Rich medium to royal blue, violet blue, and azure, sometimes mixed blues, with flecks of gold color, opaque.

Lapis will inspire loyalty between workers and also for a company. Carry lapis to gain promotion, to avoid being tempted by unwise shortcuts or risky offers, and to inspire the trust of others. Lapis is good for travelers, especially when traveling by air.

Lodestone*

Colors: Black, dark gray, opaque but can shine; male stones are pointed, the female ones are square or rounded. Buy a pair that attracts each other for perfect balance.

Draw money and success into your worklife by keeping any lodestone in your bag with a few coins; it attracts new business and a constant inflow of customers and orders if kept where the finances take place. For protection set a male stone, point outward, toward the door or the direction of hostility to absorb negative vibes.

Malachite*

Colors: Emerald to grass green with black or occasionally pale green stripes, bands, or swirls, opaque.

Malachite is good for cleansing and protecting work spaces against all the pollution and toxicity of noise, overbright fluorescent lighting, and harmful rays emitted by electrical and technical equipment of all kinds. Place malachite at the corners of a computer and near a phone to filter out negative communication; it is a good anti-virus defense. Malachite also brings strength, focus, and determination.

Moonstone*

Colors: Translucent white, cream, peach, pink, gray, and less commonly blue, all with an iridescent shimmer.

A friend to shift workers and those whose jobs involve constant traveling and irregular hours, moonstones help the body clock to adjust. Moonstones encourage intuition and imagination as well as lateral thinking. Moonstones are good for countering stress and mood swings and for connecting with natural rhythms, especially lunar ones. Make calming moon water with moonstones left in water on the night of the full moon.

Moss Agate*

Colors: Colorless with a profusion of deep green tendrils inside of the dark-colored mineral called hornblende that may make it appear green, also pale blue or a deeper green with pale blue or white inclusions, translucent to opaque.

Moss agate brings beauty to workplaces or spaces that are in less than ideal settings. It will slowly attract money and luck to an individual and firm and is good for all who work in horticulture, botany, or any form of alternative medicine, especially aromatherapy or herbalism. Moss agate also helps new businesses, especially those set up from home, to take root in the market place. Use it in a charm or mojo bag if you are trying to get the first foothold on a particular career ladder. Plant moss agate in office greenery, especially those plants you use for protection, to keep them healthy.

Obsidian

Colors: Black, dark smoky gray as Apache tears, mahogany brown, black and white called snowflake, opaque. The kind that is called Apache tears is sufficiently transparent to see light through it.

Black obsidian will calm frustrations at the incompetence or stubbornness of others; it is a natural stress absorber and a protection for your work space. Obsidian is the facilitator's stone, getting everything to run smoothly; take it to any enterprises you are organizing. Apache tears encourage optimism after a major setback such as a layoff or a business closure and are a reminder that the sun probably will shine again tomorrow.

Olivine and Peridot*

Colors: Olivine is olive green and tends to be translucent; peridot ranges from pale to a beautiful olive green or bottle green and is transparent.

Olivine as tiny crystals will attract money and good fortune into your life. A small peridot in your purse or wallet or with your cell phone will deter pickpockets and muggers. At work, olivine and peridot are helpful for any business involving direct selling or money exchange. Make one part of a prosperity charm or mojo bag; they are good for speculation.

Rose Quartz

Colors: Translucent to clear pink.

Rose quartz is excellent for maintaining peace and personal harmony in your working life. Keep it by the phone and if a phone call unexpectedly becomes confrontational, circle a rose quartz counterclockwise around the phone as you speak to absorb negativity. Rose quartz is also good for ongoing protection against intrusion or spite. Place a large piece of unpolished rose quartz with a pointed end in your personal work space; put a dish of rose quartz on the conference tables to encourage positive interactions. Make drinks for office bullies and empire builders with rose quartz water. Rose quartz dipped in water and placed on your temples will soothe a tension headache.

Rutilated Quartz

Colors: Clear to occasionally smoky quartz with golden yellow to brownish red needles that can form patterns within the crystal.

Rutilated quartz protects those who work in cities or industrial complexes. It counters hidden ageism in the workplace and strengthens older people who are unemployed or who took early retirement to explore new avenues of employment. After any reversal rutilated quartz will bring the courage to rebuild using the experience and maybe old stock or ideas to a new successful venture.

Smoky Quartz*

Colors: Smoky brown or dark gray, tinted, translucent.

Smoky quartz protects work premises from malice, ruthless competitors, and intruders and protects computers against virus attack. It guards vehicles from theft and mechanical breakdown and the driver against road rage. Use it to absorb stress and hostility and as one of your work space defensive crystals. Smoky quartz also lifts a pessimistic mood.

Sodalite*

Colors: Deep blue with white flecks of calcite; occasionally indigo, opaque.

A deeply protective stone, sodalite helps people facing retirement or a layoff. Also the stone of the wise communicator, sodalite aids all who teach, advise, or are involved in the law, government, or financial institutions to speak and act fairly and wisely even under provocation. This is another work space defensive crystal. Sodalite overcomes fears when flying.

Sugilite

Colors: Lilac to violet, dense and opaque with black, white, orange, brown, or, less commonly, blue markings.

Sugilite will preserve your integrity and self-esteem in a workplace where profit is put above people and where it is so impersonal you feel unconnected. Protective while traveling especially by car against road rage and accidents, sugilite is another good addition to a travel charm or mojo bag. It supports aid or charity workers and those in social or welfare services.

Tiger's eye*

Colors: Honey or golden brown bands, brown and gold striped; lustrous, reflecting light in a wavy band; also blue or green as the hawk or falcon's eye.

A natural luck and money bringer to the home and workplace, tiger's eye is a stone for those who work with stocks and shares, investments, in real estate, and for bankers and insurance staff. It encourages optimism and self-confidence. The falcon's eye is for all who aim high and seek the power and focus of a bird of prey.

Turquoise*

Colors: Light blue or blue green, opaque.

Turquoise has dual empowering and protective properties and will attract money and business but repel intruders if placed near entrances. It is effective for ambitious schemes and personal ambitions. Turquoise guards against accidents; as a traveler stone it is effective for sea and overseas ventures, for trains and planes, and for protection in lonely places at night.

Symbols in Divination and Dreams

The following are interpretations of traditional divinatory and dream symbols that often refer to workplace matters. Some are more geared to dreams, but you may see whole pictures such as when scrying with coffee grounds. You can also expand a single image obtained during divination so in your imagination you can see where the object is being used and by whom or where the animal or person symbol is standing and what he or she is doing or feeling. This extra information will help you to interpret the symbol in the relevant context of the question under consideration in the real world.

The meanings of symbols can be adapted to other aspects of your life. Negative dreams, for example, of being trapped, carry built-in solutions. Such a dream is alerting you that you are ready to move away from your restrictions and that the opportunity to do so is around you or coming very soon.

These are only basic ideas, drawn from a number of traditional systems and from my own extensive research into dream work. Add your own interpretations to your dream and symbol list in your journal.

Abroad Working or living abroad, if pleasurable, suggests a widening of horizons and a desire for new experiences, maybe even an unacknowledged desire to get an overseas post or at least one in another state. If you are lost in a foreign city or amongst hostile foreigners, you may fear invasion of your work space or a threat to job security by people who are unfriendly or are newcomers to the firm.

Absent or former colleagues or overseas reps This can be an indication of telepathic communication. You may hear from absent or former colleagues soon or should contact them as a link has been made. This image sometimes occurs if a former colleague has information about a job offer or information that may be helpful to you.

Actor/actress If you are starring in a play in your dream or see a stage in coffee grounds, you will soon gain recognition and reward for your hard work. If you forget your words, you may be worried about failing in a coming presentation or speech or about others finding out your inadequacies. Watching a play suggests that you may feel sidelined at work. Any acting dream is a good omen if the play has a happy ending.

Airplane An airplane may reflect a desire for distant travel or to move away from what is restricting you; a crash can indicate fears of failing in your work. If you are flying the plane, it shows you have the power to succeed if you let go of fear.

Airport Waiting to catch a plane says that you are about to embark on a new stage of your life or should take a new opportunity that will soon come your way. To be unable to find your flight gate or having to face delays shows your frustration with others or your own fears that are holding you back from desired action or change.

Alien A friendly alien represents original ideas you have that could succeed if put into practice or that you are ready to act or work on independently. If the alien is hostile you may be feeling alienated, misunderstood, or lonely at work and should maybe think of moving on or striking out in self-employment.

Ambush If you are setting an ambush, you may be angry at double-dealing or spite at work and are building up toward effective retaliation. If you are ambushed you may fear that you may be caught out over a past minor indiscretion or secret you have shared perhaps unwisely.

Anger To express anger in a dream is very positive and is often a rehearsal for an event in the days ahead. To be on the receiving end of anger suggests you may feel afraid of expressing your true feelings in a situation you would like to alter.

Ants Ants crawling over your desk and on the office floor means that you are feeling overwhelmed by a lot of small issues or problems that have built up; ants can also indicate that people are irritating you with trivial problems or petty complaints.

Anxiety Anxiety dreams where you lose luggage on trips, miss trains, or are stuck in traffic in your dream and late for an important appointment, are a simple sign of overload in your everyday world and of trying to keep to impossible work schedules.

Assassin If you are being stalked, you should seek to understand the identity of a possible enemy at work. This may be someone seeking to assassinate your good name. If you are killing someone, it is a sign that you need to be ruthless to survive the present situation or demands.

Attic If the attic is dusty and crowded with junk, it is time you cast aside regrets and guilt from past failures or try a new approach if you are stuck in a rut. If there is something or someone scary in the attic, there are legal or money matters you need to tackle, especially if you work alone.

Baby A baby is a sign of a project coming to fruition in the very near future. It also represents the need to nurture a special dream and slowly move toward attainment.

Bag If your bag is overflowing and messy, you are trying to keep too many people happy. If you lose or drop your bag and it spills everywhere, you are worried about people finding out a secret or of letting spill strong feelings you are trying to hide.

Bank (money) A sign of financial security, this image indicates that you should not worry about money. Successful bank robberies augur that a risk you are contemplating will lead to great advantage, also that you will have an opportunity to profit from someone else's mistake or carelessness. To dream of a bank safe or a vault indicates you need not worry about money as you are entering a stable financial period; an empty safe says you may be worried about a lack of savings or long-term security. Being overdrawn, meeting an angry bank manager, or failing at your bank robberies (a common dream among the self-employed) suggest that worrying about money is stopping you from working out a realistic solution to your financial problems.

Bees Bees are a sign that activities will be profitable; good news is coming, which your psyche has picked up on a very deep level. A swarm of stinging bees refers to a possible spiteful attack, perhaps from an older matriarchal figure.

Beggar If you are helping a beggar, you should be careful you are not falling for too many hard luck stories in real life or covering for colleagues once too often. If you are a beggar or are frightened by a beggar in a dream, you are feeling insecure (usually needlessly) about losing the respect of your colleagues or boss or that present success will not last.

Birds Like bees, flying birds indicate messages of good news, especially from overseas or people you have not heard from for a while. Unhappy caged birds talk of your own unacknowledged fears of being trapped in a job with no prospects; hostile flocks of birds suggest gossip and petty spite from someone senior.

Borders If you are trying to escape over the border of a country, you are feeling stifled by your work routine or being given all the boring tasks. Crossing borders in a dream talks of unexpected travel opportunities coming your way.

Boss A dream where you are boss indicates future promotion or business success; if your boss is praising you or offering more money it may be a wish-fulfillment dream, but it also can mean that your efforts have been noticed. An angry or bullying boss says that you need to stand up for yourself and not give way to colleagues or your boss when they shout or make a fuss; it can also indicate worries about getting in trouble with officialdom. Bosses can represent mothering or fathering issues; maybe you need approval too much.

Bridge A bridge represents a transition or change point in your life; it can also indicate the need to find allies or maybe a partner in launching an independent venture. It may be time to put an end to a pointless feud not necessarily of your making.

Bubble If you are in a bubble or surrounded by bubbles flying into the air, you have every reason to be optimistic as promotion or new opportunities are coming into your life. A bursting bubble talks about an earlier disappointment you need to release.

Buildings Buildings symbolize the physical self so the kind of building or its condition can indicate hidden feelings and desires. Tall buildings talk about ambitions to be fulfilled; official buildings about bureaucratic, tax, or legal matters that need to be sorted; burning buildings about a desire to get rid of something or escape from someone you feel is holding you back; and a ruined building expresses feeling worthless or manipulated by others.

Butterfly A butterfly is the universal symbol of rebirth and regeneration. Positively, it represents the need to enjoy present happiness and success without worrying about tomorrow. It can also indicate a new job after a period of unemployment. A trapped, torn, or dying butterfly can represent fragile hopes and a sense of frantically trying to hold on to a rapidly changing situation or staying too long in a job going nowhere.

Cactus A cactus in a dream represents an irritating or irritable colleague at work who keeps invading your space. If you hurt yourself on a cactus, you may need to step back from an ongoing quarrel or feud between two people you know well at work.

Calculator If a colleague or boss is using a calculator in a dream, they may have a calculating, colder side that you may not have acknowledged. Using a calculator yourself says a venture will be profitable if you check all the details and anticipate problems in advance.

Calendar A calendar on a wall (or on a desk) with lots of marks on it says you need to work out your priorities, which may mean saying no to people who always ask for help; an empty calendar says you are waiting for something to happen to activate your career and maybe should do something to hasten the event. A calendar from years back says that you need to leave some part of the past behind that still troubles you or erodes your confidence. To dream of a particular date means that it will be important to you next time it occurs. A crossed-out date says that anything planned for the morning of the dream may be cancelled or postponed.

Canoe or kayak Paddling your canoe along a river or lake shows that you are very self-sufficient and do not need the approval of others. If the canoe tips over, you may face jealousy or unexpected rivalry from someone who is usually very friendly.

Cap Wearing a cap like a baseball cap says you should relax a bit more as everything will go well; cap pulled over your eyes says you are afraid to slow down and have fun. A cap over someone else's eyes says they are quite uptight and may be hiding resentment at your popularity or success.

Car A car represents ourselves as we go about the world in our daily lives; if you are driving then you are in control of your life or a particular situation and should not let others take over or try to change your mind. If it is a fast car you want more excitement and power. A broken-down car reflects fears that things will go wrong with your future plans (maybe a warning to check whether you are up to date with your work and are filing your replies in case of dispute). If the brakes fail or the car goes out of control, it is a warning that you should be careful not to let others make decisions for you that will affect your career.

Cart If a horse is pulling the cart, people will be unusually cooperative and helpful in the days ahead, so push ahead with projects. An empty cart warns that you are giving too much to others, emotionally, practically, or financially, in your working life. A cart with a broken wheel or axle says there may be temporary delays in plans.

Celebrities Mixing with celebrities says you want recognition for what you do and maybe want to move more toward center stage instead of letting others take the credit. It can also mean that you have a talent you could develop that would bring you money and success. If you are famous in the dream, you should push ahead with a venture on which you have been holding back, creatively, work or personal success is assured.

Cell or jail Being imprisoned shows that you would like to escape from the restrictions of your life or from a person who is trying to bully or manipulate you. The cell or quiet room of a monk or nun says you need peace and quiet for a while—and maybe some advice from a wise colleague.

Cereal, breakfast Enjoying breakfast cereal in a dream promises a trouble-free day ahead. Spilling cereal says you will have to check details and times of transport and so on in order to avoid delays or minor mishaps.

Chain Linked chains indicate successful business partnerships, maybe with a relative or close friend. If you are trying to break free of the chains, you may have outgrown a mentor or student relationship that sustained you in your earlier working life. Broken chains may suggest a working relationship or partnership is falling apart and should either be mended or abandoned; broken chains also warn of an unwise office love affair.

Classroom Being in a classroom as a pupil says you will have the chance to learn a new skill or will succeed in any tests or interviews coming up. If you are having a bad time in class, then you should not let anyone at work try to make you feel stupid to boost their own ego; this is also a warning to check your facts.

Clothes Buying new clothes implies a desire to change your image. Wearing the wrong clothes at a work social event or in the office can mean that you are afraid of the disapproval of those around you. Torn clothes say petty spite or gossip is worrying you more than you acknowledge.

Comet A comet represents a sudden unexpected opportunity to shine that may be short-lived and so should be seized.

Corner If you cannot see around the corner, you are afraid for your long-term future or of having to make necessary changes in your career. If someone is hiding around a corner, check details of any plans for hidden costs or problems.

Criminal To be threatened by a criminal says you are worried about a financial commitment where you took a shortcut or did not consider the implications fully. If you are the criminal you may need to take an unconventional approach to a problem and take a chance on success.

Crossroads A crossroads is a turning point in your life involving choice. If the signs are clear, you should make a fast decision. If, however, the sign is broken or no signpost is present, you should wait until you are more certain and look for guidance. The actual places marked may be of deep significance.

Dagger A symbol of power, a dagger indicates that now is the time to thrust ahead with plans or make demands. If threatened by or stabbed with a dagger, beware treachery or malice from someone who is being over-friendly.

Delays Transport delays especially on an important journey are anxiety dreams about the incompetence or slowness of others who hold you back from achieving targets.

Desk A school desk says you are not being taken seriously and resent this. A tidy office desk promises you will get chaotic business or financial affairs, not necessarily of your making, under control very soon

Detour A detour to avoid delays or danger is very positive, showing that if you adapt your plans you will succeed. An endless detour that takes you away from your destination indicates that you must avoid being sidetracked by the objections or demands of others.

Dialing Trying to dial a number on the phone and keep getting it wrong, forgetting it, or being unable to hear the speaker or be heard is a common anxiety dream about needing help but not receiving it or not being able to get people to take your worries or opinions seriously. If you constantly get the engaged tone on the telephone, your dream is telling you that you may be relying too much on the opinion of the person you are phoning.

Diamonds A diamond is a sign that a prospective investment or financial outlay needs closer scrutiny before going ahead.

Dice Dice mean you may be worried about the trustworthiness of a person or the reliability of a job offer. If you are winning at dice you can take a risk.

Documents Signing documents says you are ready to make a major change or commitment but you must obtain guarantees or permanence; losing documents can mean you are being pressurized into changes about which you are uncertain; finding documents you have really lost at work or home is an indication of where you will find them.

Drawers If you are opening a drawer you are unwisely tempted to reveal a secret; closing a drawer says you need to put off a decision for a while. A drawer that is too full to close shows that negative feelings are spilling out perhaps as stress or minor illnesses.

Dress or dressing Dressing for a special occasion says you are concerned about making a good impression upon someone new in your life. If your clothes do not fit or you cannot get dressed properly, you are anxious about not fitting in at work.

Drowning Though this is a frightening dream, if you do not actually drown it means that you are ready to make a major commitment or to take a financial risk that should pay dividends if you do not lose your nerve and back out halfway. If you do feel you are drowning just before the dream ends, it is a sign that you are overwhelmed by responsibilities and commitments and need to reassess your priorities. A child drowning may represent a growing fear about coping with family life and career, especially if people at work are being less than helpful about your home commitments.

Dumbness Not being able to speak or, worse, still cry out for help in a dream says someone close is ignoring your protests or warnings or that you feel you are being silenced over a principle that is close to your heart.

Earthquake An earthquake is an indication of insecurity in a deal or job offer, based on warning signs you may have missed on a conscious level. Collapsing buildings indicate that there may be a financial problem you need to face if you run your own business or are overstretched financially in your private life. If you escape from an earthquake, you will be offered changes that will improve your lifestyle, often resulting from a current upheaval.

Editor If a person is editing and correcting what you have written, you may need to tackle someone who is constantly interfering with your work or repeating what you say in an exaggerated way that may cause trouble.

Electricity If you dream about electricity lines or pylons, you need to get input or seek help from others to succeed. A power cut says one line of income may temporarily be cut off but will return or be replaced if you wait and do not worry.

Elevator If you are going up in an elevator, a current career move or dream will succeed; going down means you shouldn't let others dampen your enthusiasm for a venture. Being stuck in an elevator says you are feeling trapped by a particular person or situation.

Entrance This image depends on what the entrance is to, as it represents hopes or fears of what lies ahead that should be taken further or faced. Making a spectacular entrance to a place says your efforts or talents will get recognition.

Envelope Good news is on the way with the advent of an envelope. If it is a tax or official letter envelope or a reminder to respond to any urgent financial or business correspondence, even to say you cannot pay or supply the information right now, it is a definite and positive action.

Eruption A volcanic eruption says you are worried about the suppressed fury of someone who tries to control you or that your own patience, maybe with that person, is coming to an end.

Escalator Going up an escalator indicates a smooth and more prosperous period in your life; going down says you regret leaving a job or downsizing more than you admit. A broken escalator shows a sticking point in your career or a venture that needs mending by you.

Examination If it is a medical examination, you may be worried about your health or your subconscious is reminding you a checkup is overdue. If it's a school examination, you may be afraid that you know far less than other people at work or socially.

Exit If you cannot find an exit to a building, you may have become too involved in the worries of others and need to find a way out of promises you have made that you don't want to keep.

Eye An eye means you should trust the evidence of your own eyes and not what people tell you. Check any contract or official documents carefully.

Falling One of the most universal dream symbols and scenarios, at its most positive, falling represents letting go of inhibitions or fears and opening the self to new experience. Fears of losing security and of letting go of control may be indicated if the fall ends in disaster; examine your fears carefully as dreams can offer hidden signs of valid but unacknowledged worries.

Fan, electric An electric fan means it is a time to reduce the pressures in your life or to take the heat out of a particular confrontation or work feud that no one can win.

Father Whether or not your father is alive, if the relationship with the father in the dream is good, it indicates the need for reassurance and advice from a wise father figure. A forbidding, stern father figure represents unnecessary restraints on your spontaneity and the need to reassert yourself and believe in your own competence.

First If you come in first place, either in a race or an examination or competition, you should acknowledge your ambitious side and not stand aside for others.

Flag A flag represents a need to show courage and rally support for yourself; a ripped flag says you are supporting the wrong side in an argument. A state emblem or national flag augurs that you will have profitable dealings with and maybe a visit to the country or state whose flag it is.

Floodlights Floodlights say that there are matters you need to bring out into the open; floodlights that go out suggest you are worried someone is not telling you the truth or that you will be left without support.

Floods or tidal waves If floods trap you, you are being swamped by others' emotional pressures or constant demands for your attention, help, and approval, and also by your own repressed feelings of anger or helplessness.

Flying Often associated with sex, and so maybe the deepening of an office romance, dreams of flying through the air like a bird especially with gentle landings represent the opening of opportunities and the ability to act on your dreams.

Flying a plane If you are flying a plane in your dream, your love or work life will take off in a big way before long. This also indicates travel in the near future.

Forgetting If you dream that you have forgotten an appointment or where you are going, it is a warning of overload in your life and a reminder that you need to double-check all commitments and appointments for the coming week.

Fox At the sign of the fox, use subtlety and tact to persuade others to your point of view rather than direct confrontation. Beware of fast-talking flatterers who may not be telling the truth.

Fruit To dream of eating fruit or bowls of fruit is a sign of abundance coming into your life; fruit on trees promises long-term plans and investments will be successful. If the fruit or vegetables are ripe, it is the right time to act and take opportunities or to cash in investments made earlier. Rotten fruit can indicate an untrustworthy colleague.

Gain Any gain in a dream, whether money, praise, or promotion, says your financial or work situation will likewise become more successful. If you gain the advantage illegally, you may be worried about an offer you have been made or a possible investment or loan that seems too good to be true; it is too good to be true.

Gambling Gambling dreams are all about taking risks. If you win at gambling, the risk is worthwhile; if you lose then you should be cautious.

Garbage To dream of piles of garbage in or around your workplace says that you need to clear away a lot of old unresolved though justifiable grievances that are stopping you from moving forward. If you are disposing of garbage, you have to clear up problems others have created, however unfair that seems.

Gas (propane) A gas leak means someone you trusted is gossiping about what you told them in confidence; cooking on gas, especially outdoors, promises happy times and outings with family and friends, maybe time to book some leave; a gas explosion suggests a situation or confrontation you have been avoiding needs resolving before matters get out of hand.

Giraffe A giraffe warns you not to interfere in other people's quarrels or problems as you will only get hurt; someone close may be exaggerating the truth.

Glass If you are enclosed in glass you may feel that no one is listening to your opinions. If the glass is broken, especially if you break it in the dream, your illusions may be shattered about someone trusted. Being cut with broken glass says someone may become uncharacteristically spiteful because of their own unhappiness but you must nevertheless protect yourself; throwing a glass and breaking it warns that you are getting overstressed about a situation and best let go.

Gold To dream of piles of gold says you have the power to make serious money within a few years; to have gold stolen or to be stealing bags of gold warns that you should take care of your financial affairs, especially if considering a major purchase or investment. A gold mine is a warning not to lend money or to take out a loan without checking that it is a good deal.

Golf To play or watch golf says you should not work too hard and need to take more relaxation. To win at golf says you will outsmart a business rival.

Government To dream about a government, whether national or regional, says that an official matter will turn out to your advantage; to be in the government says that extra responsibilities and rewards are coming your way professionally.

Handshake If you are shaking hands to conclude a deal, a new business opportunity in the week after the dream will prove advantageous. If you are shaking hands when you meet someone unknown, a stranger or new business acquaintance will become a good friend. To shake hands with a colleague may indicate an unspoken agreement or alliance; if a colleague or someone you know refuses your hand in a dream, he or she may prove duplicitous.

Handwriting If you cannot read the handwriting in the dream, someone is not communicating his or her genuine feelings or is keeping a secret from you. If your own writing is indistinct or unintelligible, it can indicate that you are uncertain of your own feelings and desires, so wait before speaking out or acting. If you are doing beautiful writing, you will have a chance to express yourself creatively or artistically.

Imitation To dream you are wearing imitation jewelry says that you are being offered second-best career opportunities and should not accept them even for the sake of security. If someone is imitating your movements or actions, beware of a rival who may try to steal your ideas or your job.

Inkpot or spilled ink An old-fashioned inkpot indicates important matters that should be communicated in writing, not by phone, to avoid misunderstandings. Spilled ink suggests you should check your facts and calm down before putting your thoughts or feelings down on paper or in an email you may regret sending.

Juggler A juggler represents a time of trying to balance different priorities, meeting conflicting demands. If the balls stay in the air, you will succeed; if the balls scatter, decide on one course of action or the most urgent task and focus on that until it is completed.

Jumping It is very empowering to be jumping in a dream if you leap effortlessly over objects or even buildings. This indicates that if you have confidence in your own abilities, you will succeed beyond your wildest expectations. If the objects are too high or you stumble in the dream, you may be afraid of risking failure or worried that others will be critical if you attempt something ambitious or new.

Jungle If you are walking into the jungle, you may be worried that a flirtation is going too far; to be lost in the jungle says you should take care before risking money on an uncertain venture or an expensive item you do not really need; to be swinging happily through trees tells you to trust your instincts about a decision and maybe take a risk to attain what would make you truly happy.

Kettle The kettle is a domestic symbol that shows that if matters are difficult, you need to instigate informal friendly conversations and try to resolve matters informally, rather than resorting to official channels. Listen carefully to what people are saying privately as there is a lot of change in the air.

Kingdom If you are the king looking over your kingdom or ruling it, then you will have a major opportunity for promotion or for making money, which will succeed if you have the confidence. A kingdom is a good omen for starting your own business, especially if you employ family or friends; if you cannot enter a kingdom there may be a hidden block on promotion or equality at work that needs bringing out into the open.

Knot(s) A knot in your hair or in a chain or cord means that things may not proceed as straightforward as planned and you may need to rebook or rearrange schedules. Try to clear up rumors, as people may have jumped to the wrong conclusion about a memo or information passed from an outside source and be arguing at cross purposes.

Label If you are labeling folders, objects, clothes, or piles of paper, you are trying to bring order and organization to an area of chaos in your life or to the problems of someone for whom you feel (or are) responsible for at work. This may not be easy if they do not want to help themselves.

Ladder Climbing a ladder symbolizes steps toward achieving ambitions, high ideals, and dreams and so is a very powerful sign of imminent success. Feeling fear at climbing a high ladder or clinging to one as it sways in the wind indicates a natural fear of aiming high and of failing. A ladder with broken rungs suggests that there are obstacles to success that you can overcome with patience.

Lake Swimming or boating on a lake is a very good sign of harmony in your life and of peaceful and satisfying relationships. A stormy lake says that you may be suffering from other people's disputes and should take a step backward and ensure your own peace of mind.

Lamp Finding a magic lamp means your dearest wishes will come true. Being given a lamp or switching on a lamp indicates you will recover a lost possession or missing piece of information or be paid money you are owed.

Lawyer If you consult a lawyer in your dream, you should read the small print or take advice before signing a contract or entering a formal agreement, even a verbal one.

Leader To be a leader in a dream says that you will soon be offered promotion or a leading role in a project. If you are following a leader, be sure that decisions you make are your own and not those of someone dominant who is trying to bully you.

Leaves Walking under leaves on a tree or jumping in a pile of leaves is an indication of happiness, prosperity, and success coming in small ways, one after the other. Falling leaves herald a natural change point or happiness in the fall.

Letter To receive a letter in a dream or seeing one in divination indicates good news coming by post within the week. Writing and sending a letter says you have something you need to say to a particular person that you have held back for fear of upsetting him or her, but it will bother you until you speak.

Lines, straight A straight line represents a direct course, a straightforward journey or enterprise.

Lines, wavy or broken Wavy or broken lines represent uneven progress, the need to take detours to achieve an aim.

Lizard A lizard means you should check your facts carefully as the source may not be reliable. A lizard is an early warning signal that people may change their minds or break promises of help at the last minute. As with all reptile symbols and dreams, the lizard is a warning not to trust an overcharming colleague at work or a new financial or business adviser who offers you an easy solution or a get-rich-quick scheme.

Loop Any loop in divination or a dream means that you may be temporarily diverted from your work or goal by seemingly pointless arguments and prejudices.

Magician If you are watching a magician perform magic tricks, someone at work is pretending to be more knowledgeable or competent than they are, and you should not be fooled by their fine words and illusion of expertise. A box of magic tricks warns you against taking the easy option or going along with a too-good-to-be-true offer. If you are demonstrating magic tricks and they are working, you may get away with a risky plan if you keep your nerve. If the tricks go wrong in the dream, you will be caught in white lies.

Magnifying glass If you dream you are looking at things through a magnifying glass, this is a warning that you may be worrying unnecessarily about a particular problem or person.

Market A market is a good indication if you are trying to sell something. It is also auspicious for job hunting, especially after a period of unemployment

Mask If you are wearing the mask in a dream, you may feel unable to show your true feelings because you are uncertain of the intentions and responses of others. If someone else is wearing the mask, they may have secrets they are unwilling to reveal or are playing power games with you.

Mountains A mountain dream says that there are obstacles ahead. If you are running or walking effortlessly up a mountain or on the downward path, these obstacles will easily be overcome.

Nail, finger Long nails indicate a colleague may be jealous of your relationship or success. Dirty nails suggest that you should not dismiss a prospective business partner because they are not immediately attractive or good at flattery. Broken fingernails are a sign of a promise that will be broken.

Nails, metal Banging nails into a wall or making something with nails says that you may need to be quite forceful in getting your point of view across.

Nakedness If you find yourself naked in a public place or at work, you may be afraid that you are not capable of keeping your present job or that you are not attractive or charismatic enough compared with colleagues. Usually these fears have been planted by someone who is insecure themselves and so has tried to make you feel inadequate.

Nets Nets full of fish indicate the success of a business or financial venture. Empty nets warn that you should possibly try further from home if you are looking for a new job or sales outlet.

Oasis To dream of arriving at an oasis says that you will soon find relief from ill health or a long-standing problem. If the oasis in the desert turns out to be a mirage, a source of money or business may soon dry up so make sure you have alternative sources of income or orders.

Oath To swear an oath, whether in court or at a lawyer's office, is a good indication that a legal or official matter will soon be settled to your advantage. To break an oath or refuse to swear one is a warning that you should not to be too liberal with the truth in official matters.

Obstacles Whether actual obstacles or unexpected difficulties appear in a dream, ask yourself if you really want to go ahead with a plan. Sometimes this is a way our subconscious warns us that we do not really want to make a change or leave a familiar setting.

Offer To receive an offer whether of work, a loan, or a bargain is a very good omen, indicating that luck is turning and that good luck is coming your way; you should receive a promising offer within a week or so of the dream.

Oranges Oranges are a symbol of health and of prosperity. They are good for new or existing partnerships, for applying for new jobs, and for all careers with children or the travel industry. A grove of orange trees says that it is a good time to start long-term savings or investment plans for the future.

Orchestra If the orchestra plays in harmony, success lies in joint venture or by cooperating with others, a favorable omen for partnerships of all kinds. If the orchestra is discordant, you may be trying too hard to fit in with others and may be happier following your own path.

Page, in a book An open page in a dream may offer a solution to a problem or give you necessary information if you can remember it. Record the dream as soon as you wake and try to find the book. This image also says that you can trust a new friend or colleague.

Parachute Floating down on a parachute is a good sign that if you aim high, you will not fall or fail. If a parachute does not unfold, do not rely on others to help you career or money wise.

Paralysis Being unable to move in a dream is quite normal especially as your mind tries to wake from a bad dream. Feeling unable to run away from danger or formless terrors implies that there are issues that need to be faced in your working life, also that there is frustration that the lack of money or resources is holding you back.

Pen A pen promises a letter from abroad before the week is through. A leaking pen warns not to leave correspondence where curious eyes can read it.

People People we do not know in a dream generally signify different aspects of ourselves, projected onto various characters—heroes, heroines, and villains. Observing how they behave and, most important how you react to them in the dreamscape can reveal a great deal about your current state of mind and emotions. Such dreams can also be a rehearsal for scenarios that you would like to occur or fear may happen with people you do know in real life.

Pigeon A pigeon is a trustworthy messenger or arbitrator; a pigeon augurs unexpected communication from afar.

Pins To have a lot of pins is an indication of impending good luck; if you drop them you should be careful not to break anything of value the following day.

Playing sports Playing sports means you may be living or working in a very competitive atmosphere and are finding it hard to set your own pace. Running or a cycling race indicates you have a deadline to meet or a number of pressing commitments; pace yourself rather than panicking. It is a good omen if you are winning in the sport.

Price If you are buying an item and the price is very high, it may refer to a price you are being asked to pay in some aspect of your life, maybe in terms of emotional stress or compromising your independence in return for job security or approval. Is the price too high?

Procession Taking part in a procession says that you will be given credit for successful completion of a project or for winning an important order; it also indicates success in examinations, tests, and interviews of all kinds.

Radiator A radiator warming an office says money and success will flow into your life; a leaking radiator warns that money is trickling away on a project that is not going to be profitable.

Rags A dream with rags is one of those dreams that mean its opposite. In this case rags indicate that tattered hopes will be revived, abandoned projects rekindled, broken dreams repaired, optimism restored, and general good fortune renewed.

Recurring dreams Any recurring dream indicates that you should listen to it or act on it, especially if it is a warning. The inner voice will often use recurring dreams if it is not being heard. If you dream repeatedly of a particular place, try to locate it and go there, as you may learn something there or meet someone who can help you in your future life.

Reflection To see your reflection in a mirror in a dream says that you may be following the opinions of others too closely and should allow your own originality and initiative to shine through.

Repeat To watch a program you have seen before on the television in a dream indicates you may be about to repeat an old mistake.

Road A road in a dream represents your path through life. You can tell a lot from its form, both of hidden influences on you and coming opportunities. A road with a fork represents choices; the right one can identify if a choice is a dead end or is full of potholes. An uphill road ahead indicates that you may need extra input or help for a while; a gentle incline represents a gradual increase in luck.

Rocket A rocket represents a very ambitious plan that will need tremendous impetus to launch, but will have far-reaching effects.

Rocks Rocks signify potential hazards. However, with care they can be surmounted and used to scale greater heights; jagged rocks can indicate jealousy and spite. Rocks covered by the sea suggest you will need to wait for the right moment and then go ahead without hesitation.

Running, away Running away is a straightforward escape dream, symbolizing something or someone you seek to escape from. If you are being pursued and find that you cannot run, fear may be holding you back from tackling a problem head-on. Alternatively you may be holding yourself in a destructive or emotionally draining situation or work relationship because you fear the consequences of leaving or protesting.

Saddle A saddle or a saddled horse says you may have an opportunity to work in a new location or area of expertise. Sitting in a saddle says you will gain a position of authority; saddling a horse indicates an increase in prosperity.

Samples If you are given samples of material or food or beauty products, your business or plans will grow from small beginnings with increasing profitability after the first few months. You or a family member may need to try several jobs or forms of training before they settle, but if given time will find the right career.

School A happy return to childhood school days says that you will have the chance to learn some new skill or course of study. A return to unhappy or humiliating school scenes can indicate you may lack confidence in your abilities and have been listening to the unjustifiable criticism and carping of a current authority figure such as a boss or in-law.

Scissors Cutting with scissors says that you should cut through other people's inertia or indecisions and act decisively; dropped or broken scissors can herald quarrels between two people who are competing for your attention or work time.

Sex Sex with the boss or sex with a colleague is a surprisingly common dream. This can be a wish-fulfillment dream, especially if there have been signals of attraction passing between you and the colleague in real life. However, sex with the boss often says more about your own hidden desire and ability to become very successful in your own career.

Shark A shark represents emotional predators that play on your natural kindness to gain sympathy; spiteful gossiping coworkers need to be told to find another victim before you bite back.

Shoes New shoes can indicate a new job or business opportunity; if they are uncomfortable in the dream you may have difficulty at first in settling in. Worn-out shoes suggest a particular avenue of approach in dealing with a difficult person may be exhausted; stop arguing and walk away. To lose your shoes warns that you may be making excuses to avoid a change in your life that you do not really want.

Success Success dreams can occur when things are going badly. They are a vote of confidence from your subconscious that has detected a change in fortune; if you try you will succeed.

Swimming Swimming, like floating in a dream, is an excellent dream omen, indicating that life will flow along happily and that things will happen quite naturally. Swimming to shore is an especially good omen if you have been struggling with life or worrying about the future.

Tank, fish Fish in a tank, especially gold ones, are a sign of money coming into your business or personal career. An empty fish tank says your enthusiasm for a project or person is draining away, though you may not have acknowledged this.

Thirsty To be thirsty in a dream says you are not being given enough appreciation or tangible rewards for your efforts; alternatively it is a warning that a source of income may be drying up or you need to find a new outlet for your talents.

Tongue A tongue in a dream, especially a swollen one, says that you should ignore gossip and rumors you may hear during the next week as they are totally untrue.

Traps Animal traps are a warning not to confide your secrets or confidential work information in people you do not know really well, and even then be cautious. Vermin traps say a spiteful colleague will be caught out in is or her own lies.

Treasure To find treasure is an excellent omen, not only for money inflow but for developing new talents. Burying treasure warns you not to give too many good ideas away for free.

Underwear If you see a colleague or your boss in just their underwear in a public place, they may be caught out in a compromising or embarrassing situation. If you are in your underwear in the street, you may be worried about a minor indiscretion or mistake becoming known.

Victory To dream of a victorious army, sports team, or victory parade is an excellent omen of success if you have been struggling for some time to make a business profitable or for a court case or legal matter about which you have been worried.

Walls High walls can indicate either protection or exclusion, depending on whether you are inside or outside them and whether you want to be inside or are trying to escape. Walls represent a barrier between two places or two states, such as captivity or freedom, admission or exclusion. Your feelings in the dream are crucial as to whether the walls are a positive factor in your life and should be strengthened or negative and should be knocked down.

Wasps Wasps tell you to beware a vicious-tongued colleague and avoid contact with them where possible. Killing wasps is a good indication that you are ready to stand up to a critical senior or an embittered older colleague.

Web, spider A universal symbol for the web of fate, a spider web indicates that your destiny is very much in your own hands if you remain confident and learn from the past. Being trapped in a web, with a giant spider, symbolizes feeling trapped by circumstances and the actions of others.

Web, World Wide (Internet) To be connected to the Internet often suggests that information or a contact you need will be found on the Internet; try to recall which pages you saw in your dream as these will be key ones. To catch a virus on the World Wide Web indicates someone in your life is trying to invade your privacy, especially your confidential emails, or to steal your ideas, not necessarily electronically.

Whispering Whispering in a dream or hearing whispers hints of intrigues and secrets in the real world that can lead to factions within the workplace.

Zodiac To dream of studying the zodiac says that you need to let the future unfold and not worry so much about tomorrow; this is an indication that you could be gifted in astrology if you studied it. It is always a good luck dream.

Herbs, Oils, Incense, and Smudge Sticks

You can buy the following herbs either already dried or grow your own. Incense sticks are widely available in stores and on the Internet or by other mail order, as are essential oils. You can take flowers into work and also miniature trees like the protective bay or orange.

The fragrances I have suggested are especially effective for empowerment, harmony, and protection at work. You can add to the list or substitute your own favorites, especially those that grow in your local area. Note in your journal any herb or incense empowerments you create, and keep your herb and oils rack at home well supplied so you can take in supplies of herbs to work as necessary.

Common name	Latin name and category	Properties and uses
Allspice	*Pimenta officinalis*	Incense, spice Attracts prosperity, strengthens business links with profitable out-lets, gives courage to bring about necessary changes, encourages single-mindedness of purpose Mars Fire
Aloe Vera	*Aloe vera*	Herb, plant Keeping the whole plant in the workplace attracts good luck and money, guards against accidents Moon Water

Angelica	Angelica archangelica	Flower, herb, oil Banishes hostility, provides protection, aids forward planning, encourages connection with spiritual self Sun Fire
Balm of Gilead	Commiphora opobalsamum	Herb Comforts after a loss or setback, aids harmonious workplace relationships and networking Venus Water
Basil	Ocymum basilicum	Herb, oil Encourages loyalty, reduces fears of flying, protects, attracts prosperity especially when coins are buried in the soil of a basil plant and a green candle is burned nearby Mars Fire
Bay	Laurus nobilis	Herb, oil, smudge, tree Brings loyalty, encourages profitable partnerships, increases wealth and resources, purifies the workplace Sun Fire
Bergamot	Citrus bergamia	Herb, incense, oil Cleanses inertia and unproductive atmosphere, brings success especially in real estate and financial speculation Mercury Air
Black Cohosh, also called Squawroot	Cimicifuga racemosa	Herb Overcomes stagnation, encourages creativity, brings kindness to the workplace, supports second careers especially for older women Saturn Earth

Blessed Thistle, also called Holy Thistle	*Silybum marianum*	Herb Removes malice and spite from the workplace, blesses all who work under difficulties, supports the self-employed and those coming back after job loss Saturn Earth
Carnation	*Dianthus carophyllus*	Flower, incense, oil Calms stress and restores energy and enthusiasm, encourages a happy workplace Sun Fire
Cedar/ Cedarwood	*Cedrus libani*	Herb, incense, oil, smudge (thuja), tree Reduces stress, cleanses negative thoughts, helps to let go of past regrets and mistakes, attracts prosperity, protects Sun Fire
Chamomile	*Chamaemelum nobile*	Flower, herb, incense, oil Reduces anger, irritability, and anxiety at work, prevents work-related worries intruding on self time, gradually increases wealth and resources, supports those starting a first job Sun Fire
Cinnamon	*Cinnamomum zeylanicum*	Incense, oil, spice Brings enthusiasm for work, attracts success and prosperity, increases intuitive awareness Mars Fire
Clove	*Syzygium aromaaticum*	Herb, oil, spice Keeps away hostility and envy, increases self-confidence, improves luck and finances, helps after a setback or betrayal by a colleague Jupiter Air

Devil's Shoestring	*Viburnum alnifolium*	Herb Provides good luck, encourages speculation (like kelp the root can be kept in whisky to attract money), overcomes unemployment, helps when seeking promotion or a salary increase Mercury Air
Eucalyptus	*Eucalyptus globulus*	Herb, oil, incense, tree Improves focus and concentration, banishes negativity, purifies a bad atmosphere, stops ill-intended mind games Moon Water
Fennel	*Foeniculum vulgare*	Herb, oil, incense Gives courage and stamina, protects against industrial espionage and attacks from rival firms, cleanses any overcompetitiveness or potential rivalry within the workplace Mercury Air
Fern	*Dryoptens wallichiana*	Herb, incense Attracts good fortune, provides security for all travel, supports career moves and changes, encourages original ideas Mercury Air
Frankincense	*Boswellia carteri*	Incense, oil Brings courage, joy, strength, success, successful business trips, prosperity, confidence, leadership, nobility of purpose Sun Fire
Galangal Root (also called Low John)	*Alpinia galangal*	Herb Brings good luck, drives away negativity and hostility, promotes forward planning, attracts money when used in a mojo bag Mars Fire

Geranium	*Pelargonium*	Flower, herb, incense, oil Encourages optimism and positive interactions, enhances creative thinking, helps an office romance, protects against spite or those who are overcritical, protects a workplace from external threats and hostile strangers Venus Water
Hibiscus	*Hibiscus*	Flower, herb Promotes planning, increases intuitive awareness, attracts good fortune, encourages positive workplace communication and interactions Venus Water
High John the Conqueror Root	*Ipomoea jalapa*	Herb Handle with care and keep well away from children. It is poisonous (or use Low John) Promotes good luck and speculation, encourages strength, overcomes obstacles, provides prosperity, achieves ambitions, protects against harm Mars Fire
Hyssop	*Hyssopus officinalis*	Herb Purifies and protects, counters exhaustion after overwork, counters stress and anxiety Jupiter Air
Jasmine	*Jasminum officinale*	Flower, herb, incense, oil Overcomes doubts and fears, encourages prosperity, enhances intuition and all forms of psychic awareness so excellent for planning forward, supports office romance, brings solutions to problems in dreams, benefits night workers Moon Water

Juniper	*Juniperus communis*	Herb, oil, incense, smudge, tree Supports new beginnings and opportunities, provides blessings at new workplace, cleanses the atmosphere after a quarrel or a bad-tempered outburst, protects against theft and intruders, works as antivirus near computers Sun Fire
Lavender	*Lavendula officienale*	Flower, herb, oil, incense, oil, smudge Calms anger and irritability, alleviates exhaustion, guards against unkindness and sarcasm, encourages a happy calm workplace, helps people starting work for the first time Mercury Air
Lemon	*Citrus limon*	Fruit (use the dried peel or whole fruit), flower, incense, oil, tree Brings mental clarity and improves focus. Improves memory and concentration, cleanses negative atmospheres, promotes new beginnings and initiating projects Moon Water
Lemon Balm	*Melissa officinalis*	Herb, incense, oil Reduces workplace tension and stress levels, encourages cooperation, encourages creative thinking, finds answers in dreams, promotes planning Moon Water
Lemon Verbena	*Lippia citriodora*	Herb, incense, oil Reduces anxiety and stress, increases personal charisma and powers of persuasion, cleanses negativity of all kinds, overcomes resentment Mercury Air

Lemongrass	*Cymbopogon citratus*	Herb, incense, oil Repels spite and venom, increases psychic awareness, speeds up office romances, encourages astute deductions and fast mental reactions Mercury Air
Lucky Hand Root	*Orchis*	Herb Brings good luck especially where speculation or risk is involved, promotes success, protects against harm especially when traveling Venus Water
Meadowsweet	*Spiraea filipendula*	Flower, herb Brings good fortune to any business, attracts and maintains peace, encourages optimism, protects against spite and gossip, enhances intuition Jupiter Air
Mimosa	*Acacia dealbata*	Flower, incense, oil Reduces stress, secures long-term plans and employment, brings answers in dreams, enhances intuitive powers Saturn Earth
Mint, garden	*Mentha*	Herb, incense, oil Attracts money, encourages dedication to career, banishes malevolence, protects especially while traveling Venus Water
Neroli/Orange Blossom	*Citrus aurantium*	Flower, oil Encourages loyalty, promotes fertility of every kind, supports partnerships, increases self-confidence and self esteem, counters mood swings Venus Water

Nettles	*Urtica dioica*	Herb Dried, chopped nettles are very defensive. Keep a small pot or dish on your desk for protection. Replace them regularly, scattering the old one to the winds in an open space. Mars Fire
Orange	*Citrus sinesis*	Fruit (use dried peel or whole fruit), incense, oil Alleviates stress and exhaustion, brings abundance and good luck, reduces panic in a crisis, enhances self-worth, promotes partnerships Sun Fire
Patchouli	*Pogostemon patchouli*	Herb incense, oil Reduces stress, attracts prosperity and long-term security, increases energy levels, channels energy into worthwhile projects Saturn Earth
Peppermint	*Mentha piperata*	Herb, incense, oil Reduces anger and irritability, protects while traveling, aids the fast inflow of money, cleanses negativity, increases intuitive awareness Mercury Air
Pine	*Pinus sylvestris*	Herb, incense, oil, smudge, tree Promotes happiness and protection in the workplace, encourages inspiration and originality, attracts money and new business, cleanses negative words, returns hostility to sender Mars Fire
Rose	*Rosa damascena*	Flower, herb, incense, oil, smudge Reduces stress and hyperactivity in the workplace, regains confidence after a career break or a layoff, restores good luck, increases psychic awareness, protects against

workplace bullies and autocrats,
encourages intuitive dreams, protects young women in the workplace
Venus
Water

Rosemary	*Rosmarinus officinalis*	Herb, incense, oil, smudge Increases concentration and focus, improves memory, encourages single-mindedness, initiates change, protects Sun Fire
Rosewood	*Aniba rosaeodora*	Incense, oil Reduces stress and aggressive com- petition, brings harmony and coop- eration, heals the memory of past failures and resentments that serve no purpose Venus Water
Sage/Sagebrush	*Salvia officinalis*	Herb, incense, oil *Artemisia* smudge Provides career security, brings wis- dom, protects, grants wishes, improves memory, attracts good health, attracts power, attracts lead- ership opportunities and success, cleanses negative energies when used as smudge and replaces them with powerful positive ones Jupiter Air
Sandalwood	*Santalum album*	Herb, incense, oil, tree Encourages altruism, integrity, and idealism even in a large corporation, banishes negativity and unfair com- petition, brings calm and natural rhythms even to frantic periods Moon Water
Star Anise	*Illicum verum*	Herb, incense Brings good fortune, attracts the balanced energies of the four direc- tions and elements, amplifies natu-

		ral psychic awareness, promotes planning abilities Jupiter Air
Sweetgrass	*Hierochloe odorata*	Herb, braided as smudge Calms tensions, removes negativity, encourages kindness and helpfulness in the workplace, especially toward newcomers, supports people who work from home, especially those bringing up a family at the same time Moon Water
Thyme	*Thymus vulgaris*	Herb, incense, oil, smudge Improves memory and concentration, supports all examinations, presentations, and interviews, brings courage, increases psychic awareness, especially during sleep Venus Water
Vanilla	*Vanilla aromatica*	Incense, oil, spice Encourages optimism, harmony, and loyalty, increases mental acuity, favors partnerships, especially those in which the partners are friends or relatives Venus Water
Vetivert	*Vetiveria zizanoides*	Herb, incense, oil Breaks a run of bad luck, provides antitheft, protects against all negativity, attracts money Saturn Earth

Prohibitions

I have not suggested the internal use of herbs or oils, but you should be aware of the following precautions if you do use certain herbs or oils. If you suffer from any chronic or potentially serious medical condition or have allergies and asthma, check with a pharmacist or reliable herbalist before using any herbs or oils medicinally or in baths. The lists on this page include herbs and oils not in this book. Keep smudge or incense away from children and pets, and where possible open windows or use smudge in the open air.

The following herbs and oils should be avoided during pregnancy:

aloe vera	mandrake
angelica	marjoram
autumn crocus	myrrh
barberry	parsley
basil	pennyroyal
black cohosh	poke root
caraway	rosemary
cayenne	rue
cedarwood	sage
clary sage	southernwood
fennel	tansy
feverfew	tarragon
golden seal	thuja
High John the Conqueror root	thyme
hyssop	wintergreen
juniper	wormwood
male fern	yarrow

This is not a comprehensive list, so as with any substance you use in pregnancy, check with an herbalist or pharmacist before taking anything, especially in the early months.

If you suffer from epilepsy you should avoid:

aniseed
camphor
fennel
hyssop
rosemary
sage
star anise

If you are on hormone replacement therapy, avoid:

clary sage
coriander
fennel
Spanish sage

Phototoxic oils can irritate the skin if they are exposed to the light and should be well diluted if used on the skin.

Avoid direct sunlight for six hours after using the following oils in baths:

bergamot
ginger
lemon
lime
mandarin
orange

Colors

The following colors are especially helpful for workplace power and harmony, whether used around the workplace or worn to increase a particular quality or burned as a candle in a home ritual. You can also make colored waters at home by placing still mineral water in small colored glass bottles for eight hours in daylight, starting around dawn or when you get up. You can add a crystal of the appropriate color to the bottle if you wish. Use clear quartz or fluorite for white. Store the bottles in the fridge and take them to work to drink or splash on pulse points when you need their energy. You can also use flowers, ribbons, scarves, cushions, drapes, prisms, and crystals to infuse color into the workplace.

White Use or wear white for new beginnings, for starting up new businesses, for enthusiasm and optimism, for innovative approaches and finding ways around obstacles, for successfully integrating different aspects of self and priorities, and for striving for perfection; white is good for those who work in the field seeking new markets and outlets, for sole traders, ministers of religion, employers, pioneers, and captains of industry.

Red Use or wear red for courage, for instant energy, for power, for initiating change, for getting your efforts noticed, for achieving ambitions, for effective protests against inequality and injustice, for overcoming inertia in others, and for increasing stamina; red is good for all who work in rescue or the armed services, any profession involving physical risks, and manufacturing.

Orange Use or wear orange for enhancing self-esteem and confidence, for strengthening identity, for overcoming exhaustion and establishing personal boundaries around your workspace, for negotiations and balance, for lateral thinking, and for developing your unique talents and own life path; orange is good for those who work in the media, theater or music, any field to do with art or publishing, marketing, design, and all creative ventures; it is also good for self-employment.

Yellow Use or wear yellow for sharpening logic, for focusing, for enhancing all aspects of conscious mind power, including memory, learning, mental acuity and concentration, for short-distance and short-term travel, for improving sales techniques, for strengthening determination, for clearing communication, and for overcoming debt; yellow is good for all involved with technology, commerce, retail, sales, or medicine, especially surgery and speculation.

Green Use or wear green for gradually increasing all energies, especially wealth and resources, for attracting good luck, for overcoming anxieties and panic, for improving harmony and positive relationships within the workplace; green is good for those who work in any people-related career, horticulture, agriculture, healing, beauty industry, air care industry, aid agency work, counseling, and the environment.

Blue Use or wear blue for finding a job and for promotion, for passing examinations or interviews, for learning new languages, for acquiring conventional knowledge and qualifications, for long-distance and long-term travel, for leadership opportunities and success in legal matters, for driving long distance; blue is good for careers in law, government, politics of all kinds, administration, management posts, education.

Purple Use or wear purple for planning, for developing your intuitive people- and situation-reading skills, for protection in the workplace, for neutralizing negative earth energies, for becoming skilled at interpreting symbols and dream material and visualization, and for maintaining ideals and integrity even in a competitive atmosphere; purple is good for all who work in alternative medicine or spirituality and fair-trade enterprises.

Pink Use or wear pink for kindness and courtesy in workplace interactions, for counteracting bullying and sarcasm, for patience when results are slow or people uncooperative, for first jobs and workers returning after a setback or career break, for peacemaking, and for tolerance; pink is good for careers working in customer services, with children and babies, pregnant women, and new mothers, all health care, and with victims of abuse and inequality attempting to regain self-love and trust.

Brown Use or wear brown for steadily accumulating profit and preventing an uncontrolled outflow of money, for accuracy especially in detailed work, for wise caution in financial and property dealings, for perseverance, for keeping within a budget, for learning new skills especially later in life, for older workers and those who have retired, and for keeping established businesses in profit; brown is good for careers in banking, real estate and government, financial matters, renovation and restoration, building, work with animals, and all practical jobs and crafts.

Gray Use or wear gray for keeping a low profile, for maintaining confidentiality, for working in the background, for negotiating delicate or potentially explosive matters, for finding compromise solutions that will satisfy everybody, for calming stress, and for keeping in touch with the underlying mood and possible changes in the workplace; gray is good for careers in detective, insurance, and fraud investigation work, work with politically or financially sensitive material, as an adviser, all maintenance work of equipment, and as the facilitator behind a high-profile figure.

Useful Reading

The books in this section are listed alphabetically by author but are grouped within subject areas. This is by no means a comprehensive list, but each title represents an excellent introduction or sound source of information on its particular topic. It is recommended to also check out other sources and titles by subject.

Animals, Power

Andrews, Ted. *Animal Speak: The Spiritual and Magical Powers of Creatures Great and Small*. St. Paul, MN: Llewellyn, 2002.

Eason, Cassandra. *Psychic Power of Animals*. London: Piatkus, 2003.

Aromatherapy and Oils

Higley, Connie and Alan, and Pat Leatham. *Aromatherapy A to Z*. Carlsbad, CA: Hay House, 2002.

Worwood, Valerie Ann. *The Fragrant Heavens*. London: Bantam Doubleday/Transworld, 1999.

Worwood, Valerie Ann. *The Fragrant Mind*. London: Bantam Doubleday/Transworld, 1996.

Astrology

Gurtman, Ariel, and Kenneth Johnson. *Mythic Astrology, Archetypal Powers in the Horoscope*. St. Paul, MN: Llewellyn, 1995.

Mann, Tad. *The Round Art*. London: Vega; New York: Sterling, 2003.

Oken, Alan. *Complete Astrology*. New York: Bantam Doubleday Dell Publishing, 2002.

Parker, Julia and Derek. *Guide to Astrology*. London: Dorling Kindersley, 2000.

Auras, Color Therapy

Andrews, Ted. *How to See and Read the Aura*. St. Paul, MN: Llewellyn, 2001.

Brennan, Barbara Anne. *Hands of Light: A Guide to Healing through the Human Energy Field*. New York: Bantam Books, 1987.

Wauters, Ambika. *Homeopathic Color Remedies*. Berkeley, CA: The Crossing Press, 1999.

Coffee-Ground Reading

Mizumoto, Sandra, and Sandra Posey. *Café Nation, Coffee Folklore, Magic and Divination*. Santa Monica, CA: Santa Monica Press, 2000.

Sophia. *Fortune in a Coffee Cup: Divination with Coffee Grounds*. St. Paul, MN: Llewellyn, 1999.

Crystals

Conway, D. J. *Crystal Enchantment*. Berkeley, CA: The Crossing Press, 2003

Eason, Cassandra. *An Illustrated Guide of Healing Crystals*, London: Vega; New York: Sterling, 2003.

Galde, Phyllis. *Crystal Healing Secrets*. St. Paul, MN: Llewellyn, 1991.

Gienger, Michael. *Crystal Power, Crystal Healing*. New York: Sterling, 1999.

Divination and Psychic Development

Eason, Cassandra. *Complete Guide to Divination*. Berkeley, CA: The Crossing Press, 2003.

Eason, Cassandra. *Complete Guide to Psychic Development*. Berkeley, CA: The Crossing Press, 2003.

Radin, Dean. *The Conscious Universe, The Scientific Truth of Psychic Phenomena*. New York: Harper Collins, 1997.

Dreams

Ball, Pamela. *10,000 Dreams Interpreted*. New York: Random House, 2000.

Browne, Sylvia. *Sylvia Browne's Book of Dreams*. New York: E P Dutton, 2002.

Feng Shui

Englebert, Clear. *Feng Shui Demystified*. Berkeley, CA: The Crossing Press, 2003.

Hobson, Wendy. *Simply Feng Shui*. Slough, England: Quantum, 2000.

Herbs

Culpeper, Nicholas. *Complete Color Herbal*. Slough, Berkshire, England: Quantum, 2003.

Cunningham, Scott. *Encyclopedia of Magical Herbs*. St. Paul, MN: Llewellyn, 1997.

Mabey, Richard. *The Complete New Herbal*. London: Penguin, 1991.

I *Ching*

Baynes, C.F., R. Wilhelm (trans), and Vary F. Baynes (trans). *I Ching or Book of Changes*. Princeton, NJ: Princeton University Press, 1967.

Karcher, Stephen (trans). *I Ching: The Classic Chinese Oracle of Change with Concordance*. London: Vega; New York: Sterling, 2002.

Stein, Diane. *A Woman's I Ching*. Berkeley, CA: The Crossing Press, 1997.

Tzu Lao, and Robert C. Henricks. *Lao Tzu's Tao Te Ching*. New York: Columbia University Press, 2000.

Incense, Smudge

Cunningham, Scott. *Complete Book of Incense, Oils and Brews*. St. Paul, MN: Llewellyn, 1993.

Eason, Cassandra. *Smudging and Incense Burning*. Slough, Berkshire, England: Quantum, 2001.

Kavasch, Barrie E., and Karen Baar. *American Indian Healing Arts: Herbs, Rituals and Remedies for Every Season of Life*. London: Thorsons, 2000.

Intuition

Day, Laura. *Practical Intuition: How to Harness the Power of Your Instinct and Make It Work for You*. New York: Broadway, 1997.

Hall, Judy. *Intuition Handbook, Access Your Hidden Power and Transform Your Life*. New York: Sterling/Vega, 2003.

Magic and Ritual

Eason, Cassandra. *Practical Witchcraft and Magical Spell Casting*. Slough, Berkshire, England: Quantum, 2001.

Telasco, Patricia. *Shamanism in a 9 to 5 World*. Berkeley, CA: The Crossing Press, 2000.

Numerology

Crawford, Saffi, and Geraldine Sullivan. *Numerology, the Power of Birthdays, Stars and Numbers*, New York: Ballantine Books, 1998.

Goldschneider, Gary, and Joost Elffers. *The Secret Language of Destiny, a Personology guide to finding your destiny*, New York. Penguin USA, 1999.

Pendulums

Bailey, Arthur. *Anyone Can Dowse for Better Health*. Slough, Berkshire, England: 1999.

Conway, D.J. *Little Book of Pendulum Magic*. Berkeley, CA: The Crossing Press, 2001.

Schirner, Marcus. *The Pendulum Workbook*. New York: Sterling Publications, 1999.

Resources

Most companies will supply a mail order service via the
Internet. Any contact details not included in the following list
were unavailable at the time of publication. Contact me at
www.cassandraeason.co.uk.

Aromatherapy Oils

Australia
Sunspirit Essential Oils
P.O. Box 85
Byron Bay
New South Wales, 2481
Phone: 612-6685-6333
Website: sunspirit.com.au

United Kingdom
Shirley Price Aromatherapy
Essentia House
Upper Bond Street
Hinckley
Leicestershire, LE10 1RS
Phone: 01455-615466
Website: www.shirleyprice.co.uk

United States
Aroma for Life
Hoffman Consulting LCC
2316 Somerset Drive
New Orleans, LA 70131
Phone: 504-392-2862
Website: www.aromaforlife.com
Charms, amulets, mojo materials,
and mojo bags

Lucky Mojo Curio Company
6632 Covey Road
Forestville, CA 95436
Phone: 707-887-1521
Fax: 707-887-7128
Email: order@luckymojo.com
Website: www.luckymojo.com

Feng Shui Supplies

Australia
Anjian
P.O. Box 870
Mount Waverley, Victoria 3149
Phone: 61-3-9544-9918
Email: info@anjian.com.au
Website: www.anjian.com.au

Other Metaphysical Supplies

United Kingdom
Exotic and Oriental Ltd.
51 St. Luke's Street
Barrow in Furness
Cumbria LA 13 9RR
Phone: 00-44-1229-832-439
Fax: 00-44-0870-138-1655
Email: guangong@firenet.uk.net
Website:
www.exoticandoriental.co.uk

United States
Dragon Gate Palace
Email: cindy@dragon-gate.com
Website: www.dragon-gate.com
Very extensive online store

Herbs and Spices

Australia
Global Herb Supplies
Corner of Byrnes and Eccles Street
Cairns, Mareeba
Queensland, 4880
Phone: 617-4092-2882
Email: health@globalherbalsupplies.com

Canada
Forget-me-Not Herbs 'n' Wildflowers
R.R. #2, 1920 Beach Road
Oxford Mills, Ontario K0G 1S0
Phone: 613-258-1246
Email: forgetmenot@achilles.net

United Kingdom
Herb Mail Order Service
Haelan Center
42 The Broadway
London N8 9DT
Phone: 0208-340-4258
Website: www.haelan.co.uk

United States
Lingle's Herbs
2055 North Lomina Avenue
Long Beach, CA 901815
Phone: 800-708-0633
Email: info@linglesherbs.com

Herbal Bath Products

Australia
Earth, Water, Fire
P.O. Box 3107
Bracken Ridge, Queensland 4017
Phone: 617-805-3107
Email: info@earthwaterfire.com.au

United Kingdom
Moonthistle
8 Alma Street
Falkirk, Central Region, FK2 7HB
Phone: 07732-397978
Website: moonthistle.co.uk

United States
Herbal Allies
63 Clove Road
Wantage, NJ 07461
Phone: 973-702-3451
Email: info@herbalalliesinc.com

Smudging Equipment, Smudge Sticks, Smudge Herbs, Incenses, Tools

Australia
Eartharomas Earthcraft
Magpie Flats Herb Farm
273/295 Boyle Road
Kenilworth, Queensland 4574
Website: www.eartharomas.com.au

United Kingdom
Dreamcatcher Trading
118 Murray Road
Sheffield, South Yorkshire, S11 7GH
Phone: 0114-268-7654
Email: info@dreamcatchertrading.com

New Moon Occult Shop
P.O. Box 110
Didcot, Oxon OX11 9YT
Phone: 01235-819744
Email: sales@newmoon.demon.co.uk

United States
Arizona Gateway Trading Post
Mail-HC 37
Box 919-UPS 14265
N. Highway 93
Golden Valley, AZ 86413
Phone: 928-767-4702
Email: agtp@citlink.net

Tibetan Incense Company
53 South 200 East
Kanab, Utah 84741
Phone: 435-874-9644
Email: Russell@tibetanincense.com

Wish Boxes

United States
California Astrology Association
P.O. Box 8005
Canoga Park, CA 91309
Fax: 818-340-9193
Website: www.calastrology.com
Abyssinian prosperity and Chinese
Li Yuan Temple wish containers,
plus other metaphysical supplies.

Natalie Lynn Company
925 Walnut Street
Traverse City, MI 49686
Phone: 800-497-4108
Email: service@wildwisdom.net
Website: www.wildwisdom.net
Prosperity boxes and a range of
other metaphysical goods.

Index

Living, essence of, 264
Li Yuan, 212
Lodestone, 217–18, 272
Low John, 303
Luck, 210–11. *See also* Charms; Wish
    boxes
Lucky Hand root, 216, 306
Lunches, 181–82

M

Magic
    elements and, 85–87
    spell casting, 80–88, 89–92
    technological, 88–92
    visualization vs., 79–80
    white, 81
Malachite, 101, 273
Marsh trigram, 169–70
Meadowsweet, 306
Meetings
    colors and, 70
    scheduling, 197–99
Mercury, 242
Mice, 247–48
Midnight, 184–85
Miles, Michael, 210
Mimosa, 306
Mind, stilling the, 42, 46–48
Minerva, 248
Mint, 306
Mirrors, 98
Mojos, 214–20
Monkeys, 247
Mood Aura, 52–53, 55, 56, 67
Moon
    influence of, 186
    phases of, 186–88
    zodiac and, 188–93
Moonstone, 72, 101, 273
Moss agate, 273
Mountain trigram, 168–69

N

Names
    calculating number of, 200–201
    power, 203–5

Naps, 182
Neroli, 306
Nettles, 105, 307
Nine, meaning of, 203
Noon, 181–83
Numerology
    dates and, 199, 206
    email and, 200, 206
    examples of, 204–5, 206–9
    meaning of numbers in, 201–3
    names and, 200–201, 203–5
    phone numbers and, 205–6
    Pythagorean system of, 197
    time of day and, 197–99, 200

O

Obsidian, 100, 274
Oils
    defensive, 106–7
    descriptive listing of, 300–309
    precautions for, 309–11
Olivine, 274
One, meaning of, 202
Orange (color), 62–63, 312–13
Orange (fruit), 307, 311
Orange blossom, 306
Owls, 248–49

P

Patchouli, 307
Peacocks, 249
Pelicans, 249–50
Pendulums
    asking yes/no questions with,
        18–20
    chi flow and, 126–28
    choosing, 15
    discovering responses of, 16–18
    dowsing with, 25–32
    flowcharts and, 20–21, 25
    holding, 16
    negative earth energies and,
        112–13
    principle behind, 13–14
    sample readings of, 21–25, 27–29
    testing responses of, 18

Wind and wood trigram, 167–68
Winter energies, 195–96
Wiseman, Richard, 210
Wish boxes, 211–14. *See also* Ill wishing
Wolves, 253–54
Workplace
    animal management in, 259–61
    collective aura of, 53–54, 66–73
    colors and, 312–14
    elements and, 117–21
    energy balancing in, 115–32
    interactions in, 66–70, 259–61
    protection in, 94–114
    stress and, 1–2
Writing, automatic, 137–40

Y
Yang, 158, 159, 176–77
Yellow, 63, 215, 313
Yin, 158, 159, 176–77

Z
Zodiac
    charms, 223–27
    moon and, 188–93

Other books by Cassandra Eason

The Complete Guide to Divination
How to Foretell the Future Using the Most
Popular Methods of Prediction

6 x 9 inches, 330 pages
$14.95 paper (Can $23.95)
ISBN 1-58091-138-2

The Complete Guide to
Psychic Development
100 Ways to Tap into Your
Psychic Potential

6 x 9 inches, 344 pages
$14.95 paper (Can $20.95)
ISBN 1-58091-150-1

The Complete Guide to Labyrinths
Tapping the Sacred Spiral for Power,
Protection, Transformation, and Healing

6 x 9 inches, 336 pages
$14.95 paper (Can $22.95)
ISBN 1-58091-126-9